IMAGES
of America

SODDY-DAISY

On the Cover: The classic expressions of church members, young and old, can be cherished forever with the preservation of images like this one. Pictured are friends and members of the Daisy Baptist Church celebrating their annual homecoming on September 17, 1939. For more pictures and information on this particular homecoming, please see page 55. (Courtesy of First Baptist Church Soddy-Daisy.)

IMAGES
of America

SODDY-DAISY

Sonya A. Haskins and
Cathy A. Hawkins

ARCADIA
PUBLISHING

ISBN 978-0-7385-4236-2

Published by Arcadia Publishing
Charleston, South Carolina

Printed in the United States of America

Library of Congress Catalog Card Number: 2005935602

For all general information contact Arcadia Publishing at:
Telephone 843-853-2070
Fax 843-853-0044
E-mail sales@arcadiapublishing.com
For customer service and orders:
Toll-Free 1-888-313-2665

Visit us on the Internet at www.arcadiapublishing.com

For Vivian, who thought I was her doll and loved me as dearly, and for Mary, who punched me, sat on me, jumped with me, and eventually liked me.
—Sonya Haskins
For my grandchildren, remember to run life's race with patience and pursue the heavenly vision with love.
—Cathy Hawkins

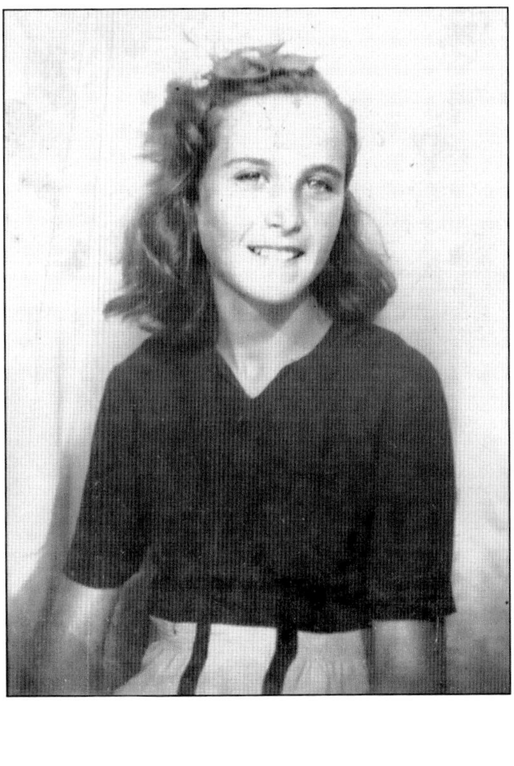

In loving memory of Linnie Mae Johnson.

CONTENTS

ACKNOWLEDGMENTS

There are many people who helped make this book possible. We are extremely grateful to those who allowed us to come into their homes, businesses, and churches to scan images. A courtesy acknowledgement of these individuals is given following each image.

We would especially like to thank Ellis and Linda Sutherland, David and Clara Bowman, Nancy Perkey, Barbara Levi, Janice Newman, Scott Brogdon, Buck Johnson, David Loftis, and Marquita Barker for the help they provided. These individuals allowed us to scan images, referred us to other people, and/or helped verify historical information.

Without professional photographers such as Scott Brogdon and avid amateur photographers such as Kay Williams and her sister, Doris Rogers, many events, buildings, and people would be lost in history. It is because of the dedication of individuals like these that we have many of the images preserved in this book. We thank all photographers for capturing memories on film.

A sincere note of appreciation also goes to those who have taken the initiative to write down stories, compile scrapbooks, and keep family mementos. Like the photographers who preserve history through pictures, those who write down the stories of the past are making sure history is not lost. One of these historians is Steve Smith, who has written a nice series of books on Soddy-Daisy history entitled *The Good Old Days*.

Allen Branum, police chief of Soddy-Daisy, was extremely helpful in finding photographs of the police and fire departments. His hospitality and recommendations were greatly appreciated.

We would like to thank Courtney Johnson and Sarah Haskins. These young ladies devoted numerous hours during the creation of this book doing childcare and research. In the face of hardship, Courtney has maintained a positive attitude and continues to try to help others. Sarah frequently helped tend to the needs of her younger siblings, Micah, Christopher, Daniel, and Hannah. Shelby Edwards also helped with childcare. For their help we are grateful.

Finally we would like to thank our editors at Arcadia Publishing, particularly Maggie Bullwinkel, for approving this project and for helping us make it the best book possible for the Soddy-Daisy community.

INTRODUCTION

Soddy-Daisy originated as two small communities along the base of Walden's Ridge (also called Soddy, Daisy, Flattop and Montlake Mountains, depending on your location). Though maps and postal addresses now say "Soddy-Daisy," any accurate history of the city would not be complete without an explanation of how two communities came to exist as one. For this, we must first go back to the beginnings of Tennessee and to the individual stories of Soddy and Daisy.

In the late 18th century, American pioneers were eager for land and anxious to explore. Despite increasing tension with British authorities ruling North Carolina at the time, settlers began to stream across the Appalachian Mountains and settled in what is now Upper East Tennessee (but what was then part of North Carolina). There were small settlements cropping up all over the area by the time the Declaration of Independence was signed in 1776.

Finally the states gained independence from England, and then several years later the "overmountain men" (settlers west of the Appalachian Mountains) gained independence from North Carolina. Tennessee was admitted as the 16th state in the Union in 1796.

Hamilton County was established in 1819, and the first white settlers we have a record of were creating homes in Soddy around that same time. In 1828, the Mount Bethel Presbyterian Church, later called Soddy-Daisy First Presbyterian Church, was established. It is quite obvious at that point that the settlers intended to stay, despite attacks by and fights with the local Native Americans who had claimed the lands as home for generations.

As early as the 1820s, coal was being mined in Soddy. The only earlier coal mines probably existed in Sale Creek. Tennessee's greatest mineral deposit is coal, but there was not a great demand for it until after the Civil War, when industries began using coal more as fuel. Around 1867, the Soddy Coal Company began operation. The company consisted of about 15 Welshmen, and the town began to grow—with the first stores, houses, and schools.

There has been much discussion about where Soddy obtained its name. This question will probably never be answered with 100-percent certainty, but since the question will be asked, we will address it. It does appear that the name is some form of the Native American word "Tsati," which has been given various meanings. The earliest translations we are aware of are "sweet water" and "little sod house." (If the first "t" is silent, one can see that the rest of the word does sound like "Soddy.")

Though the history hasn't been quite as well preserved as Soddy's, there were surely settlers living in the area we now call Daisy in the early 19th century. A post office named Poe's Cross Roads, after postmaster Samuel P. Poe, was even established here on June 30, 1846. When the Cincinnati Southern Railway came to the area, the growing town was named Daisy after the daughter of Col. Thomas Parks, vice-president of a newly established coal company in Daisy.

Daisy later became known as the location of some of the richest clay in America. The invention of the clay turpentine cup and its inventor, Charles Krager, are traced back to Daisy as well.

For the later part of the 19th and the first half of the 20th century, Soddy and Daisy existed end to end along a stretch of beautiful valley approximately 15 miles long and three miles wide.

Those who are natives to the area still know which end is which, and it is likely that natives will pass this heritage on to their own children, who know that Granny lives in Soddy, but their aunt lives in Daisy.

With that said, the stories of Soddy and Daisy are not only unique individually, but the stories intermingle, as do now the citizens and the history being created even today. In 1969, the two towns incorporated under the hyphenated name Soddy-Daisy, and in 1986, the city was featured in Gov. Lamar Alexander's Homecoming 1986 celebrations.

There are still remnants of our heritage all over Soddy-Daisy, but the tangible artifacts and visible mementos are slowly disappearing. Descendents of Welsh immigrants or Cherokee Indians also continue to be a reminder of our past, but even these individuals are becoming more difficult to locate as families move away or marry into families with other backgrounds.

The images presented in this book are not intended to portray a thorough history of Soddy-Daisy. The book is meant to be a sentimental history—a look at history through the eyes of those who took the time to preserve the moment with a camera. The photographs preserve the memories that the people who lived here 30, 40, or even 100 years ago thought were worth preserving. We are pleased to present you with this collection of pictures, documents, and stories (in the captions) on each page. It is our desire that everyone who is interested in the history of Soddy-Daisy will now have a better understanding of where we came from and the people who brought us here.

One

Buildings and Street Scenes

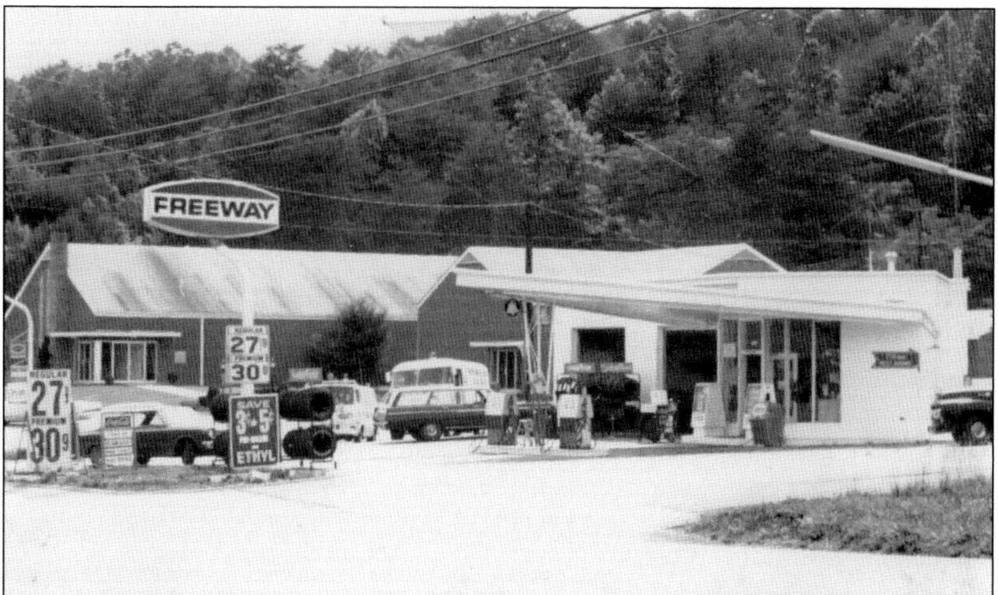

A sign outside the D. X. Station advertises regular gasoline for only 27.9¢ per gallon and premium gasoline for only 30.9¢ per gallon in this postcard from the early 1960s. Those are prices most of us would love to pay today. This gasoline station was located right next to the Daisy Church of God on Dayton Pike in Daisy. (Courtesy of Ronnie "Hawkeye" Hawkins.)

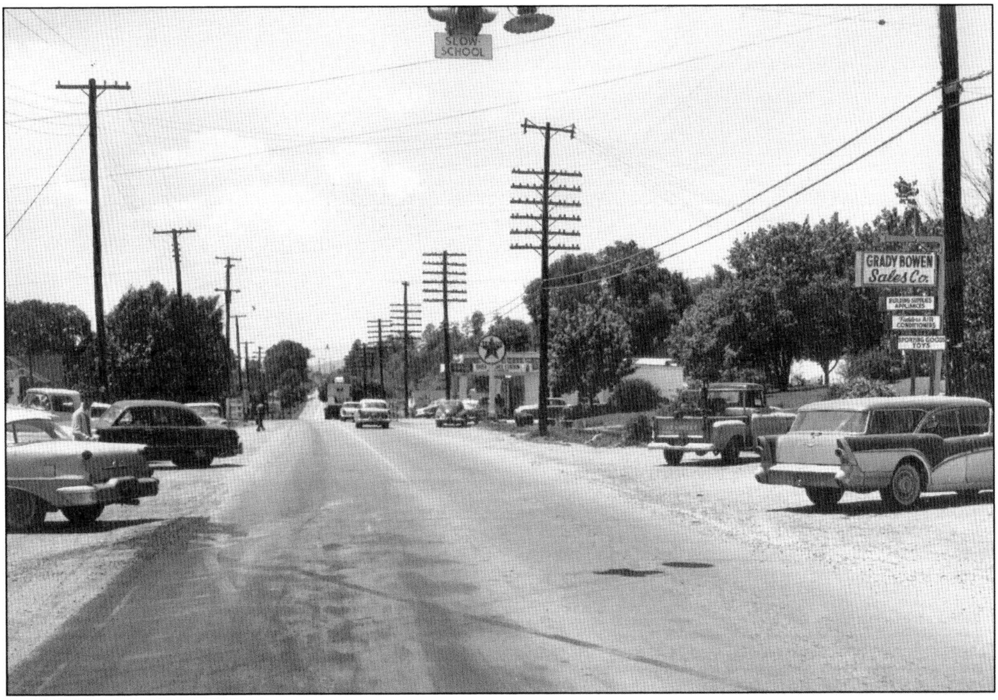

These photographs were taken in downtown Daisy on May 16, 1959, after an automobile accident. They were taken from the same location, but photographer Kenneth B. Kile faced south to take the top photograph and north to take the bottom photograph. If you look closely, you can see Daisy Clothing Store, Daisy Hardware, Smith's Drugs, the Texaco station, and a variety of vintage cars, trucks, and telephone poles on Dayton Pike. (Courtesy of Virgil Loftis.)

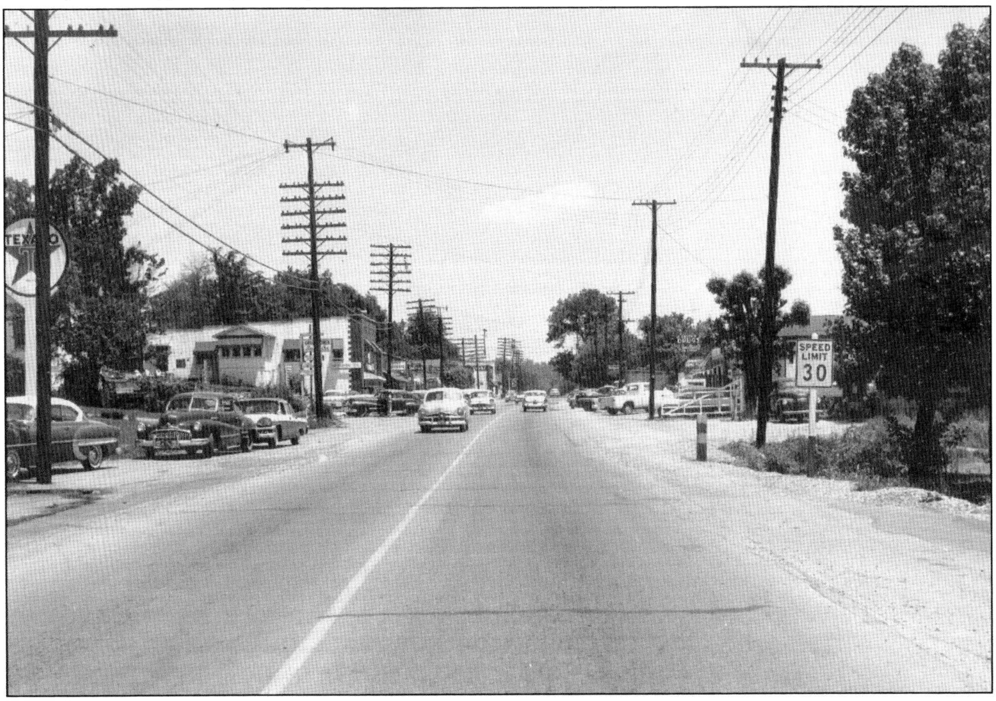

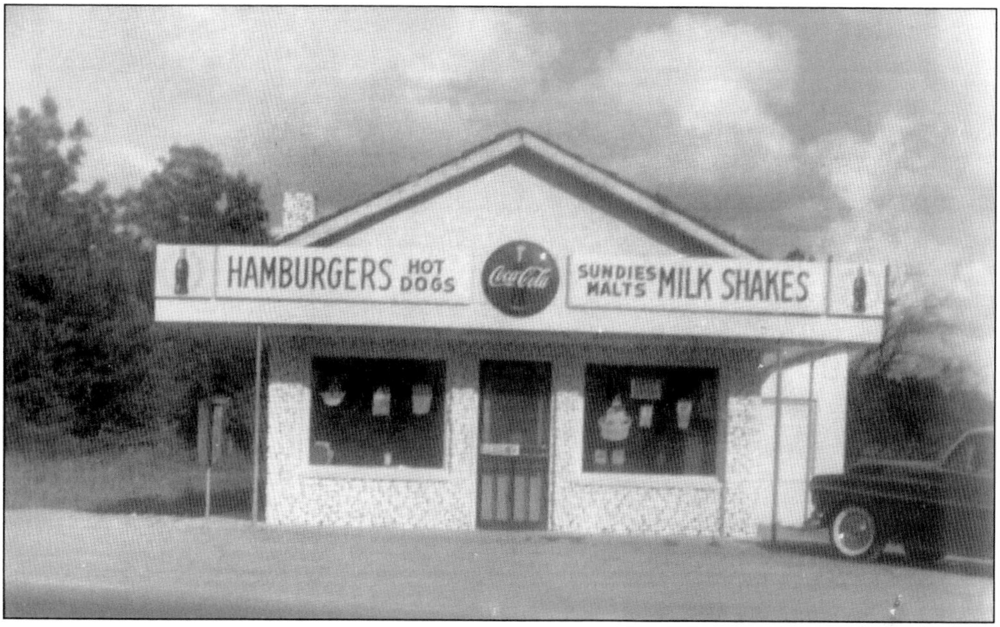

This building started out as a small rock structure built by Arthur and Jim Elliott with two gas pumps out front in the early 20th century. The store has gone through several owners and has been used for different purposes, but the most popular might always be the Jot 'Em Down, a little restaurant where patrons could enjoy hamburgers, hot dogs, milk shakes, malts, and "Sundies." (Courtesy of A. B. and Frankie McRee.)

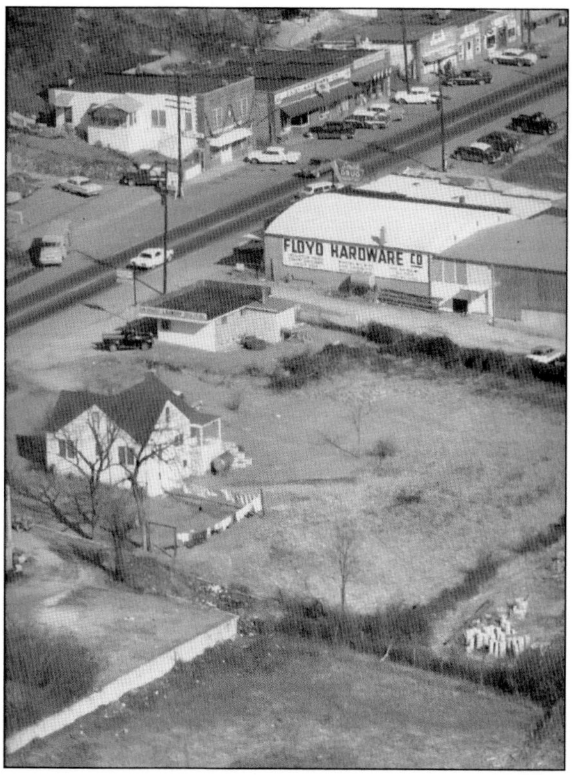

In this aerial shot of Daisy *c.* 1950, one can see Daisy Hardware and Floyd Hardware almost across the street from each other. Also visible are numerous automobiles, several other small stores across the street from Floyd Hardware, and a home with laundry hanging on the line to dry. (Courtesy of Rob Floyd.)

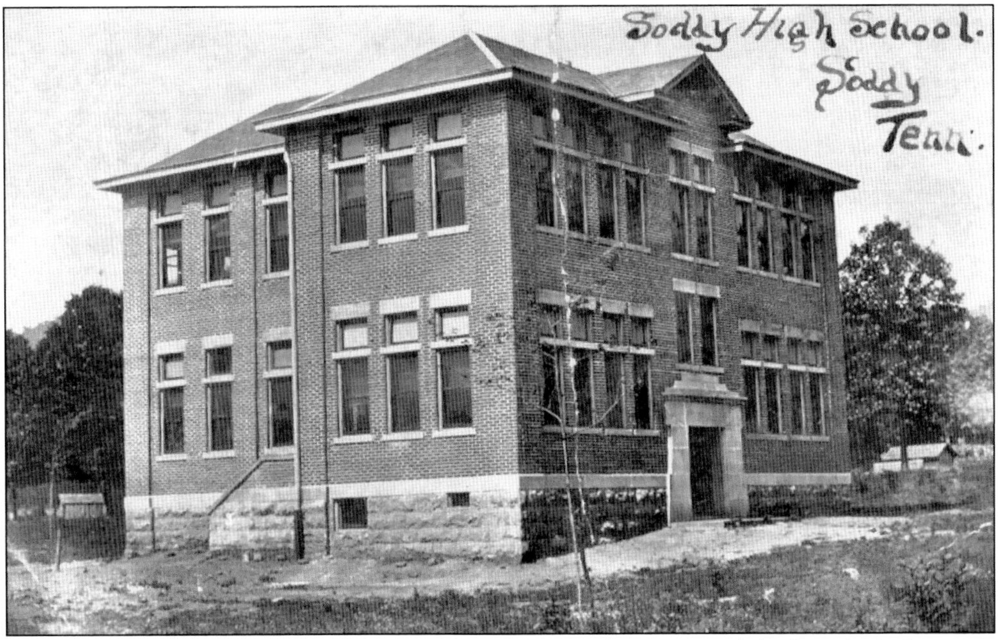

Public records by J. B. Brown, county superintendent and secretary of the board of education, indicate that the first high school in Soddy was to contain five recitation rooms, a basement, and assembly hall. It was also steam heated, which was quite modern for the time. The school opened on October 7, 1907, and the first graduating class was in 1909. The last class graduated from Soddy High School in 1936. (Courtesy of Scott Brogdon.)

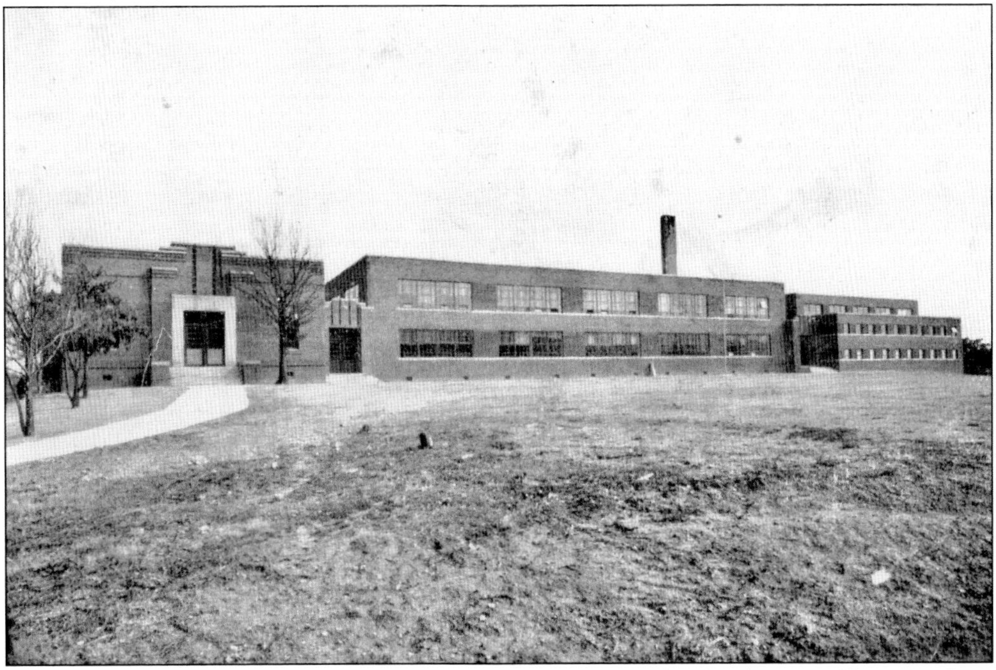

In 1937, students began attending the newly built Soddy-Daisy High School, pictured here. Students from Soddy and Daisy attended this high school until a new solar-savvy school was erected on Sequoyah Road and opened in the 1983–1984 school year. (Courtesy of Madge Lockhart.)

Two

FAMILIES, FRIENDS, AND NEIGHBORS

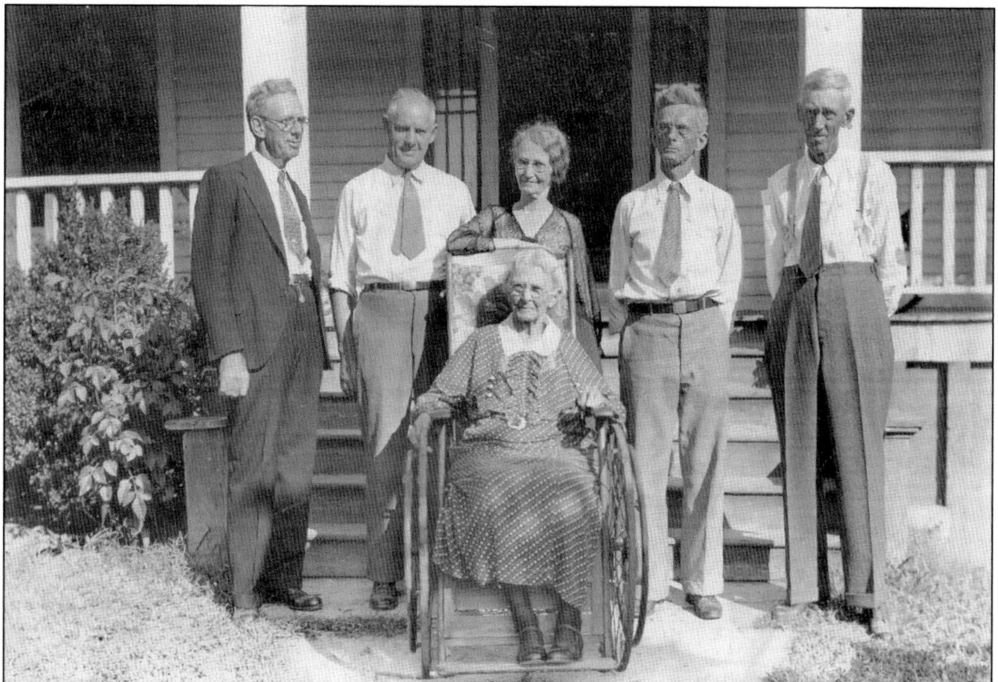

Mary Ann Varner Card, in the wheelchair, is surrounded by her living children. Standing from left to right are Walter, Warren, Marion, Lew, and Matthew. Mary Ann married Charles Card and was 100 years old when this photograph was taken in 1940. (Courtesy of Tom and Barbara Levi.)

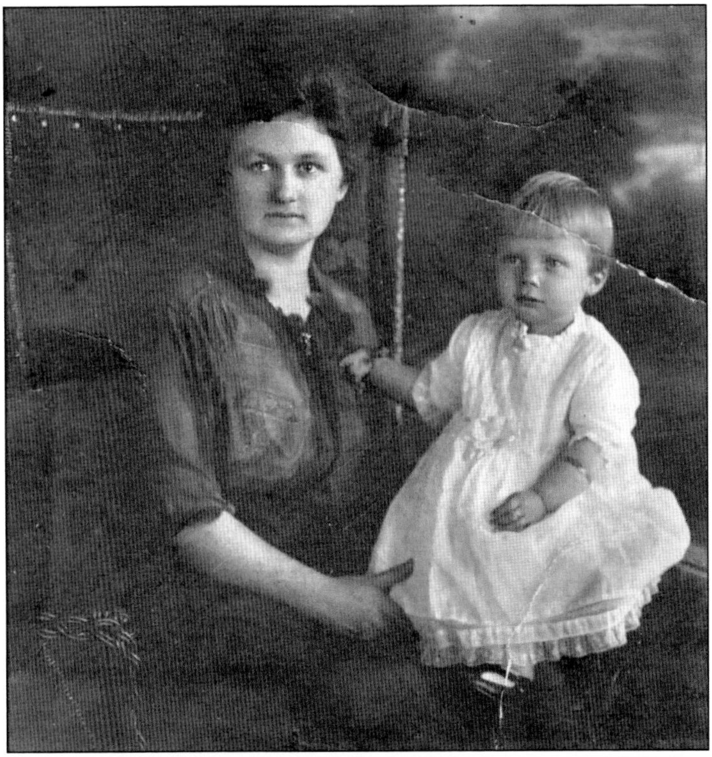

Marie Elizabeth Coleman sits on the lap of her mother, Maude Coleman, c. 1917. Though the family moved to Arkansas when Marie was young, they soon returned to Soddy. Marie was then raised by her aunt, Gertrude Coleman. Marie graduated from Soddy High School in the late 1930s and married Eugene Copeland on October 31, 1939. Eugene and Marie raised three children, Larry, Catherine, and Frank. (Courtesy of Frank and Donna Copeland.)

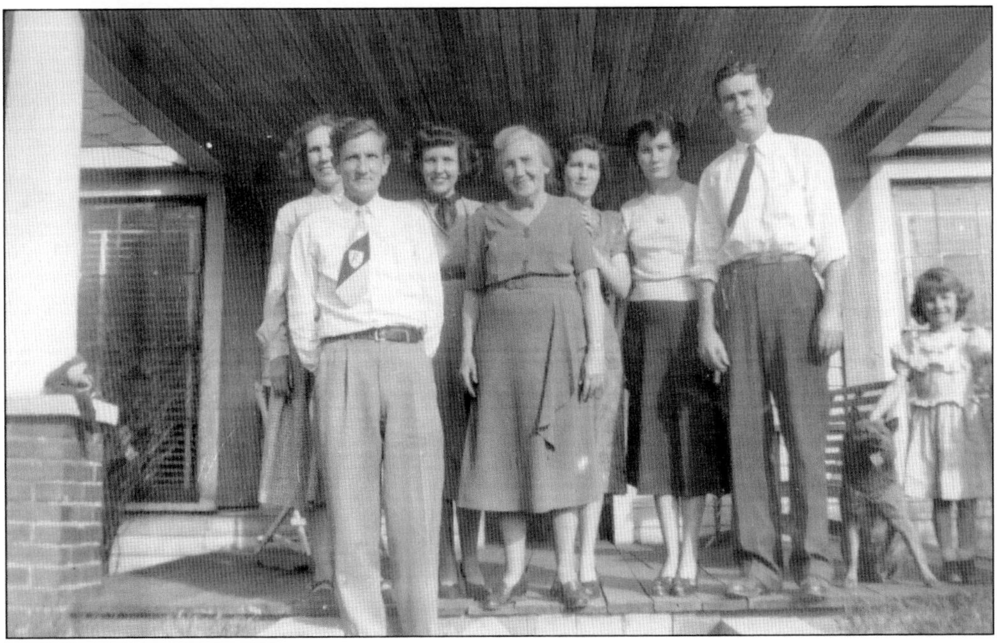

The Martin family gathers for a picture on the front porch, still a popular location for photographs as it was in the mid-20th century, when this was taken. From left to right are (first row) R. C. Martin, Lula Jane Martin, and Hugh Martin; (second row) Dorothy Martin Card, Sarah Martin Rigney, Ruth Martin Sanders, and Mary Edna Martin Clift. The little girl is Kay Martin. (Courtesy of Norris and Mary Clift.)

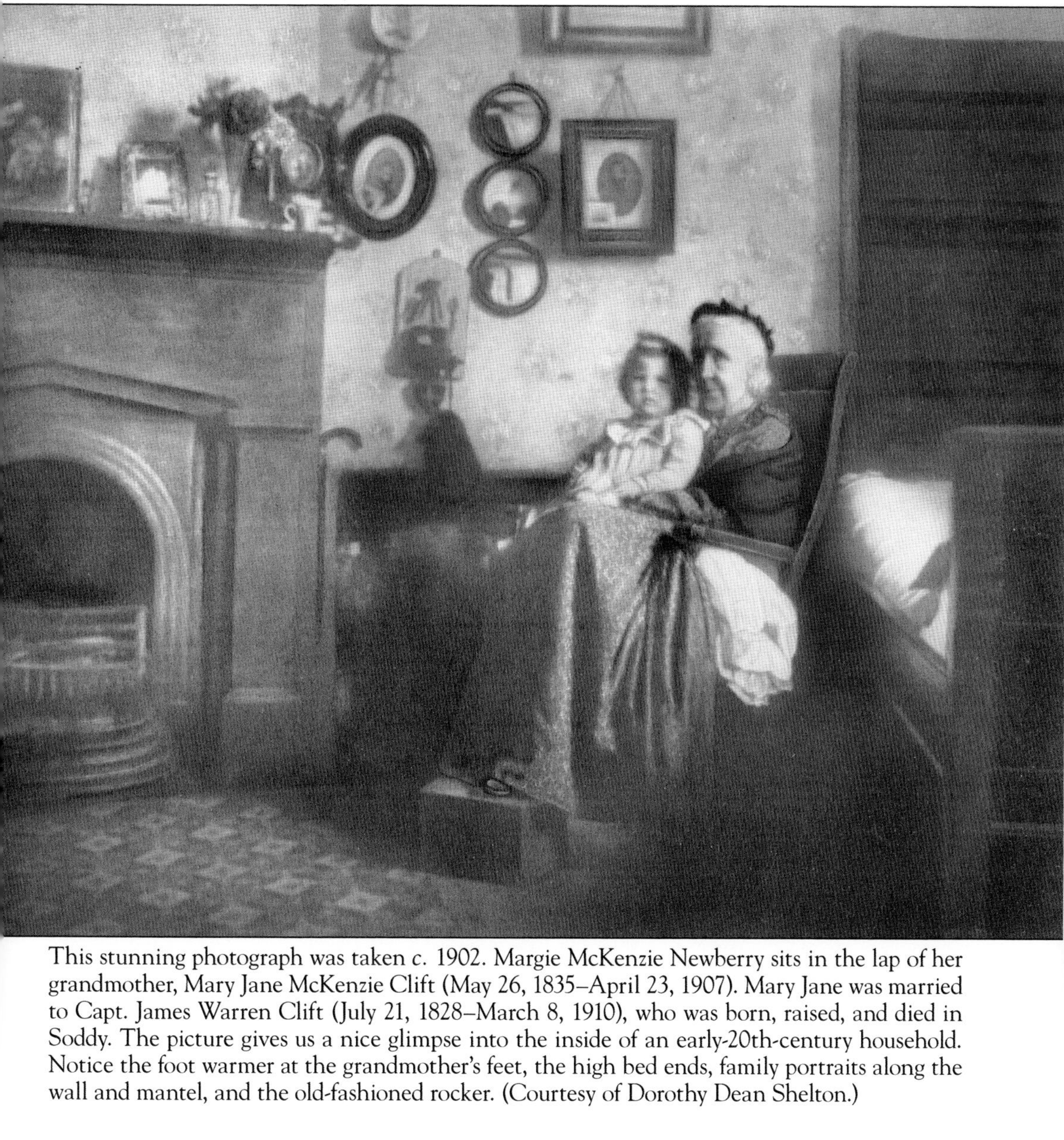

This stunning photograph was taken *c.* 1902. Margie McKenzie Newberry sits in the lap of her grandmother, Mary Jane McKenzie Clift (May 26, 1835–April 23, 1907). Mary Jane was married to Capt. James Warren Clift (July 21, 1828–March 8, 1910), who was born, raised, and died in Soddy. The picture gives us a nice glimpse into the inside of an early-20th-century household. Notice the foot warmer at the grandmother's feet, the high bed ends, family portraits along the wall and mantel, and the old-fashioned rocker. (Courtesy of Dorothy Dean Shelton.)

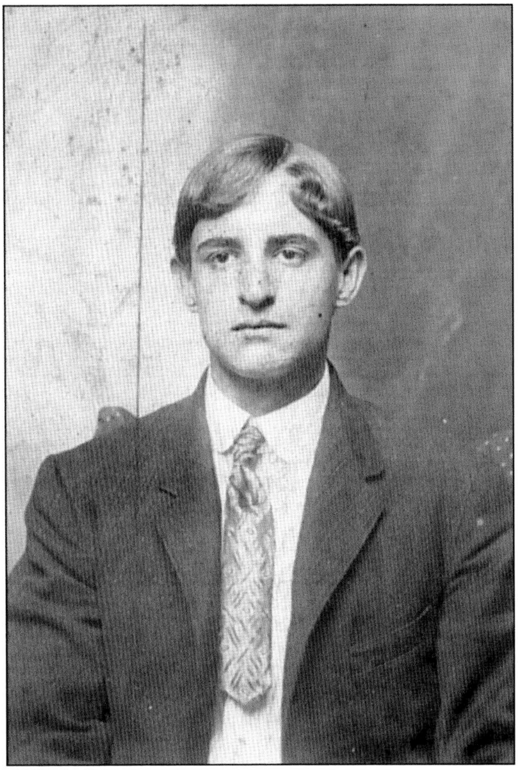

Edmund James Copeland Jr. was born in 1888. He had several jobs in the early 20th century, including working for the Durham Coal Company. Copeland traveled to Chicago during the Depression and worked as a telephone lineman. Then he returned to Soddy and retired from the Kingsboro Silk Mills. Copeland married Lena McGill (born 1893) and had several children: Eugene, Jim, Lorella, "Babe," and "Tootie." (Courtesy of Frank and Donna Copeland.)

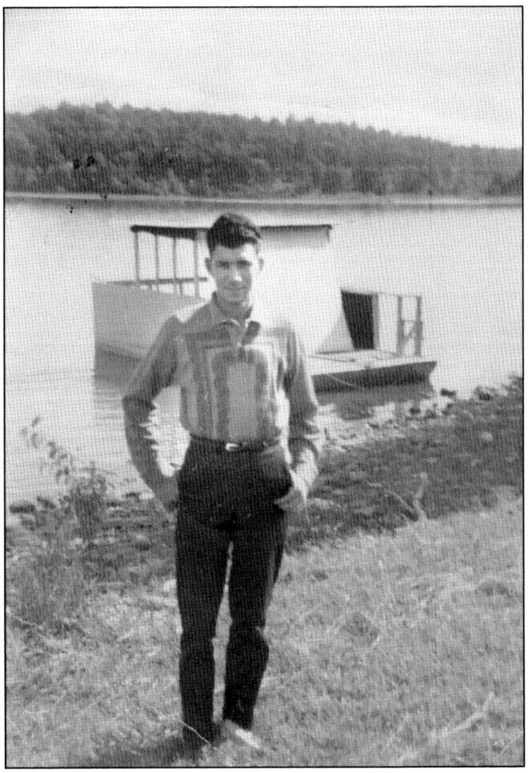

George Franklin Burton, 18, stands in front of Soddy Lake in August 1955. When George sent the film to be processed, it took longer than usual. George later found out the developer had been holding the print with hopes of using it in a photography contest. Notice the houseboat behind George. (Courtesy of Viola Burton.)

Viola Burton, age 19, holds her second child, George. Though her first child and two other babies died, Viola raised five other children, including George. Like many couples of the early to mid-20th century, Viola married young. She was only 15, and her husband, Herschel Burton, was 17. Viola finished school through the sixth grade and then cared for her home, husband, and children. (Courtesy of Viola Burton.)

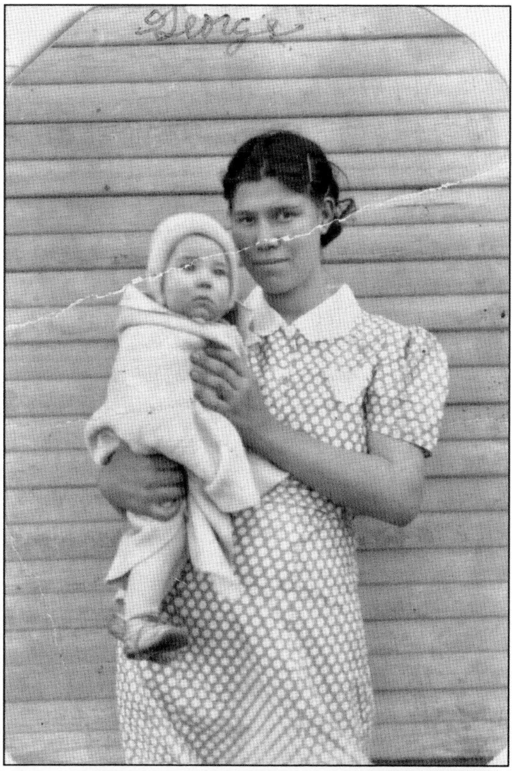

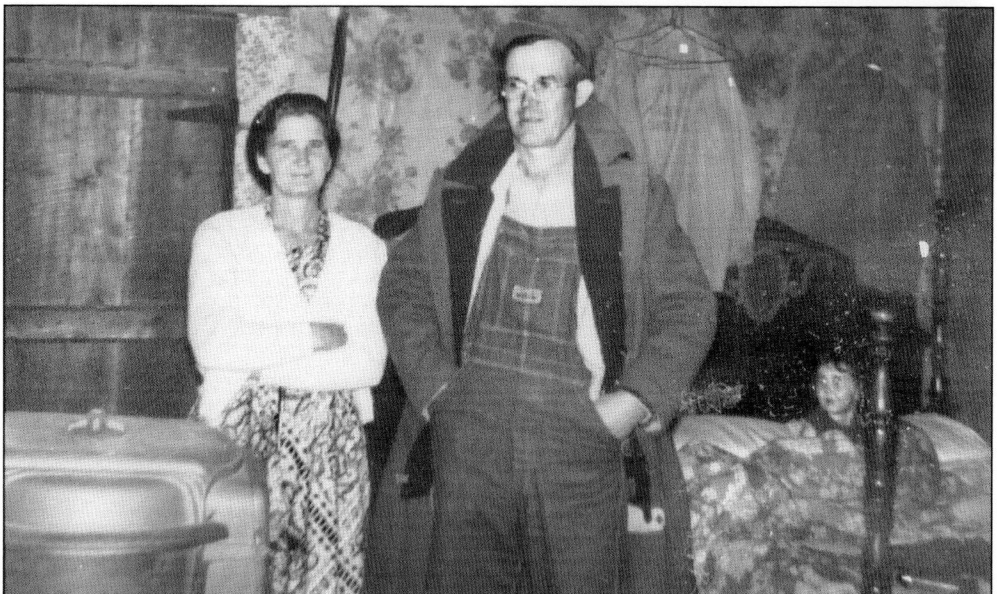

Pictured here c. 1957, Winnie Hendon Sutherland (May 13, 1913–August 9, 1998) and Luther Sutherland (April 10, 1911–October 14, 1980) raised seven children in their small home at Lewis' Chapel. Their children are: Linnie Mae (October 18, 1933–June 15, 2001), Wallace (July 16, 1935–August 25, 2002), Magaline, Anna Lee, Ellis, Ivan Edward (September 3, 1946–January 14, 1951), and Audrey Ellen (February 23, 1955–May 2, 1966). (From the authors' collection.)

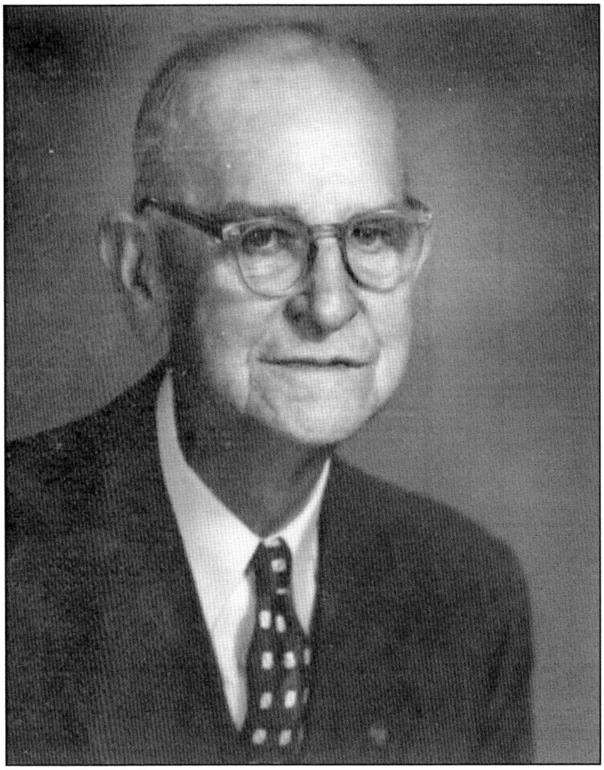

Thomas Henry Newberry was a merchant partner in Newberry-Denton General Store. During the early 20th century, miners frequently shopped at the store and kept a running line of credit. When the stock market crashed in 1929 and the Great Depression set in, many people were unable to pay their bills at the store. Newberry sold out his share and moved to Florida, but returned two years later to enjoy his remaining years in Soddy. (Courtesy of Dorothy Dean Shelton.)

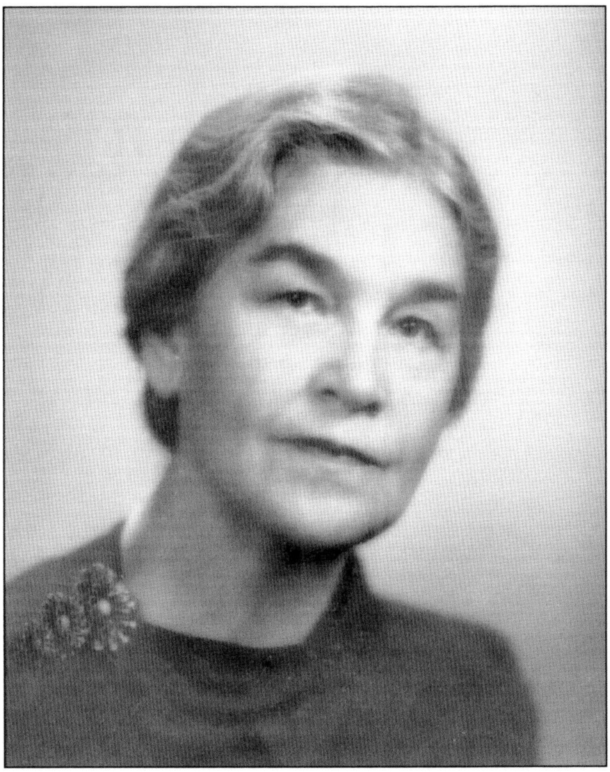

Aldine Clift (1873–1940) married Thomas Henry Newberry (1876–1955) in 1898. The couple had six children, but one died at seven years of age of pneumonia. After Aldine graduated from Soddy High School and married Thomas, she took care of her home and family and was active in the Soddy Presbyterian Church. (Courtesy of Dorothy Dean Shelton.)

Mary Ann Varner was the mother of several young children during the Civil War. When Yankees came through the area and confiscated cattle, produce, and other items from local residents, one of Mary's older sons hid in an apple tree. Since he refused to obey the Union soldiers' order to get down, they shot him, and he died. Mary Ann is shown here c. 1930. She died in 1942 at the age of 102. (Courtesy of Tom and Barbara Levi.)

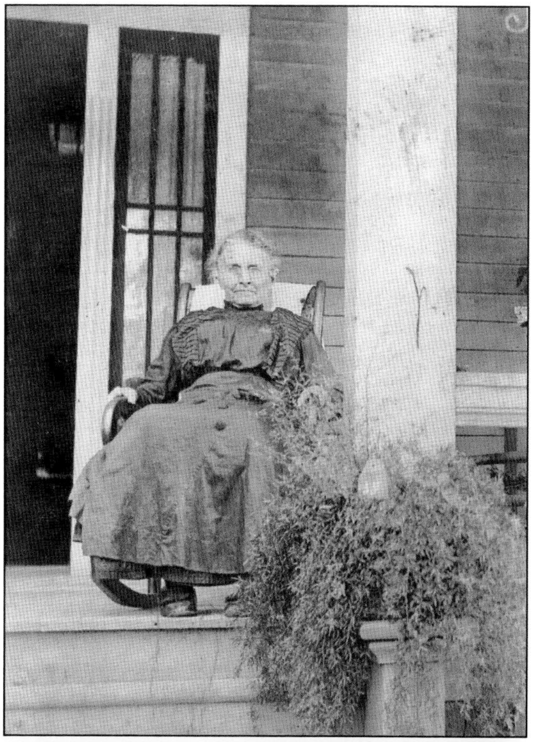

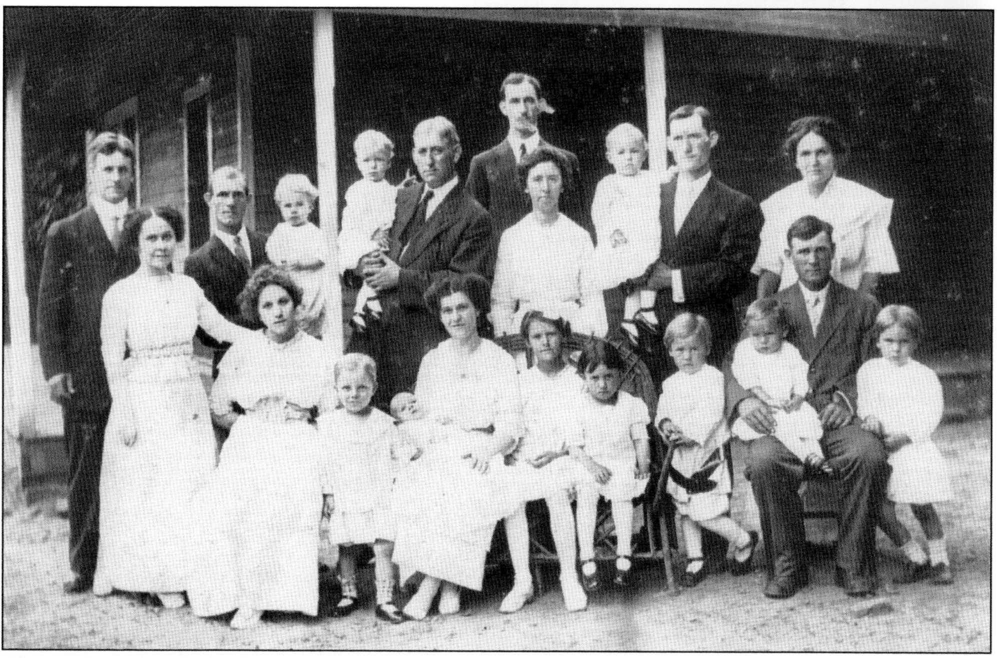

The McRee family had several youngsters added to the family within a few years, making this family portrait particularly special, since the little ones' facial expressions and clothing are now forever preserved. Among the family members in this c. 1914 photograph are Mr. and Mrs. Joe Dick, Arthur Brooks McRee Sr., Arthur Brooks McRee Jr., Gertie McRee, and Dick Boling. (Courtesy of A. B. and Frankie McRee.)

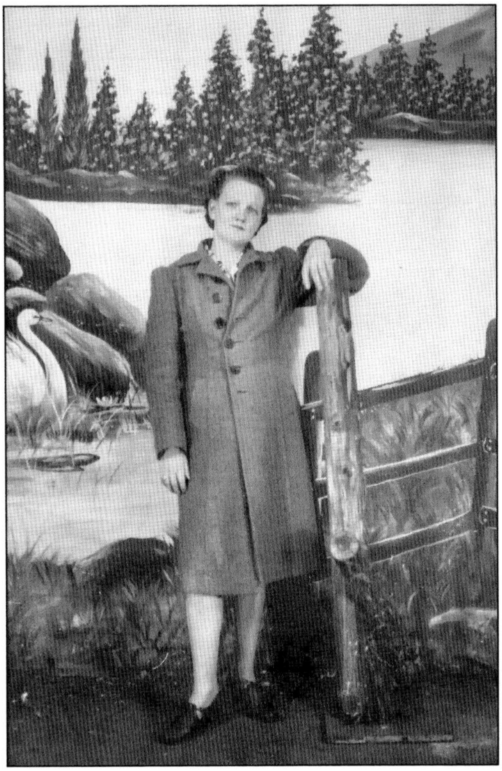

Bonnie I. Sneed Cothran is pictured here c. 1940 in a portrait studio set-up that was common in the mid-20th century. This studio was probably in Chattanooga. Bonnie was married to Walter E. Cothran, and the couple had five children: Frankie, Ruby, Clara, Nancy, and Robert. (Courtesy of David and Clara Bowman.)

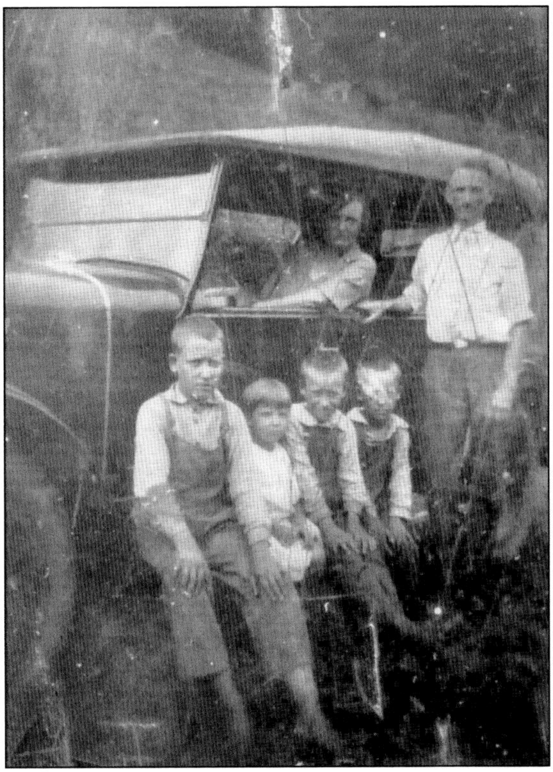

Bert Crites stands beside the car while his wife Nora Norris Crites sits inside. The Crites' children from left to right are Elmer Bert, Ruth Ann, Ray, and Roy. Though it appears that Nora is sitting on the driver's side, this is a tintype and the image is reversed, so she really is sitting in the passenger seat. (Courtesy of Scott Brogdon.)

Ruth Etta Elliott (October 17, 1927–August 9, 2004) was approximately 15 years old when this photograph was taken. Ruth attended Soddy-Daisy High School and eloped with Frank Schmid Jr. when she was 16. The couple had two children, William Lee and Mary Elizabeth, and many years later proudly celebrated their 50th wedding anniversary. For 30 years, Ruth worked at the Hamilton County Courthouse as a supervisor in the clerk's office. (Courtesy of Tom and Barbara Levi.)

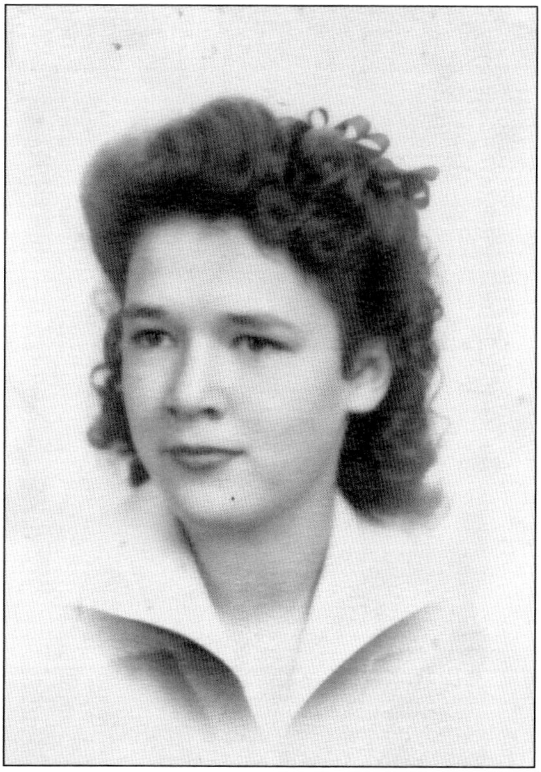

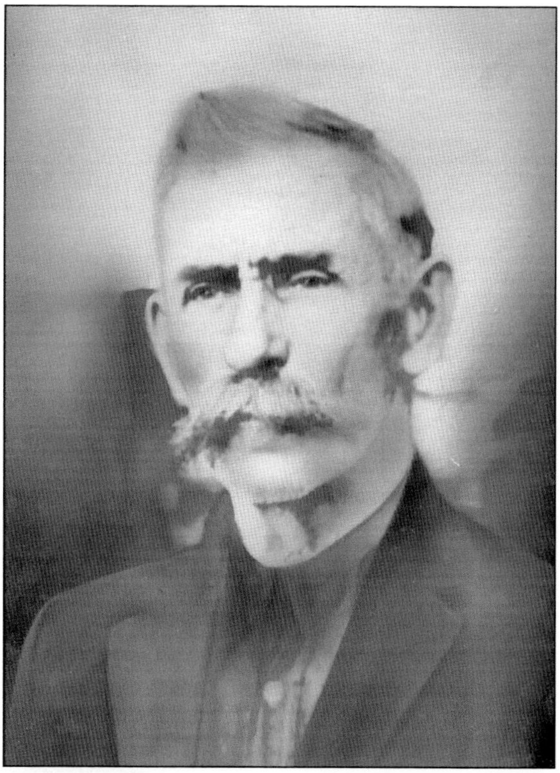

Andy Clayton (1845–1929) was a coal miner of Welsh descent. Clayton immigrated to the United States from Wales with 15 or 20 other families in the late 1860s. The settlers came to the region to find coal-mining work. Clayton and his wife told their children and grandchildren about seeing their "first horseless carriage" in Chattanooga in the late 19th century. (Courtesy of Rosa Lee Hambrick.)

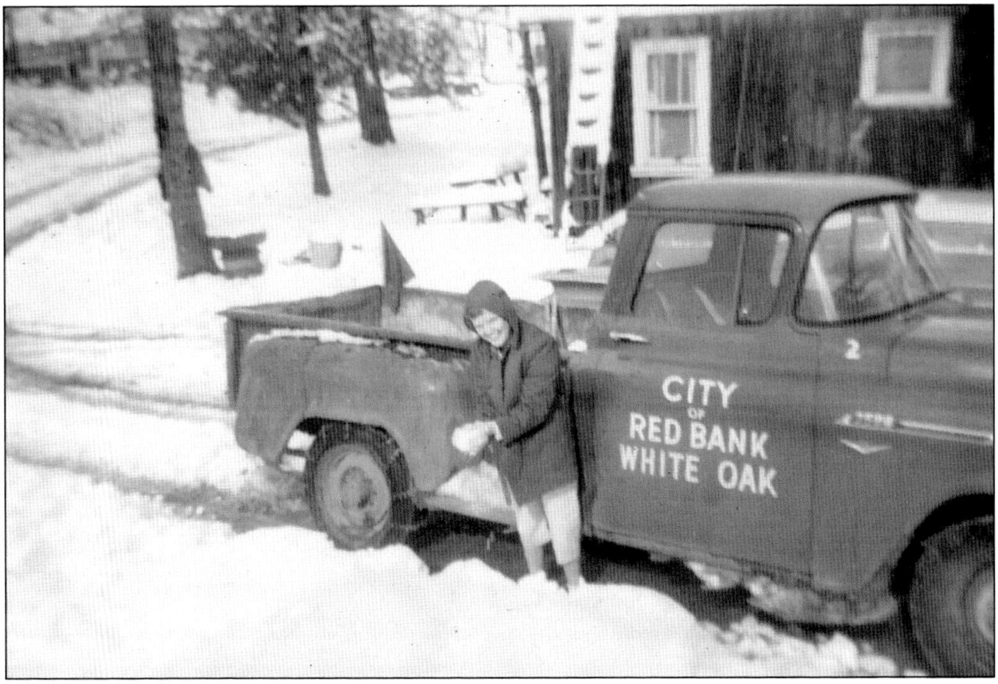

Clara Cothran Brown makes snowballs in front of a city truck during the big ice storm of March 1960. There were people in the area, particularly on the mountain, who were without electricity for three weeks due to this debilitating storm. Clara's husband, Elmer Clay Brown Sr., was a grader for the City of Red Bank/White Oak. (Courtesy of David and Clara Bowman.)

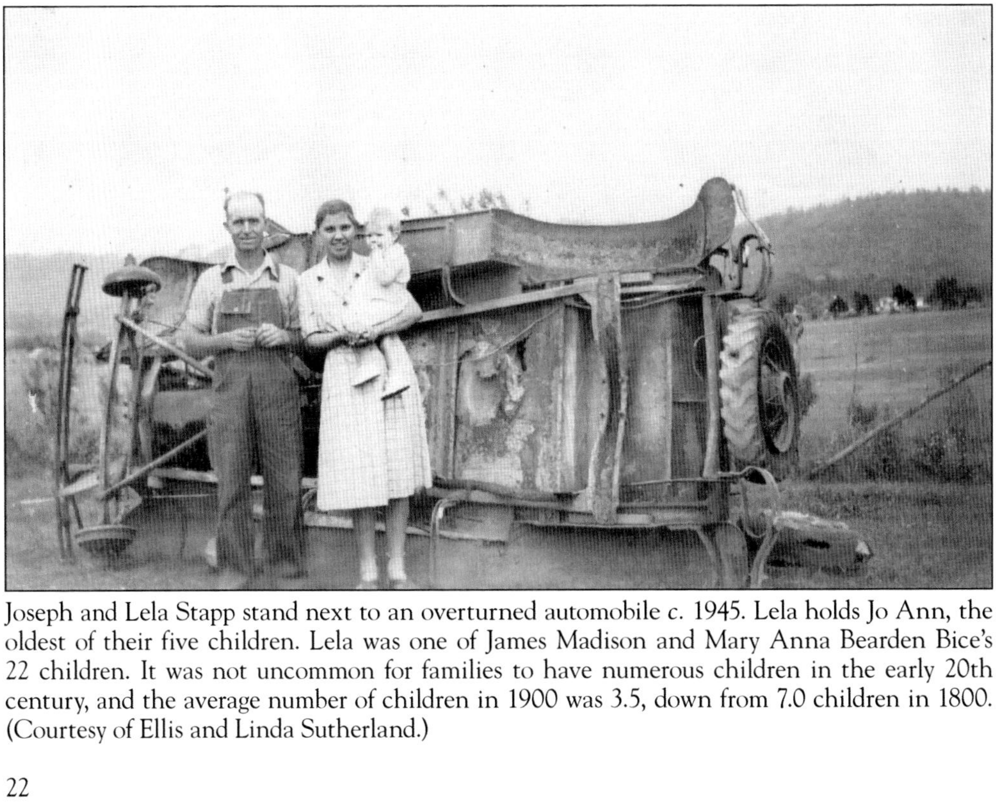

Joseph and Lela Stapp stand next to an overturned automobile c. 1945. Lela holds Jo Ann, the oldest of their five children. Lela was one of James Madison and Mary Anna Bearden Bice's 22 children. It was not uncommon for families to have numerous children in the early 20th century, and the average number of children in 1900 was 3.5, down from 7.0 children in 1800. (Courtesy of Ellis and Linda Sutherland.)

John Monroe Hawkins (1905–1976) and Willie Mae Elder (1909–1969) were walking on Market Street in Chattanooga when a street photographer snapped this photograph *c.* 1937. John and Willie Mae were both married previously and had a combination of seven children, including a baby who died when only 10 hours old. The family is proud of its Native American heritage, as Willie Mae's grandmother was a full-blooded Cherokee. (Courtesy of Ronnie "Hawkeye" Hawkins.)

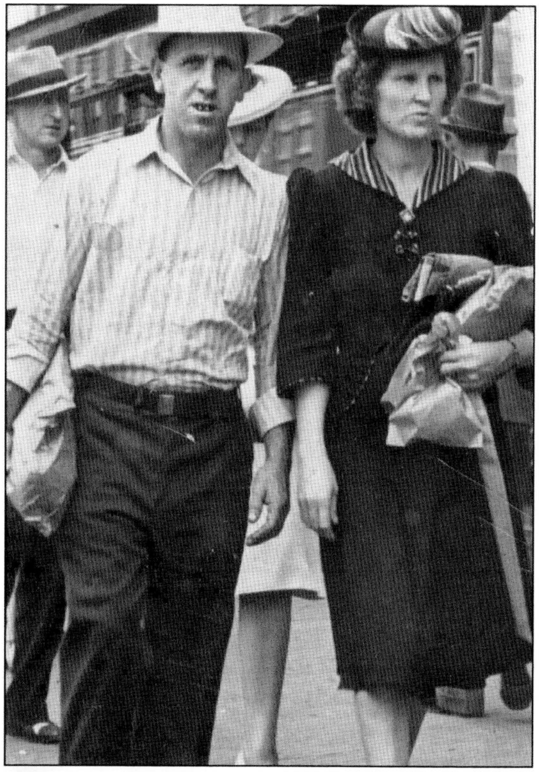

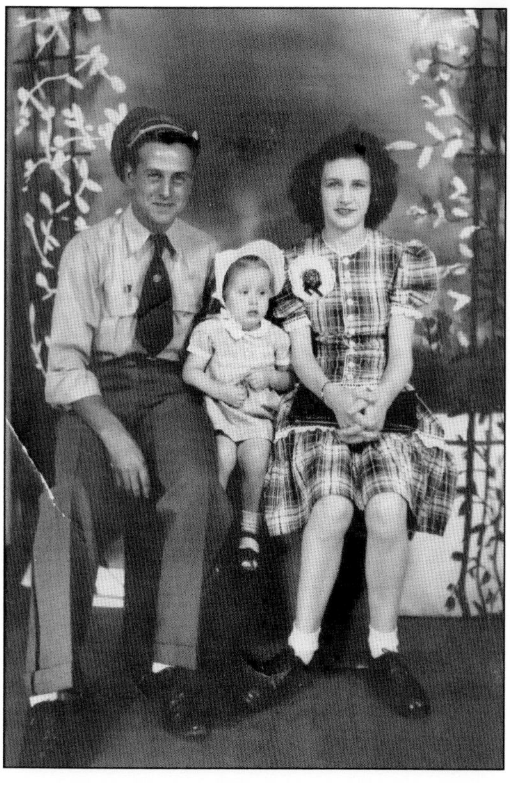

When Ken Lovelady was 15 and Dorothy was 16, they traveled to Georgia to be married by a justice of the peace. To maintain their household, Ken drove a commuter bus into Chattanooga in the morning, drove a tractor trailer during the day, and drove the last commuter bus load out in the evening. Ken is pictured here in his bus uniform with Dorothy and their first child, Linda. (Courtesy of Ellis and Linda Sutherland.)

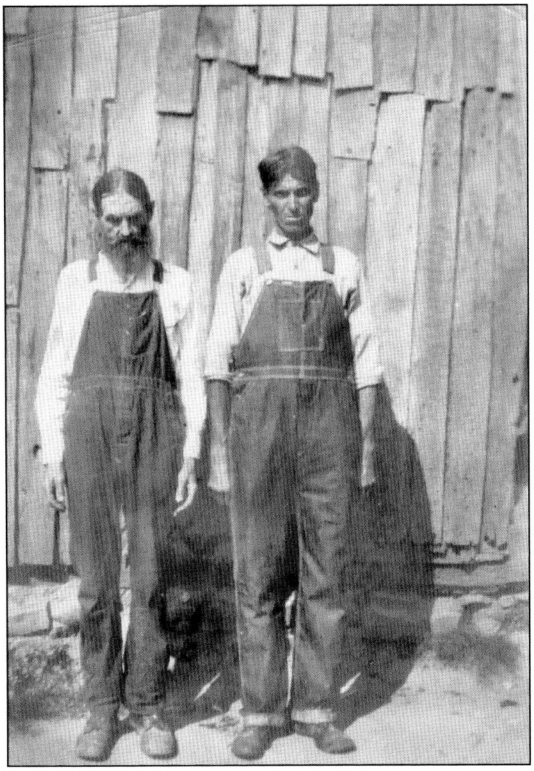

Henry Swagner (left) stands with his son, Martin, probably in front of a barn or other building on their homestead on Raven's Cliff in the early 20th century. Martin Swagner (December 16, 1880–April 20, 1971) married Lizzie Turner (December 21, 1884–December 14, 1968), and the couple had 13 children: girls Lelies, Marty, Nora, Bessie, and Ellen, boys Azberry, Joe, Johnnie, and Victor, and four children who died at an early age. (From the authors' collection.)

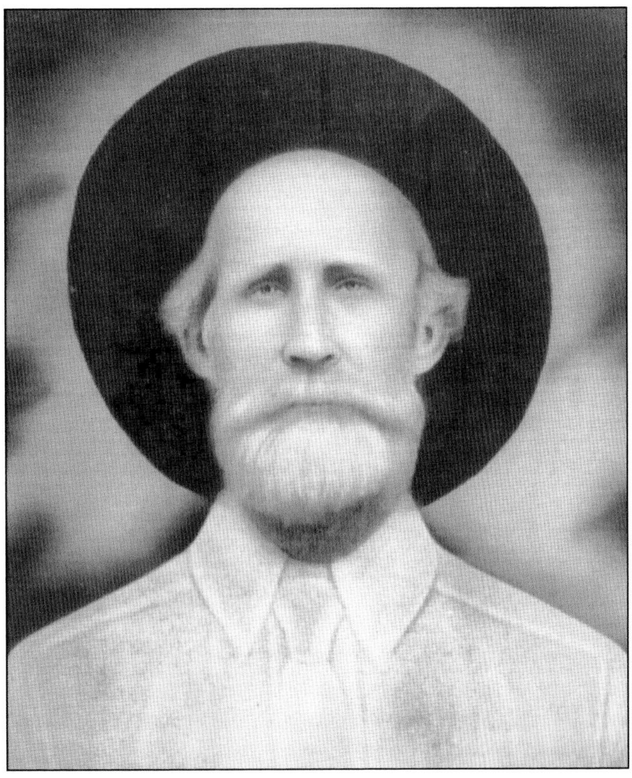

James "Perk" Sutherland (1851–1918) married Mary Keedy (1859–1926). The couple had 11 children: Jim, George, John, Loy, Arthur, Janie, Annie, Gertie, Fred, Emma, and Will. (Courtesy of Ellis and Linda Sutherland.)

Rosella Marie Lovelady (1920–2005) married Joseph Theodore Neighbors and raised three sons: James, Jerry, and Danny. The couple also had a son, Joseph, who was stillborn. Rosella lived with her family behind Lometa's Florist in Daisy. She retired from 3M Manufacturing in Chattanooga. Fortunately for those interested in the past, Rosella preserved history by keeping a lot of family photographs and even recording extensive notes. (Courtesy of Ellis and Linda Sutherland.)

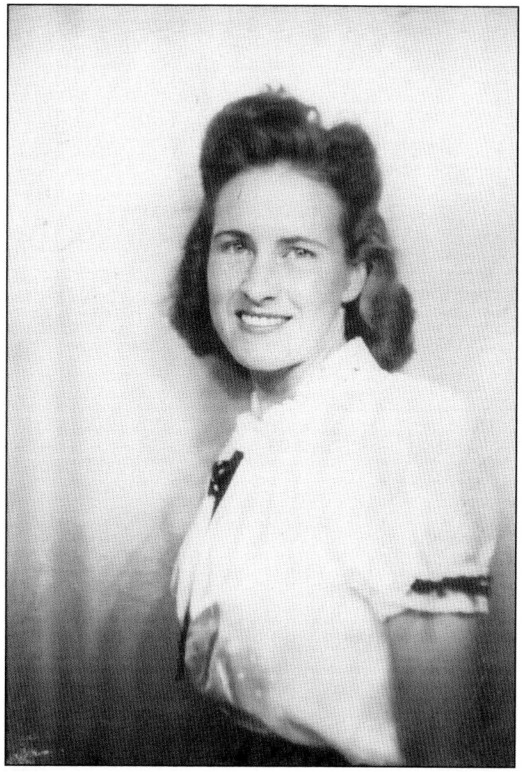

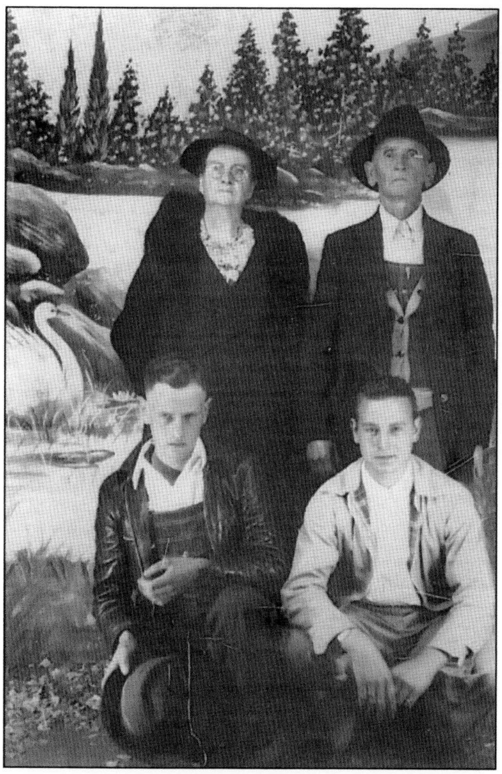

Pictured here from left to right are (first row) Sevier Lovelady and Prior "Ken" Lovelady, and (second row) Cora Bell Curtis Lovelady and Daniel Adam Lovelady. The back of this photograph contains a note addressed to Sevier that says, "This was made in January 1943. Mama sent it . . . thought you would have to go in service also. That is why everyone looks so sad." (Courtesy of Ellis and Linda Sutherland.)

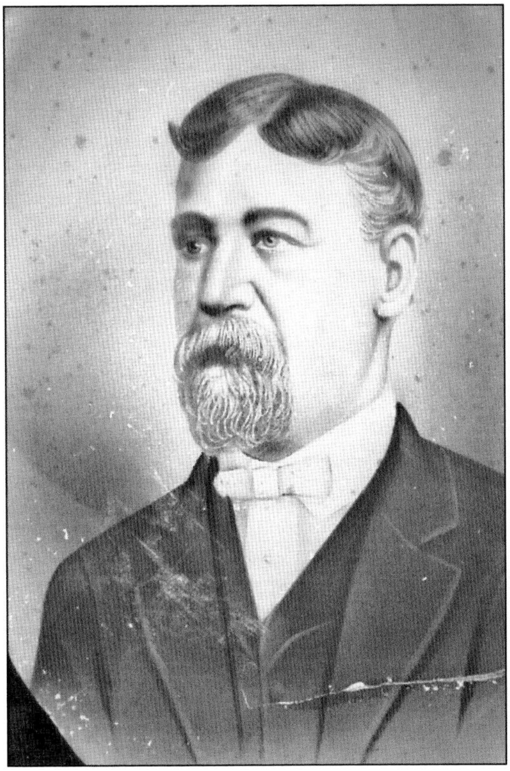

Edmund James Copeland Sr. was born in Wales in 1853 and immigrated to the United States in 1894. After living in Pennsylvania and Whitwell, Copeland moved to Soddy, where he worked for Durham Coal Company. Edmund was a troop leader (chief officer) in the Soddy lodge of the Improved Order of the Red Man, which was like a Masonic organization. (Courtesy of Frank and Donna Copeland.)

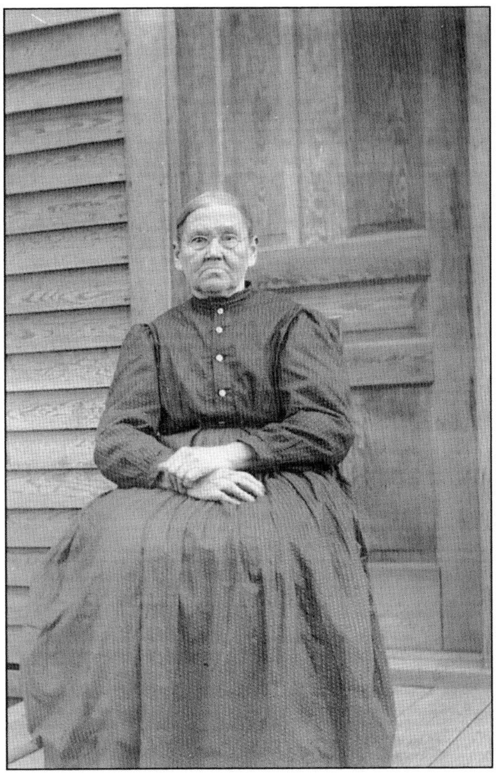

Rebecca Lewis Lovelady was born January 28, 1839, and died January 29, 1927. She married James Lovelady (1835–February 13, 1898) and the couple raised six children on Mowbray Mountain. Their children are William, Lewis, John, Fannie, Sarah, and Daniel. (Courtesy of Ellis and Linda Sutherland.)

Dale Brown Price, who went by "D. B.," worked as a railroad depot agent for the Southern Railroad in Soddy. Price sent messages for people by telegraph since the Western Union was located in the depot. Amazingly he worked for the railroad for 50 years without missing a day of work. (Courtesy of Tom and Barbara Levi.)

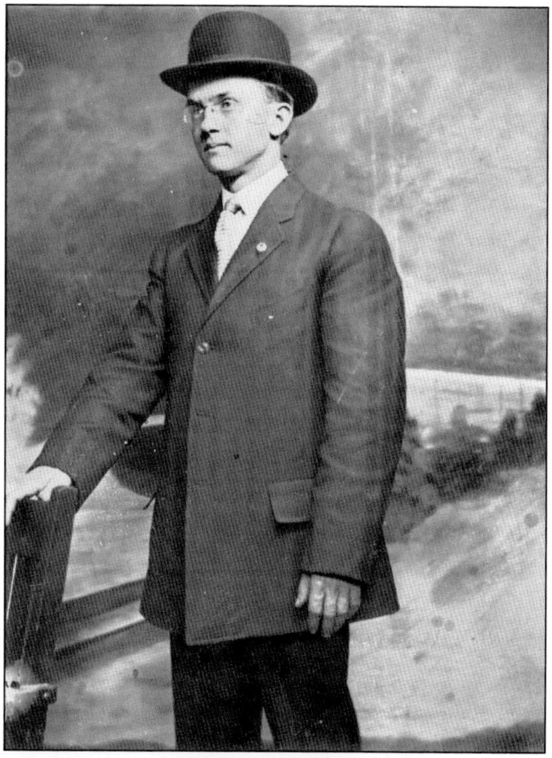

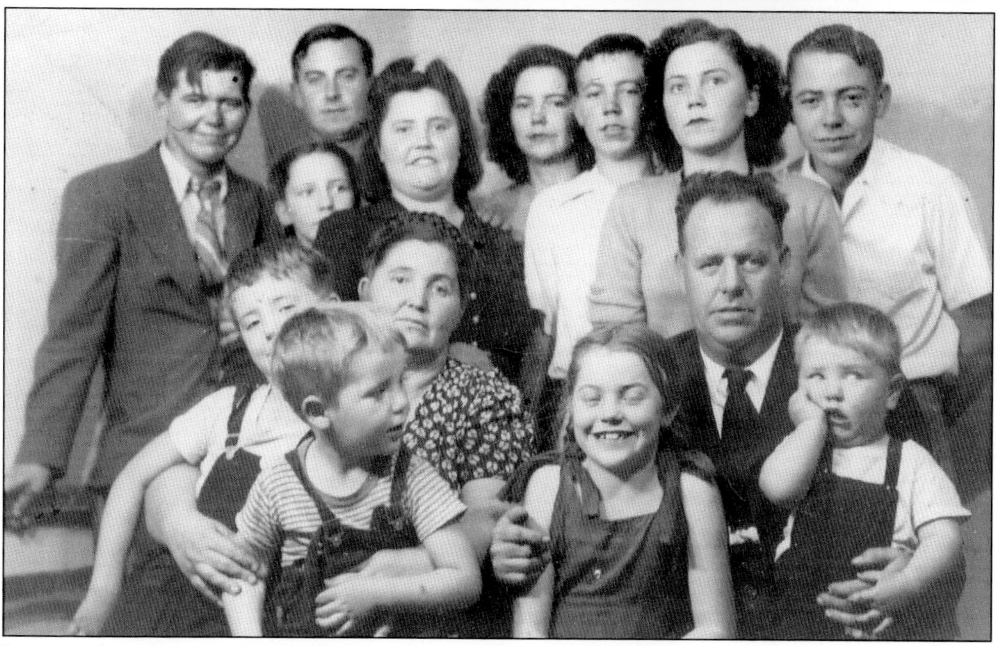

James Arlie Clements (1902–1966) and Leva Ollie Sparks (1904–1988) were married on July 4, 1919. The couple raised 12 children, with whom they are pictured here. The children, in order of birth, are Madge Pauline, Charles Wallace, George Dean, Betty June, Shirley Belle, Benny Ray, James Arlie Jr., Dorothy Arada, Rosalie Lane, John Flavius, Jerry Sparks, and Larry Lloyd. (Courtesy of Tom and Barbara Levi.)

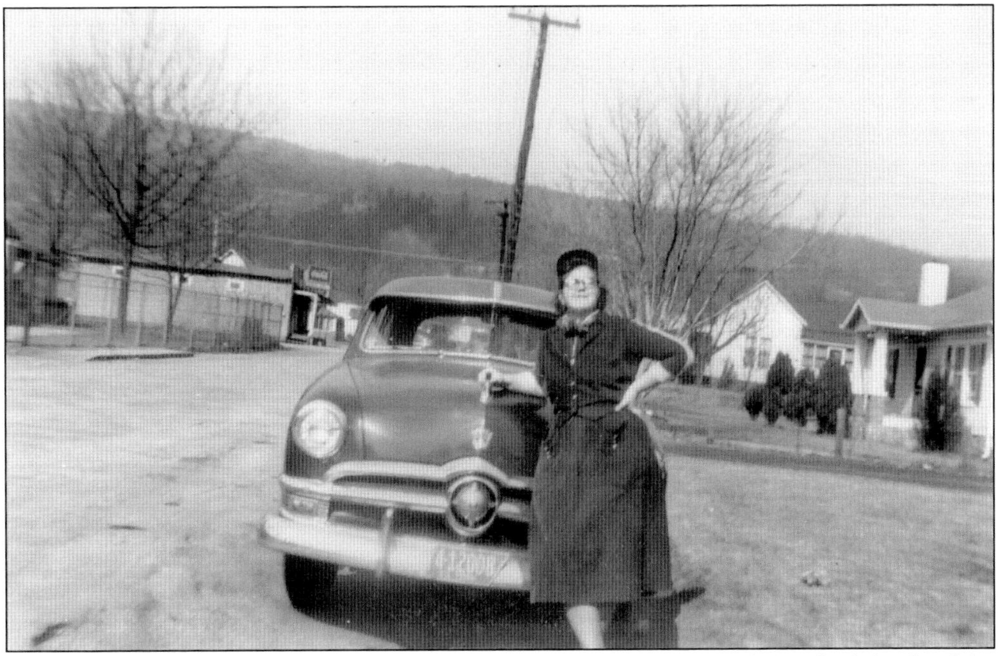

Doris Rogers, who passed away in 2000, stands beside her dad's 1950 Ford. On the left side of the photograph in the background, one can see the side of Neely's Grocery, where residents could purchase food, material, animal feed, candy, and other sorts of general store items. (Courtesy of Kay Rogers Williams.)

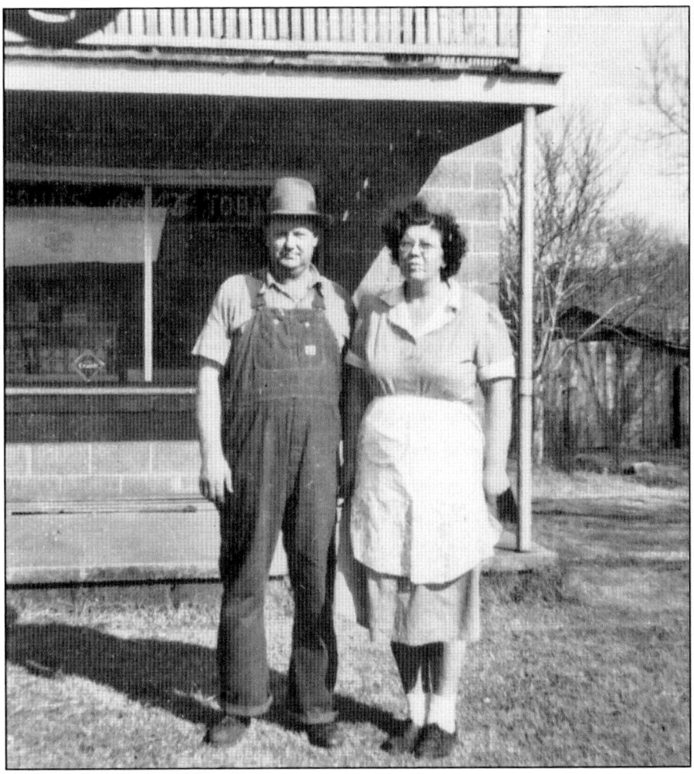

After their marriage in 1930, Jonah and Estelle Rogers moved into a small tar-paper shack on the grounds of Kingsboro Silk Mills. The couple had three children. Jonah started building a house on Bean Street and the family moved into their new home around 1946, shortly after World War II. It was only a couple of years later that Jonah opened Rogers' Grocery. (Courtesy of Kay Rogers Williams.)

According to an article in the *Chattanooga Times* dated March 13, 1947, Walter (January 20, 1909–August 13, 1963) and Lelies Swanger Johnson (November 16, 1908–July 5, 1985) were among the first families to have electricity in the Mowbray community. The article stated, "Electric power lines brought lights and radios and other twentieth century devices to make this winter a memorable one for the remote community." (Courtesy of Vivian Gamble.)

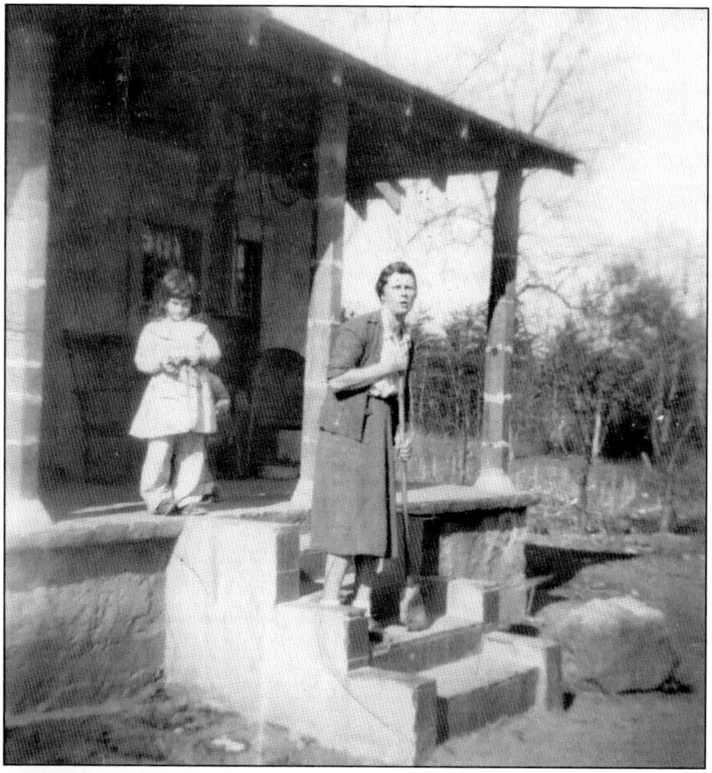

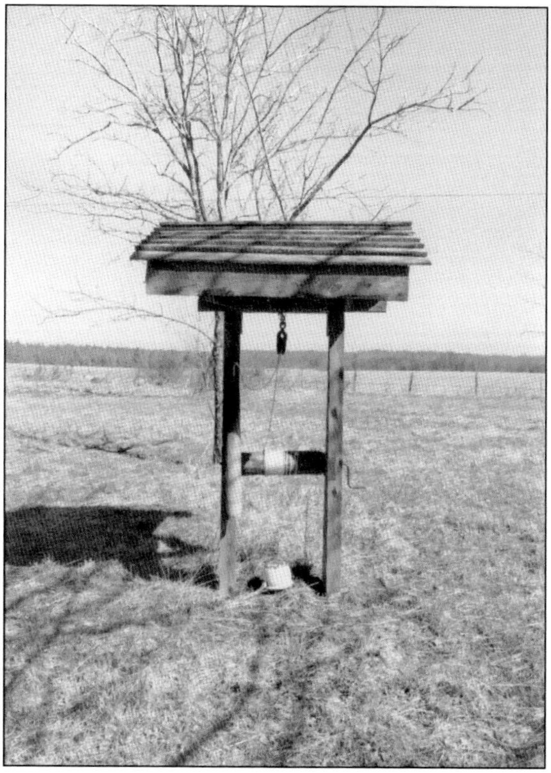

In the top photograph, Lelies Johnson sweeps her front porch, while her daughter Genevieve observes. Lelies had 13 children in their three-room (kitchen, living room, and bedroom) house. Since they had no indoor plumbing, the family used an outhouse, and a well like the one shown at left was the family's water source. Hanging to the left, you can barely see the metal container that was dropped in to obtain water. (From the authors' collection.)

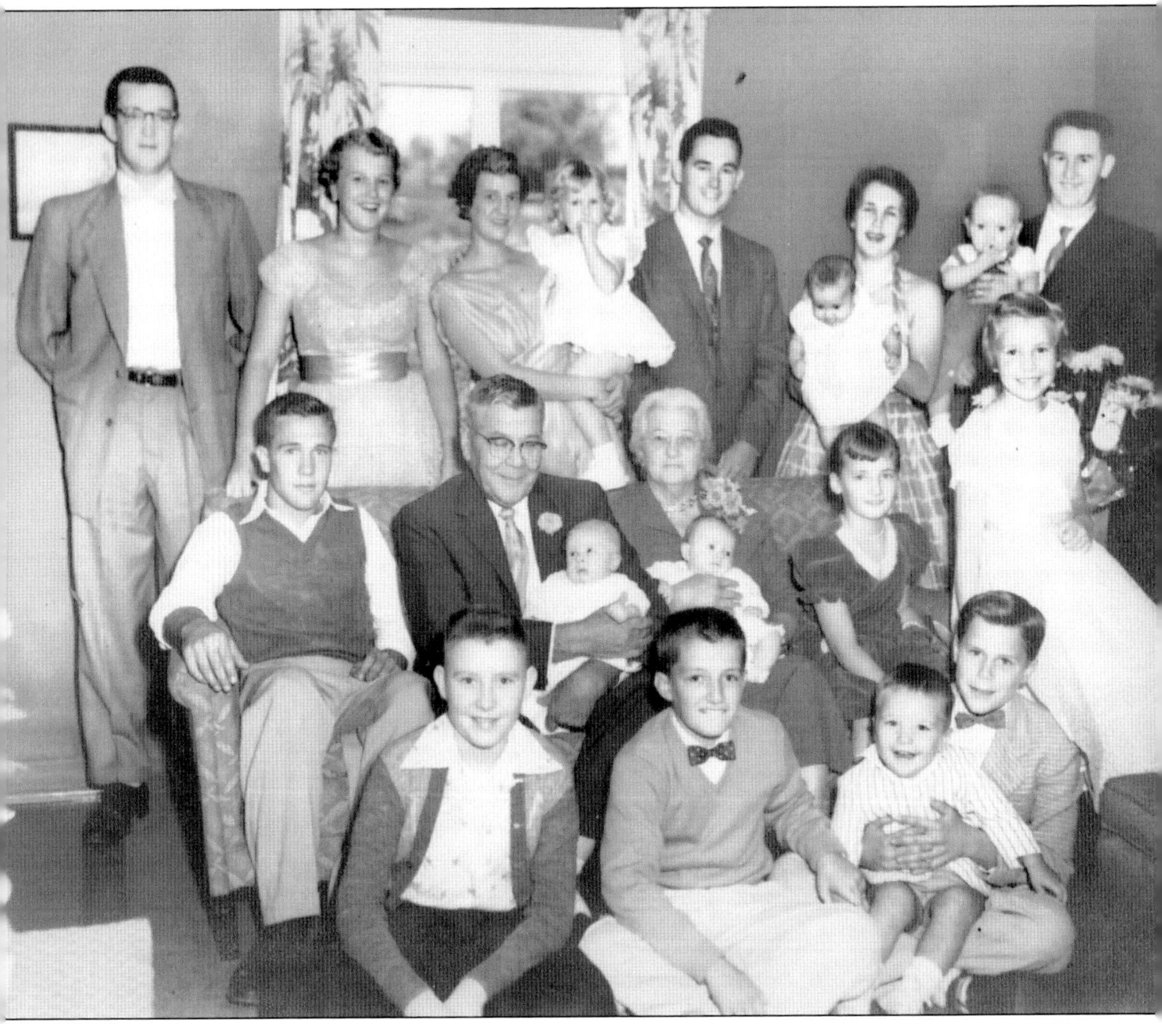

Joseph Benjamin (J. B.) Elliott and Gussie Hallett Elliott were married October 3, 1906. Here they celebrate their 50th anniversary in 1956 surrounded by family. From left to right are (first row) Jack Elliott, Billy Schmid, Greg Levi, and Morris Elliott; (second row) Carlos Don Elliott, J. B. Elliott (holding Sam Elliott), Gussie Hallett Elliott (holding Karen McRee), Mary Schmid, and Mary Elliott; (third row) Gene Elliott, Martha McRee, Mary Jo West (holding Mary Ellen West), A. B. McRee, Barbara Elliott Levi (holding Kristi Levi), and Jimmy McRee (holding Joe McRee). (Courtesy of Tom and Barbara Levi; photograph by Southland Studio.)

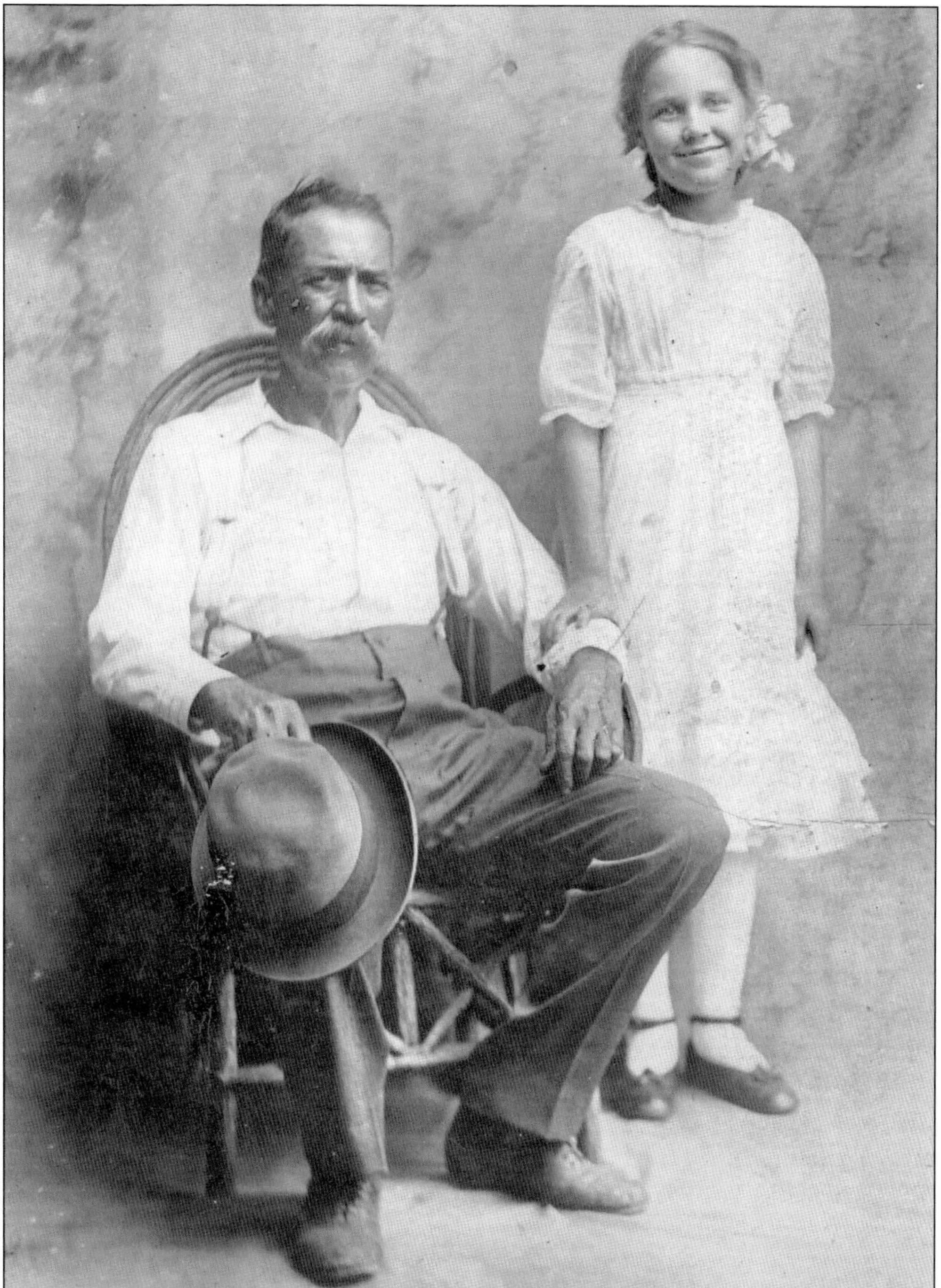

Rachel Burns is shown here with her grandfather, Joe Elliott. The family had moved to Soddy from Copperhill, where copper ore had been discovered in the 1820s. The area had the largest metal-mining operation in the southeastern United States until 1987. Due to over-mining and irresponsible mining behavior, thousands of acres were killed by acid rain. As an adult, Rachel married Ansel Jordan. (Courtesy of Tom and Barbara Levi.)

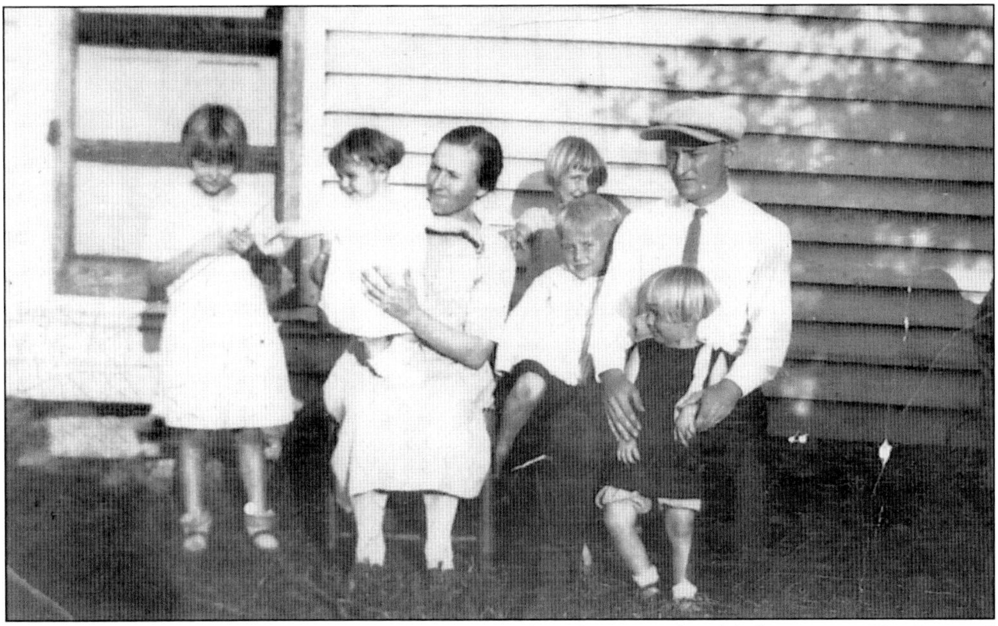

Ira (1898–1943) and Molly (1899–1994) Lively lived in the part of Soddy known as "Ducktown." The couple had 10 children, but one died at nine months of age, and a daughter, Anna Lee, died of Bright's disease when she was four. Ira and Molly are shown here with (left to right) Martha Louise, Anna Lee, Frances Lucille, James Thomas, and Rosa Lee. (Courtesy of Rosa Lee Hambrick.)

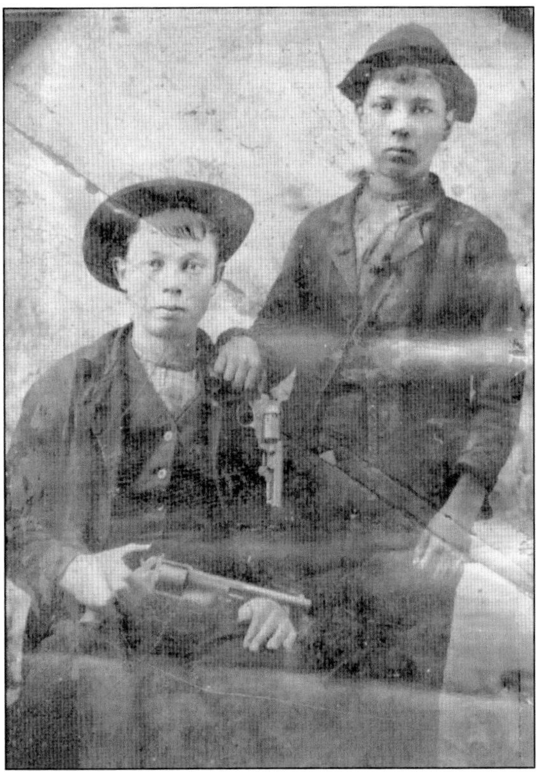

Tom Jacob Levi (seated) is captured in this tintype c. 1870 with his brother, Richard Brooks Levi. Since even young boys helped support the family during the late 19th century, it is likely that Tom had either already begun working in the coal mine or did soon after this was taken. After he retired from mining, Tom served as a janitor for Soddy Elementary. (Courtesy of Tom and Barbara Levi.)

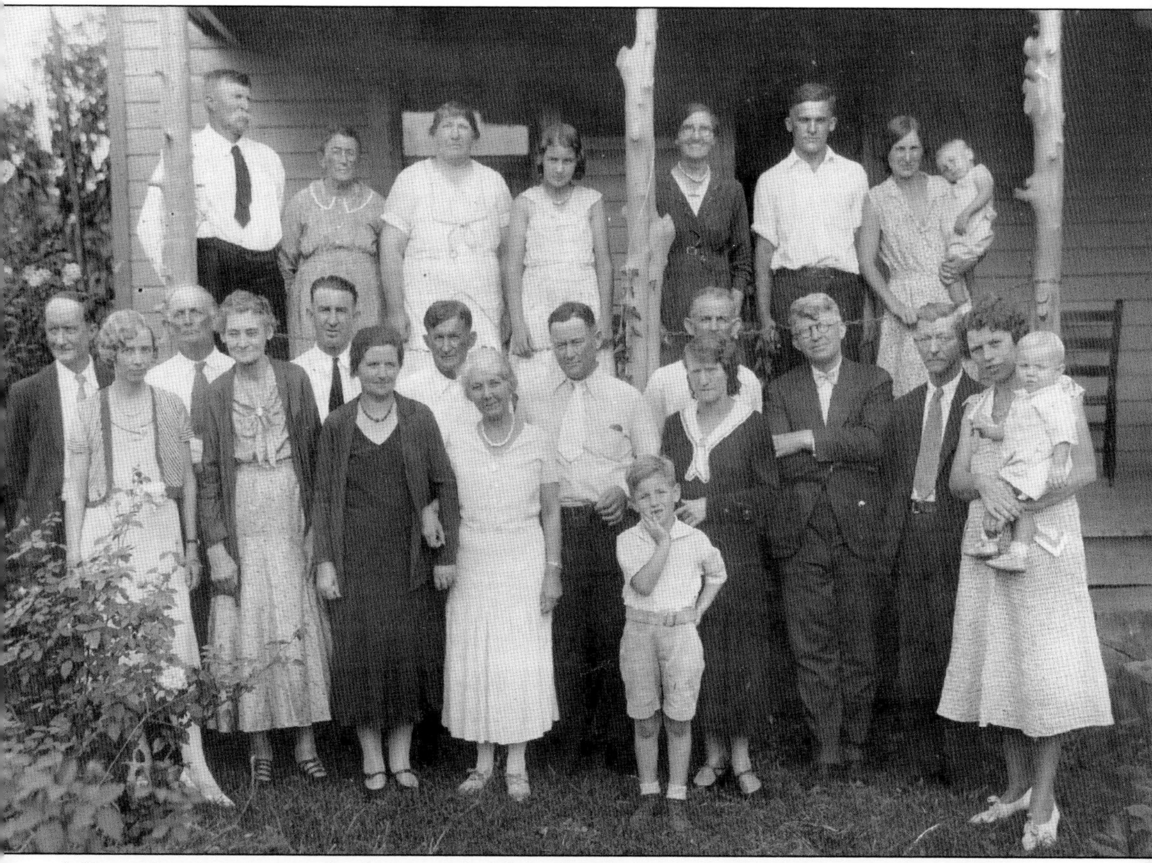

A Daisy family poses on the front porch of the family home on Bean Street in the summer of 1932. Pictured here from left to right are (first row) Mrs. Eichorn, Mrs. Johnson, Mrs. Davenport, Edith Poe, John Jim Lewis, and unidentified; (second row) George Eichorn, Lyle Johnson, Jim Lewis, Ro Martin, Doc Richie, Sam Miller, Preacher Davenport, Bert Poe, and Georgia Lewis (holding Earnie Lewis); (third row) John Smith, Mary Smith, Ora Smith, Agnes Lewis, Clementine Smith Miller Hensley, and three unidentified people. Notice that though the house looks rather modern with siding and glass windows, the front porch poles are unfinished wooden logs. (Courtesy of Bill and Patsy Hensley.)

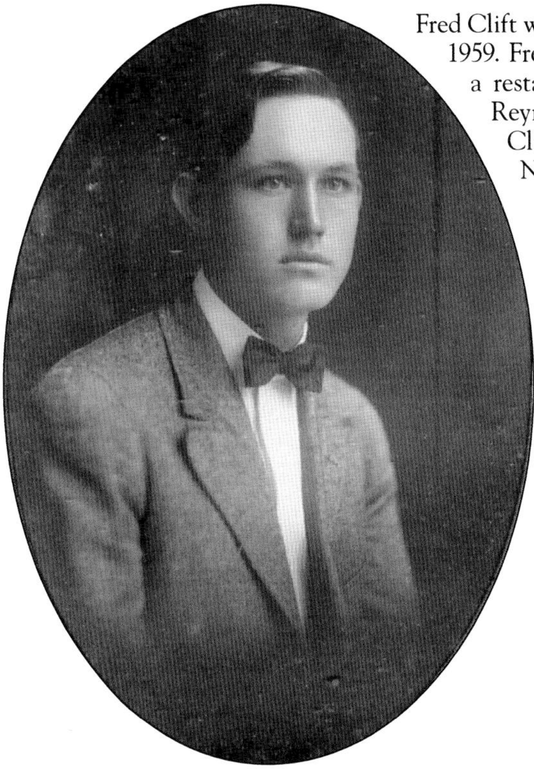

Fred Clift was born in September 1897 and died in June 1959. Fred worked as a coal miner but later opened a restaurant in Chattanooga. He married Edith Reynolds in 1917, and they had one son, Norris Clift. The family lived in Soddy. (Courtesy of Norris and Mary Clift.)

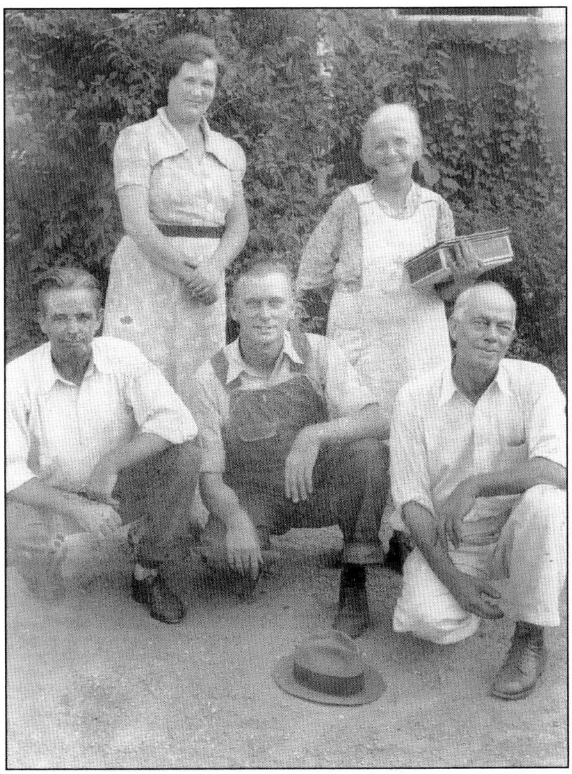

Workers from Soddy Elementary School gather outside for a photograph c. 1942. Arrie Templeton and Louise Templeton (second row, left to right) both worked in the cafeteria. The first row is, from left to right, Sam Parton, George Lasley, and Tom J. Levi. Levi was custodian for the school. (Courtesy of Tom and Barbara Levi.)

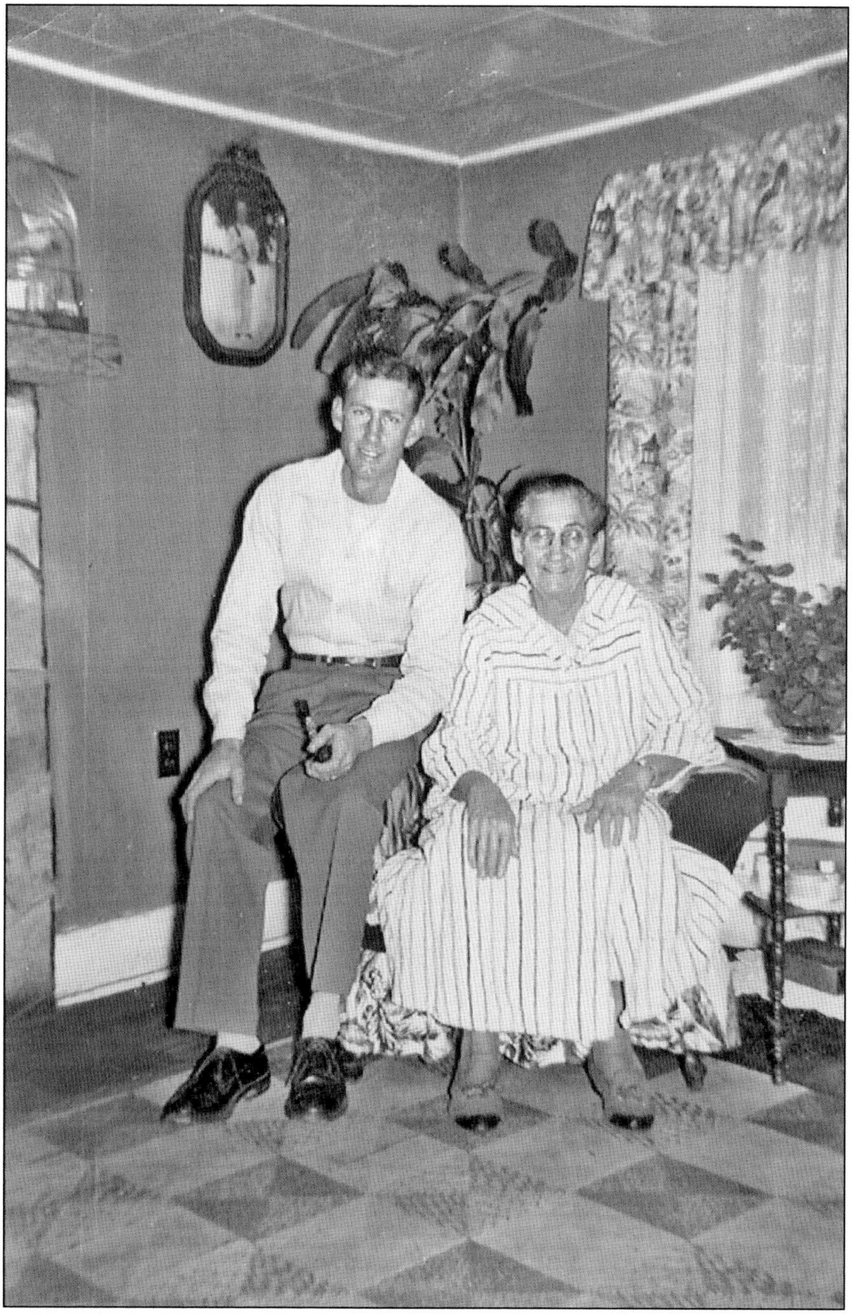

Emma Lou Daughtrey (1888–1955), wife of Luther M. Daughtrey (1878–1944), was the mother of 10 children: Graden, Homer, John Henry, Clifford, Edwin, Bertha, Frank, J. D., Bruce, and Luther Jr. Bruce and Luther Jr. died as infants, and Edwin, who was Clifford's twin, succumbed to an illness when he was only 18 months old. Emma was a very generous woman, and her family recalls how she would always keep extra food on the cook stove for hoboes who would come to her house from the nearby railroad tracks. Emma is pictured here in the living room of her Loop Road home with her youngest son, J. D. Daughtrey (1925–1984). J. D. is the father of Donald, James, Janice, and Michael. (Courtesy of Janice Daughtrey Newman.)

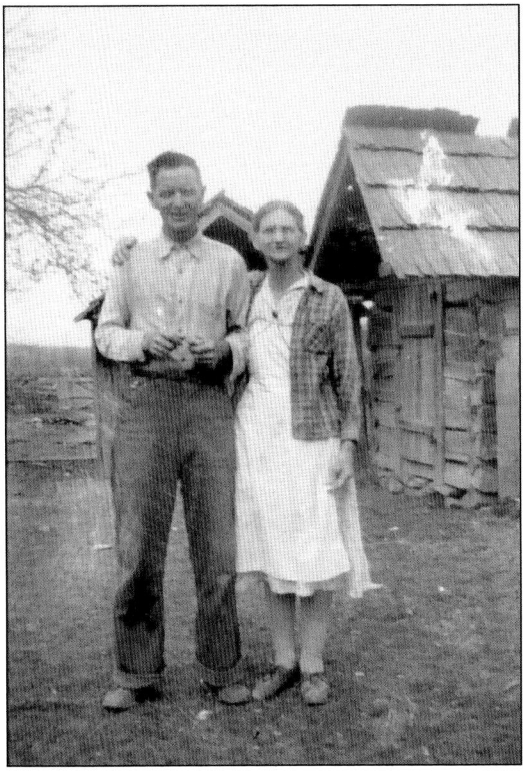

Norris (June 22, 1889–March 26, 1980) and Maybell Bowman (May 16, 1891–October 3, 1960) Hendon married in January 1906 when he was 16 and she was 14. The couple had 13 children: Edith, Willie, Kitty and Winnie (twins), Thelma, Sylvia, Quinten, Franklin, Calvin, Genevia, Etta Jo, Wayne, and Leonard. Their descendants still live throughout the Soddy-Daisy area and across the United States and include the authors of this book. (From the authors' collection.)

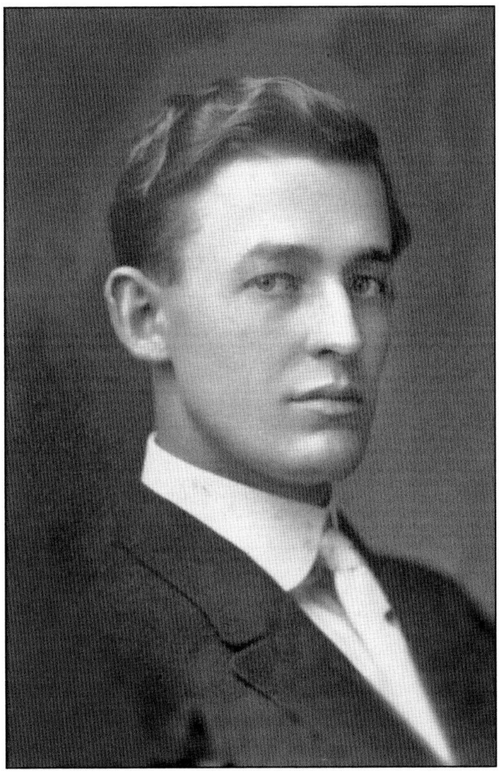

Prior to 1913, when Rev. J. B. Kenna became the first stationed pastor of the Soddy-Daisy United Methodist Church, the church was on a circuit of churches, meaning that circuit-riding preachers would come through the town, preach, then move on to a church in the next town. Reverend Kenna, pictured here, encouraged membership and church growth throughout his service to the church, which ended in 1917. (Courtesy of Buck Johnson.)

Three

EDUCATION

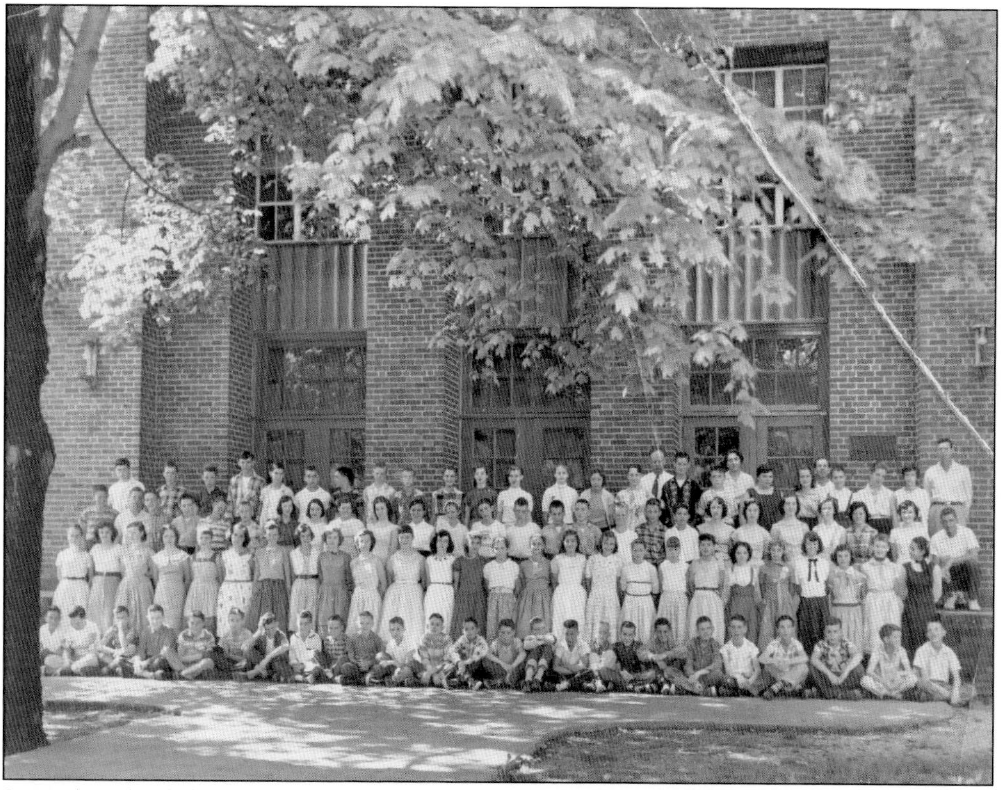

Seventh and eighth graders pose in front of the auditorium at Soddy Elementary c. 1957. Kneeling on the stoop on the far right is teacher Buck Johnson. Standing directly behind Johnson is shop teacher Donald Downey. Mr. and Mrs. Smith are in the fourth row, and in the middle right of the fourth row is teacher Ansel Jordan. The eighth graders in this photograph would go on to join students from Daisy Elementary at Soddy-Daisy High School. (Courtesy of Frank and Donna Copeland.)

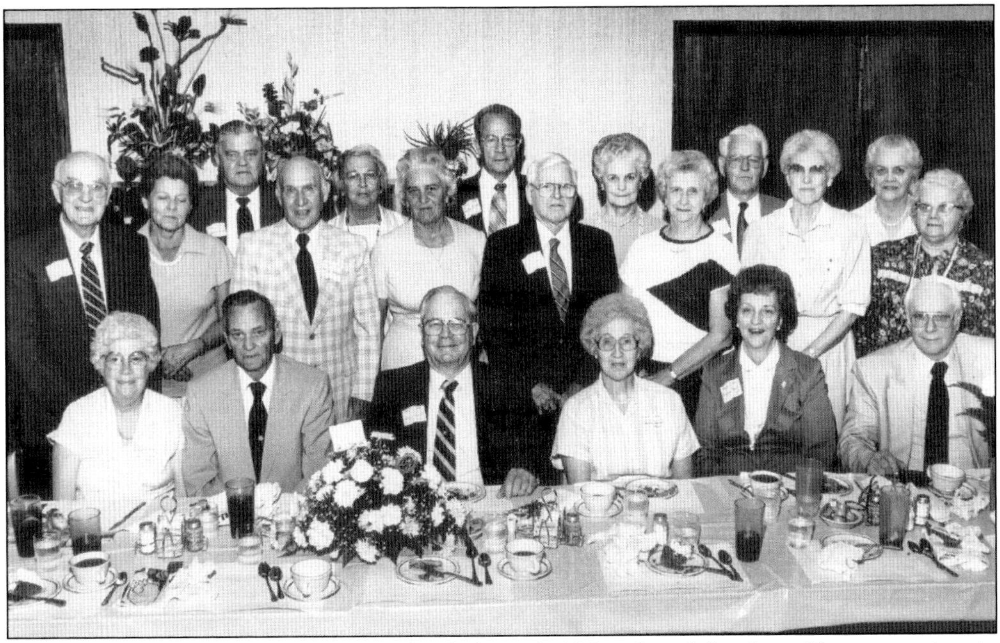

Members of the Soddy-Daisy High School class of 1936 gathered for their 50-year reunion in May 1986. Among the attendees pictured here are Marvin Gross, Marle Coleman Copeland, Ottis Penney, Jack Varner, Ceretha Johnson Grant, Natta Lee Elliott, William Daughtrey, Imogene Igou Logue, James Smith, Joe Ed Elliott, Cooper Frazier, Martin Gross, Belle Correll Daughtrey, and Ruth Swingle. (Courtesy of Frank and Donna Copeland.)

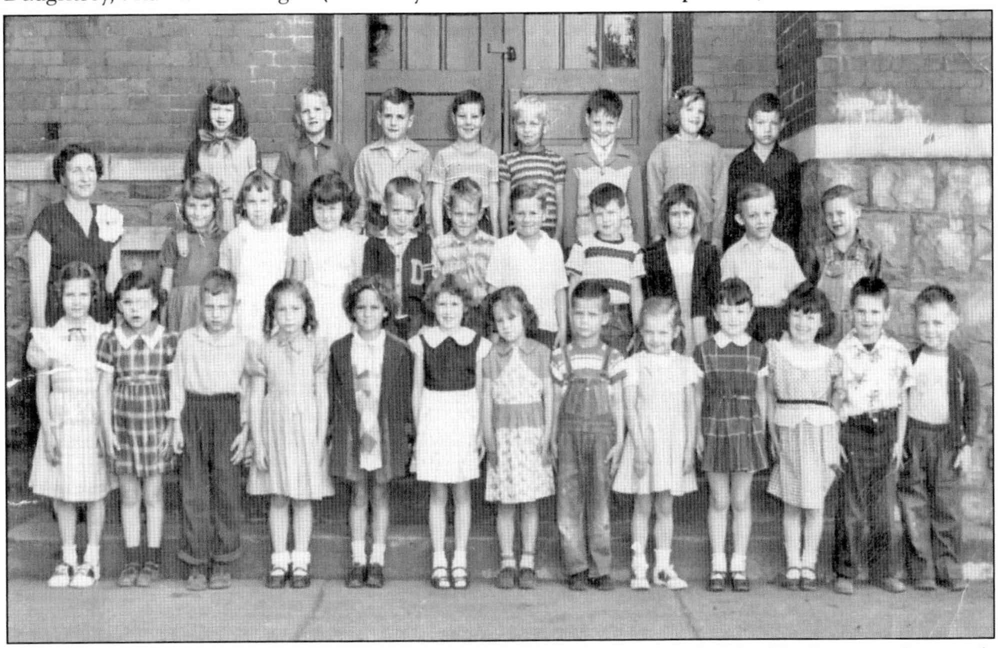

Students in Winnie Sue Smith's first-grade class stand in front of the double doors at the north end of the Daisy Elementary School building during the 1953–1954 school year. Notice the little boy in the middle row with a *D* on his sweater. The monogram was probably for Daisy. (Courtesy of Ronnie "Hawkeye" Hawkins.)

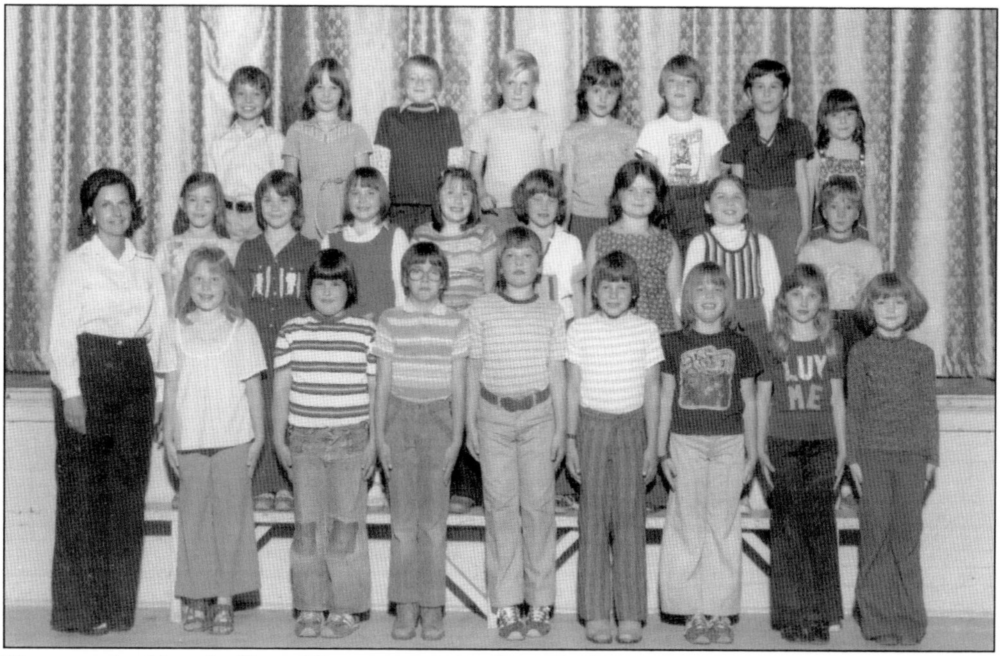

The main building for Daisy Elementary School was built in 1912. It was used until 1980, when elementary students from Daisy began attending a new school on Sequoyah Road. These second graders in Mrs. Cross's 1977–1978 class were one of the last groups of students to use the old school. The Municipal Building now stands where the old Daisy Elementary School once was. (From the authors' collection.)

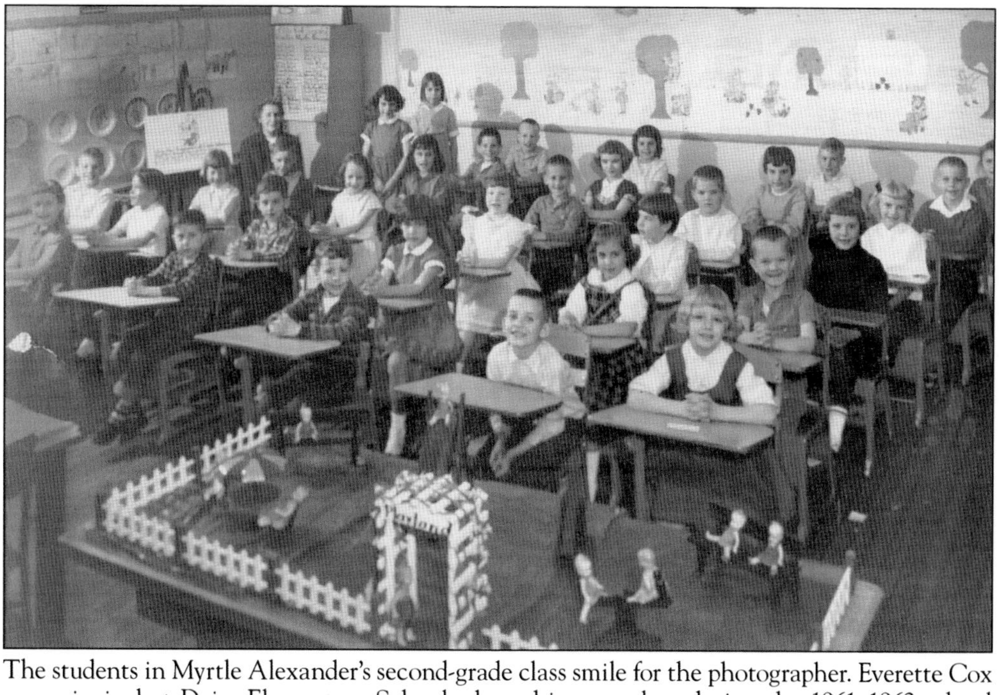

The students in Myrtle Alexander's second-grade class smile for the photographer. Everette Cox was principal at Daisy Elementary School when this was taken during the 1961–1962 school year. (Courtesy of Mike McGill and Scott Brogdon.)

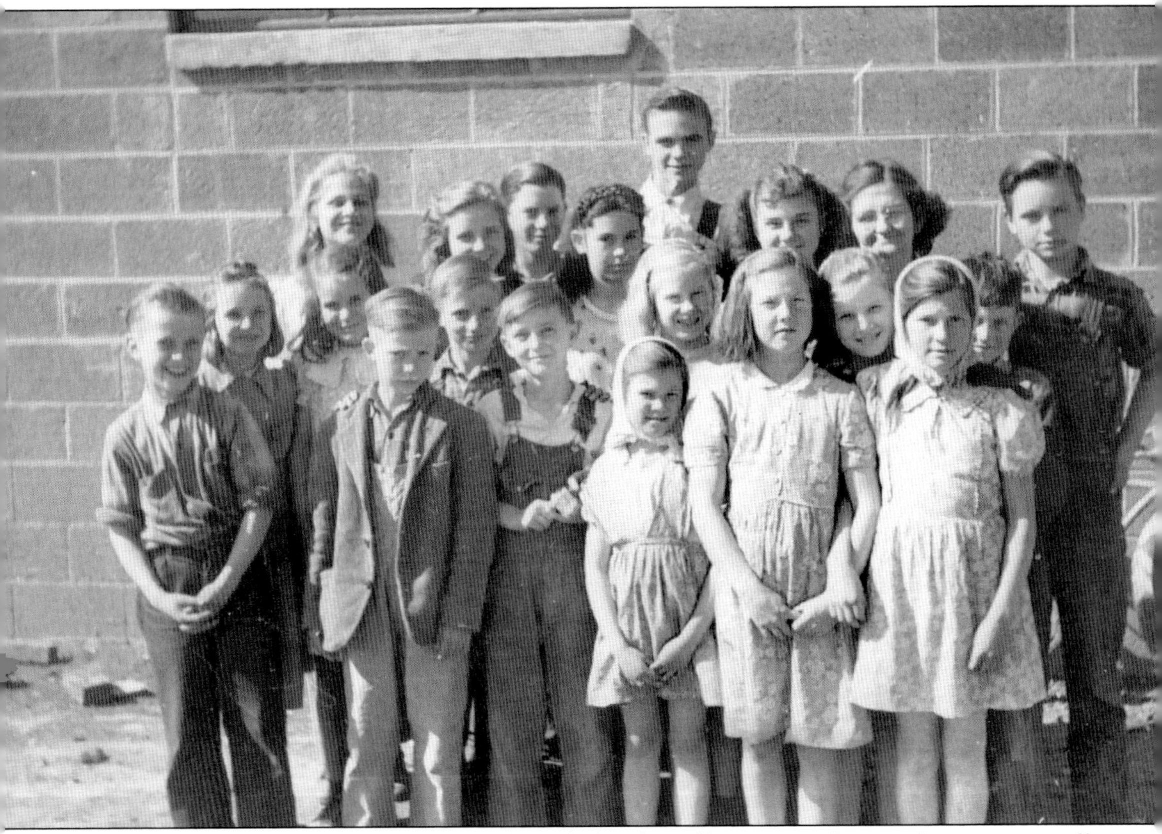

Many students at Lewis' Chapel School traveled to the valley to visit relatives, shop, or eventually live. Lewis' Chapel School students in this photograph are Leslie Green, Wilma Sims, Joyce Harvey, Corline Brown, Jonnie Harvey, Reecie Green, James Lewis, Polly Fay Hensley, Unis Grant, Lodema Sims, Allene Harvey, Rosa Lee Harvey, Fremon Grant, Hershel Grant, Jimmie Harvey, Leon Grant, Josephine C., Atooa Harvey, and Clifford Hall. The teacher was Mrs. Jackson. (All the names listed here have been spelled as they are on the back of the school photograph.) Notice the bicycle in the background of the photograph. Without school busses, students had to either ride a bicycle or, more commonly, walk to school. This photograph was taken in April 1948. (From the authors' collection.)

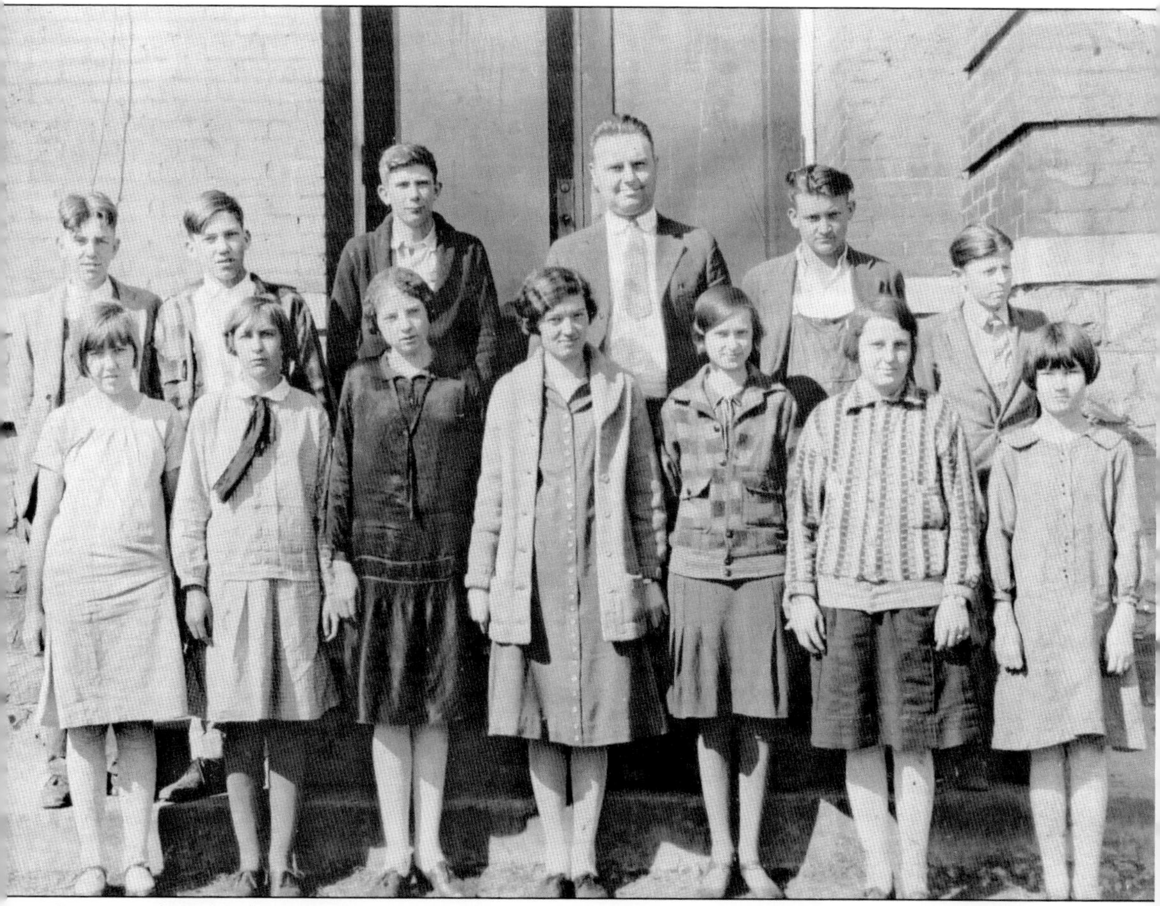

Daisy High School graduates pose for this attractive 1930 photograph. From left to right are (first row) Ruth Sullivan, Elizabeth Smith, Effie Wilson, Ms. Bigger (teacher), Mildred Yarnell, unidentified, and Mary Edna Martin; (second row) Herman Lewis, Bruce Cox, Bruce Scott, Ernest Eldridge (teacher), Leon Thomas, and Ed Hardin. Most native residents recognize the name of Ernest Eldridge, who coached basketball at Soddy-Daisy from 1920 to 1964, winning 840 games and losing only 256. Eldridge himself graduated from Soddy High School in 1913 and, 13 years later, married former classmate Nena Hixson. Eldridge fought in World War I, after which he returned to graduate from the University of Chattanooga in 1920. It was then that he accepted a position at Daisy High, and his name continues to come up as a cornerstone of the Soddy-Daisy athletic program, an outstanding member of the community, and a teacher/coach who was dedicated to his students. (Courtesy of Norris and Mary Clift.)

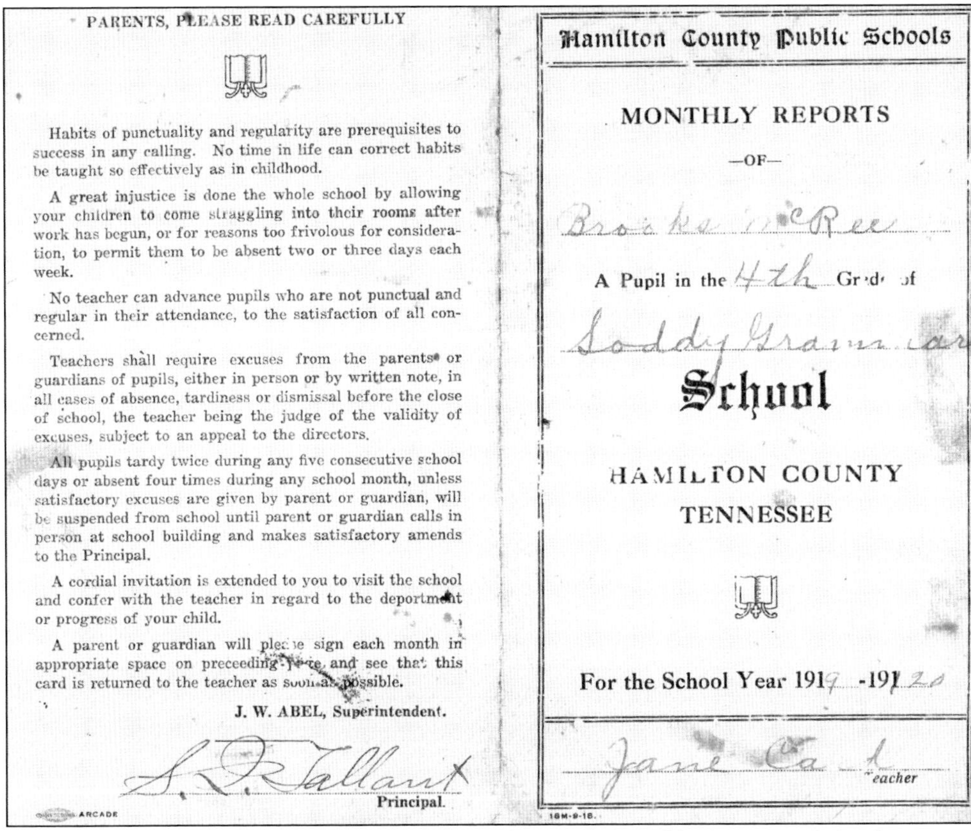

PARENTS, PLEASE READ CAREFULLY

Habits of punctuality and regularity are prerequisites to success in any calling. No time in life can correct habits be taught so effectively as in childhood.

A great injustice is done the whole school by allowing your children to come straggling into their rooms after work has begun, or for reasons too frivolous for consideration, to permit them to be absent two or three days each week.

No teacher can advance pupils who are not punctual and regular in their attendance, to the satisfaction of all concerned.

Teachers shall require excuses from the parents or guardians of pupils, either in person or by written note, in all cases of absence, tardiness or dismissal before the close of school, the teacher being the judge of the validity of excuses, subject to an appeal to the directors.

All pupils tardy twice during any five consecutive school days or absent four times during any school month, unless satisfactory excuses are given by parent or guardian, will be suspended from school until parent or guardian calls in person at school building and makes satisfactory amends to the Principal.

A cordial invitation is extended to you to visit the school and confer with the teacher in regard to the deportment or progress of your child.

A parent or guardian will please sign each month in appropriate space on preceeding page, and see that this card is returned to the teacher as soon as possible.

J. W. ABEL, Superintendent.

S. R. Tallant
Principal.

ARCADE

Hamilton County Public Schools

MONTHLY REPORTS

—OF—

Brooks McRee

A Pupil in the 4th Grade of

Soddy Grammar

School

HAMILTON COUNTY
TENNESSEE

For the School Year 1919-1920

Jane Ca[illegible] Teacher

16M-9-18.

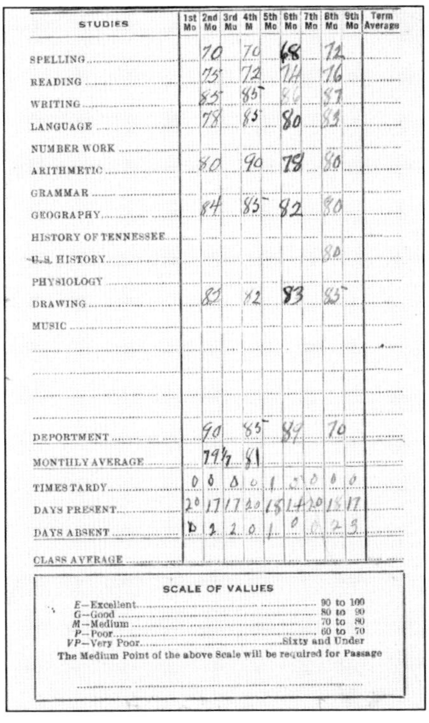

STUDIES	1st Mo	2nd Mo	3rd Mo	4th M	5th Mo	6th Mo	7th Mo	8th Mo	9th Mo	Term Average
SPELLING		70		70		68		72		
READING		75		72		74		76		
WRITING		85		85		86		87		
LANGUAGE		78		85		80		83		
NUMBER WORK										
ARITHMETIC		80		90		78		80		
GRAMMAR										
GEOGRAPHY		84		85		82		80		
HISTORY OF TENNESSEE										
U.S. HISTORY								80		
PHYSIOLOGY										
DRAWING		85		82		83		85		
MUSIC										
DEPORTMENT		90		85		89		70		
MONTHLY AVERAGE		79½		81						
TIMES TARDY	0	0	0	0	1	0	0	0	0	
DAYS PRESENT	20	17	17	20	18	14	20	18	17	
DAYS ABSENT	0	2	2	0	1	0	0	2	3	
CLASS AVERAGE										

SCALE OF VALUES

E—Excellent .... 90 to 100
G—Good .... 80 to 90
M—Medium .... 70 to 80
P—Poor .... 60 to 70
VP—Very Poor .... Sixty and Under

The Medium Point of the above Scale will be required for Passage

Brooks McRee's Soddy Grammar School report card from the 1919–1920 school year emphasizes that students should be punctual and attend regularly. "A great injustice is done the whole school," the report card states, "by allowing your children to come straggling into their rooms after work has begun." McRee studied subjects common for fourth graders in the early 20th century, including spelling, reading, writing, arithmetic, and geography. He also had the privilege of a drawing course. (Courtesy of A. B. and Frankie McRee.)

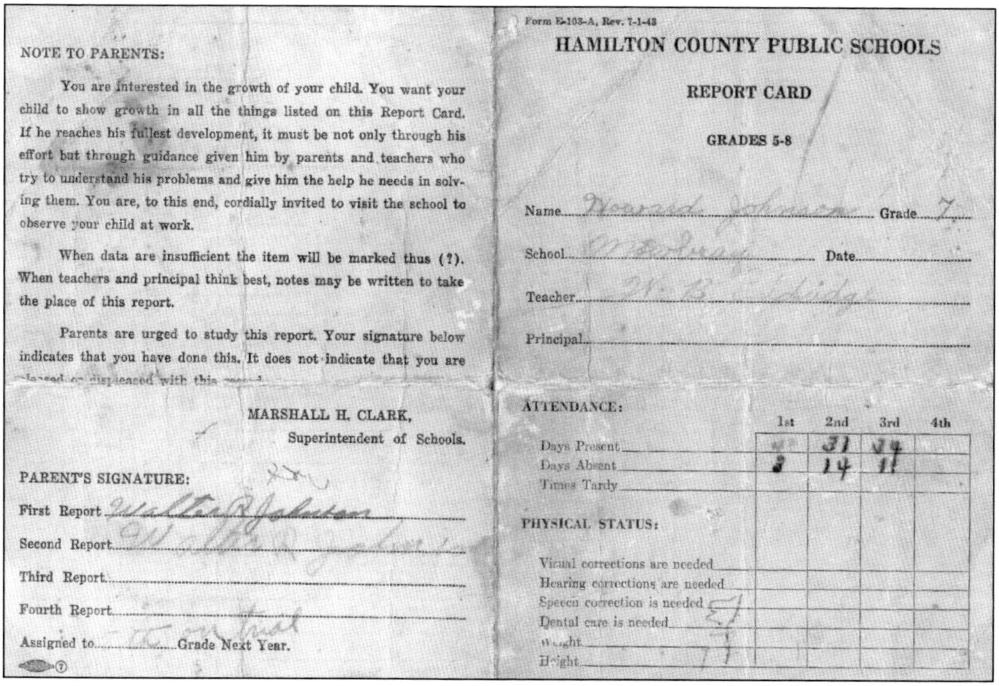

NOTE TO PARENTS:

You are interested in the growth of your child. You want your child to show growth in all the things listed on this Report Card. If he reaches his fullest development, it must be not only through his effort but through guidance given him by parents and teachers who try to understand his problems and give him the help he needs in solving them. You are, to this end, cordially invited to visit the school to observe your child at work.

When data are insufficient the item will be marked thus (?). When teachers and principal think best, notes may be written to take the place of this report.

Parents are urged to study this report. Your signature below indicates that you have done this. It does not indicate that you are pleased or displeased with this report.

MARSHALL H. CLARK,
Superintendent of Schools.

PARENT'S SIGNATURE:

First Report Walter R Johnson

Second Report W Walter R Johnson

Third Report

Fourth Report

Assigned to 8 on trial Grade Next Year.

Form E-103-A, Rev. 7-1-43

HAMILTON COUNTY PUBLIC SCHOOLS

REPORT CARD

GRADES 5-8

Name Howard Johnson Grade 7

School Mowbray Date

Teacher W. B. [illegible]

Principal

ATTENDANCE:

	1st	2nd	3rd	4th
Days Present		31	34	
Days Absent	3	14	11	
Times Tardy				

PHYSICAL STATUS:

Visual corrections are needed
Hearing corrections are needed
Speech correction is needed
Dental care is needed
Weight
Height

According to the back of his 1945 Mowbray School report card, seventh grader Howard Johnson was assigned to the eighth grade "on trial," possibly due to numerous absences. Though he started the eighth grade that fall, Howard's father made him quit school to cut timber and earn money that would help feed the large family. Howard lived on Mowbray Mountain with his parents and 12 siblings. (From the authors' collection.)

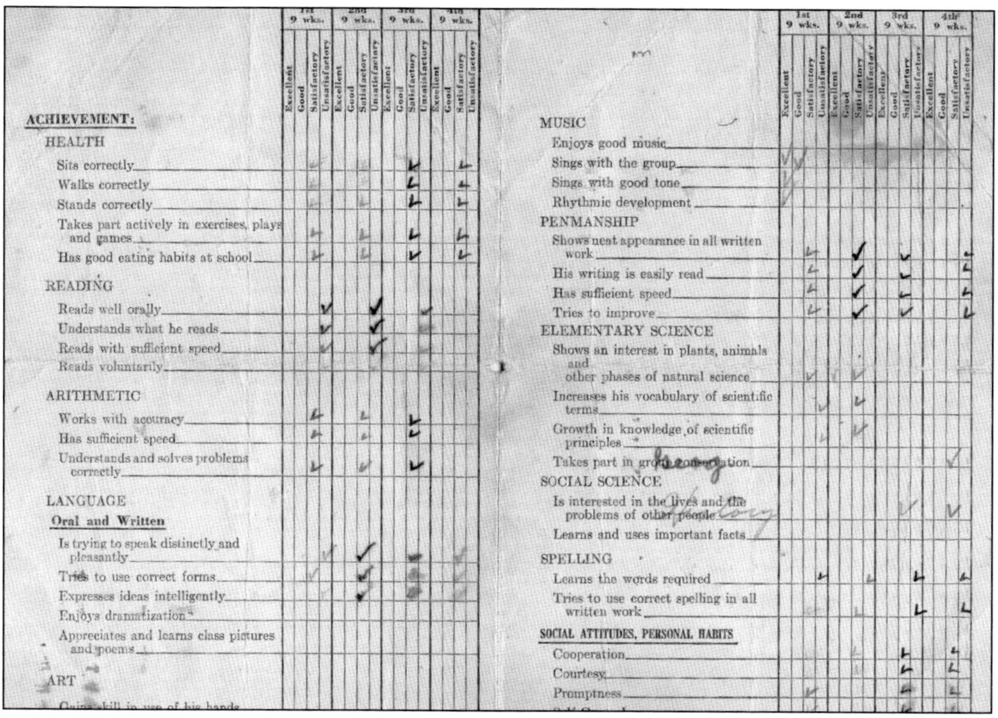

1st 9 wks. 2nd 9 wks. 3rd 9 wks. 4th 9 wks.
Excellent Good Satisfactory Unsatisfactory

ACHIEVEMENT:

HEALTH
Sits correctly
Walks correctly
Stands correctly
Takes part actively in exercises, plays and games
Has good eating habits at school

READING
Reads well orally
Understands what he reads
Reads with sufficient speed
Reads voluntarily

ARITHMETIC
Works with accuracy
Has sufficient speed
Understands and solves problems correctly

LANGUAGE
Oral and Written
Is trying to speak distinctly and pleasantly
Tries to use correct forms
Expresses ideas intelligently
Enjoys dramatization
Appreciates and learns class pictures and poems

ART
Gains skill in use of his hands

MUSIC
Enjoys good music
Sings with the group
Sings with good tone
Rhythmic development

PENMANSHIP
Shows neat appearance in all written work
His writing is easily read
Has sufficient speed
Tries to improve

ELEMENTARY SCIENCE
Shows an interest in plants, animals and other phases of natural science
Increases his vocabulary of scientific terms
Growth in knowledge of scientific principles
Takes part in group conversation

SOCIAL SCIENCE
Is interested in the lives and the problems of other people
Learns and uses important facts

SPELLING
Learns the words required
Tries to use correct spelling in all written work

SOCIAL ATTITUDES, PERSONAL HABITS
Cooperation
Courtesy
Promptness

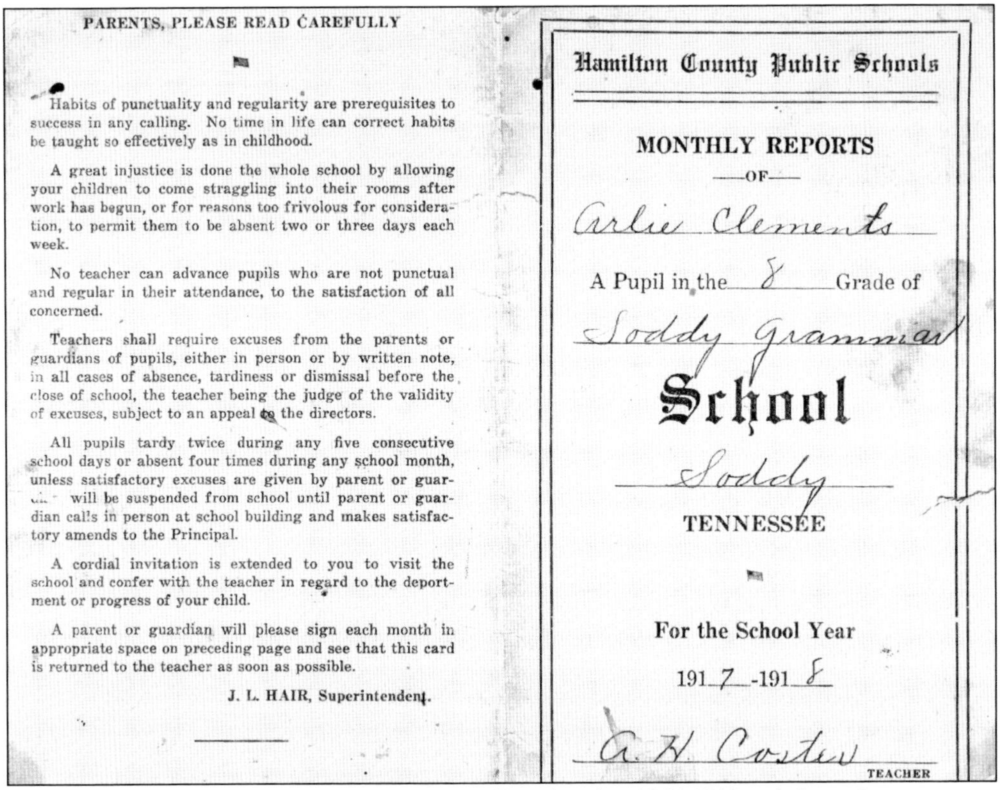

PARENTS, PLEASE READ CAREFULLY

Habits of punctuality and regularity are prerequisites to success in any calling. No time in life can correct habits be taught so effectively as in childhood.

A great injustice is done the whole school by allowing your children to come straggling into their rooms after work has begun, or for reasons too frivolous for consideration, to permit them to be absent two or three days each week.

No teacher can advance pupils who are not punctual and regular in their attendance, to the satisfaction of all concerned.

Teachers shall require excuses from the parents or guardians of pupils, either in person or by written note, in all cases of absence, tardiness or dismissal before the close of school, the teacher being the judge of the validity of excuses, subject to an appeal to the directors.

All pupils tardy twice during any five consecutive school days or absent four times during any school month, unless satisfactory excuses are given by parent or guardian will be suspended from school until parent or guardian calls in person at school building and makes satisfactory amends to the Principal.

A cordial invitation is extended to you to visit the school and confer with the teacher in regard to the deportment or progress of your child.

A parent or guardian will please sign each month in appropriate space on preceding page and see that this card is returned to the teacher as soon as possible.

J. L. HAIR, Superintendent.

Hamilton County Public Schools

MONTHLY REPORTS

—OF—

Arlie Clements

A Pupil in the 8 Grade of

Soddy Grammar

School

Soddy

TENNESSEE

For the School Year

1917-1918

A. H. Coster

TEACHER

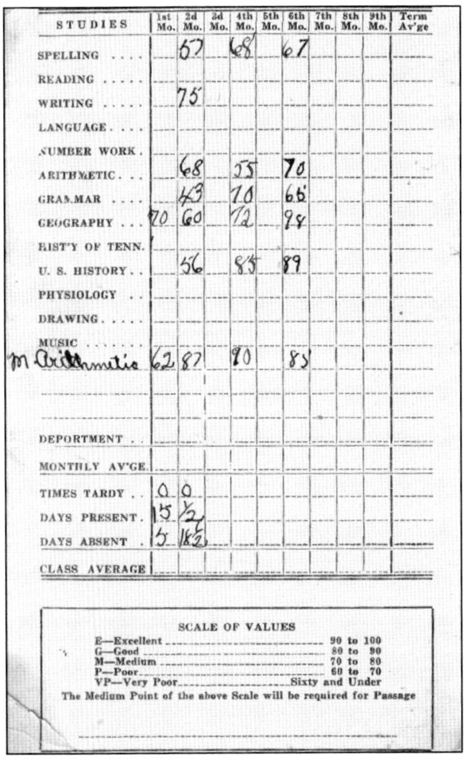

STUDIES	1st Mo.	2d Mo.	3d Mo.	4th Mo.	5th Mo.	6th Mo.	7th Mo.	8th Mo.	9th Mo.	Term Av'ge
SPELLING		57		68		67				
READING										
WRITING		75								
LANGUAGE										
NUMBER WORK										
ARITHMETIC		68		55		70				
GRAMMAR		43		70		65				
GEOGRAPHY	70	60		72		98				
HIST'Y OF TENN.										
U. S. HISTORY		56		85		89				
PHYSIOLOGY										
DRAWING										
MUSIC										
M Arithmetic	62	87		90		85				
DEPORTMENT										
MONTHLY AV'GE.										
TIMES TARDY	0	0								
DAYS PRESENT	15	½								
DAYS ABSENT	5	18½								
CLASS AVERAGE										

SCALE OF VALUES

E—Excellent .... 90 to 100
G—Good .... 80 to 90
M—Medium .... 70 to 80
P—Poor .... 60 to 70
VP—Very Poor .... Sixty and Under

The Medium Point of the above Scale will be required for Passage

Based on his 1917–1918 eighth-grade report card, Arlie Clements missed a lot of school (23 days out of the 39 recorded), and his grades reflect that fact. Arlie studied U.S. history and geography in addition to spelling, writing, arithmetic, and grammar. Just one year after being an eighth grader at Soddy Grammar School, Arlie married Leva Ollie Sparks on July 4, 1919. Charles Wallace Sr., one of the couple's 12 children, opened Clement's Antiques in 1938 while he was still in high school. The antiques store, located on Dayton Boulevard, is still a unique, family-run store full of treasures. (Courtesy of Madge Lockhart.)

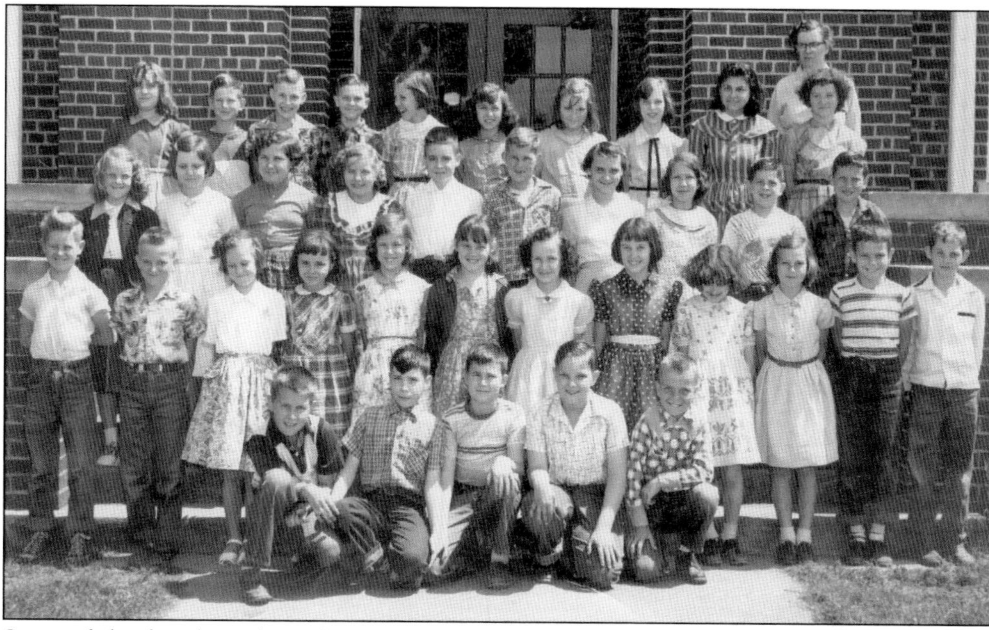

Some of the fourth-grade students appear bashful and others seem quite comfortable in this school photograph at Gann's Middle Valley Elementary *c.* 1955. The school was built in 1937 when Arthur L. Rankins was superintendent. Board of Education members were Anna Lacey (chairperson), Mrs. Will Shepard, John Allen, J. B. Brown, E. Y. Chapin, and Dr. E. S. Blair. (Courtesy of Ellis and Linda Sutherland.)

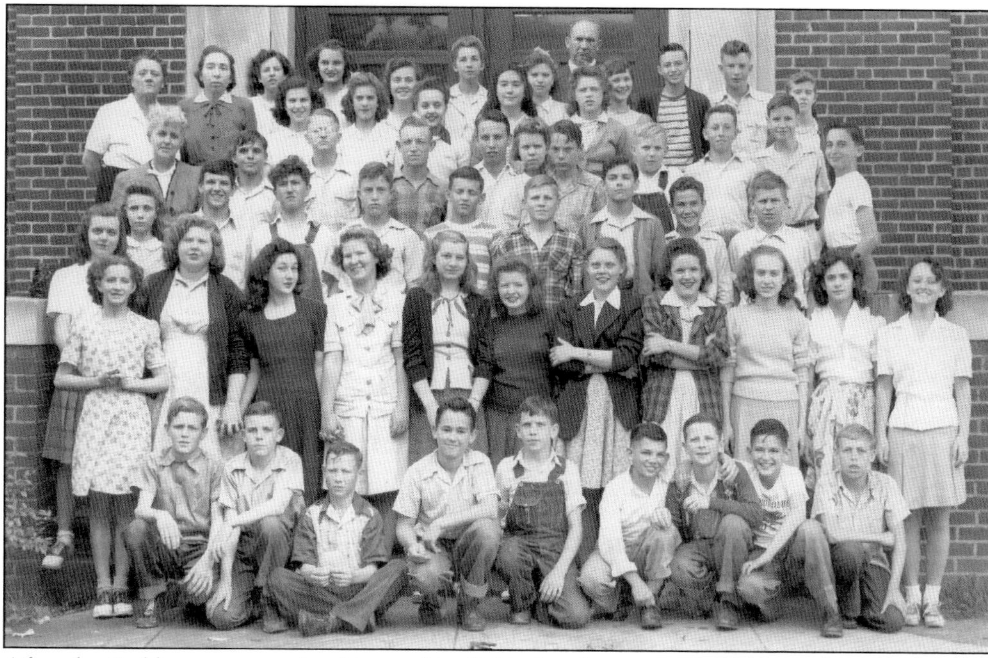

After the Soddy grammar school burned in 1944, the elementary students used the junior-high portion of the building, while the junior-high students attended the high school until a new junior high was built. Judging from the faces on these junior high kids at the high school *c.* 1945, the students look completely content with the situation. (Courtesy of A. B. and Frankie McRee.)

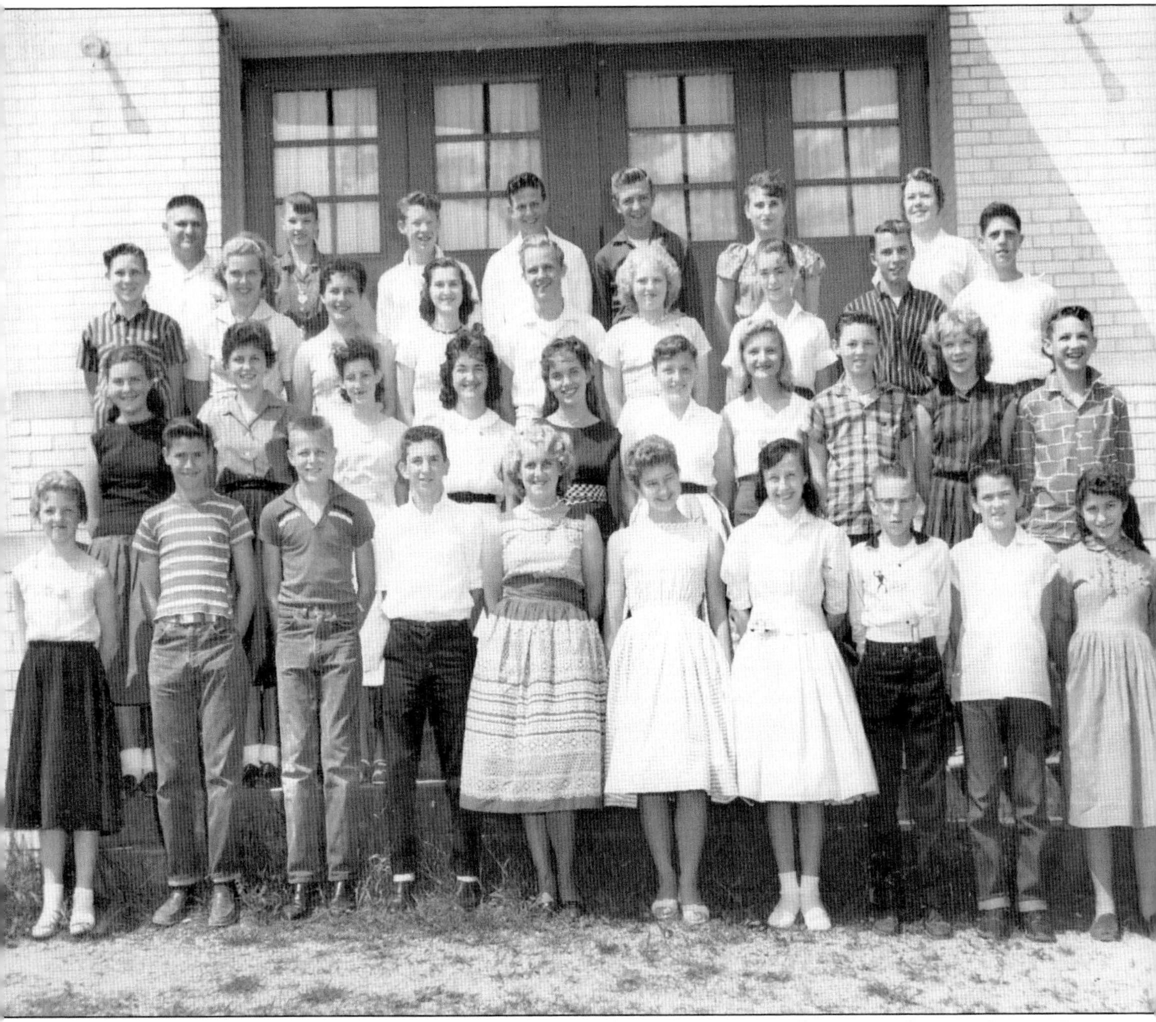

According to the Hamilton County Board of Education minutes for November 1949, members recognized the need for a school in the Green Pond area. According to the minutes, this school would "serve a number of children now attending Gann's Middle Valley, Soddy Elementary, and Daisy Elementary. Daisy is badly overcrowded, with 779 students enrolled in the second month of this school term." Approximately 10 years later, seventh graders at the new school, John H. Allen Elementary School, had this photograph made. From left to right are (first row) Linda Morgan, Ray Woodall, Eddie Griffith, Charles Howe, Patricia Gravett, Phyllis Ricketts, Linda Lovelady, Jerry Sneed, James Christian, and Alma Sue Thompson; (second row) Helen Lee, Linda Stewart, Millie ?, Frances Wilcox, Judy Brownfield, Wanda Sledge, Mary Frances, David Mathis, Charlotte ?, and Roy Lee; (third row) Frankie Swafford, Wanda Gann, Judy Penny (or Penney?), Jean Gallion, R. L. Ard, Joyce Humble, Earlene Leffew, Freddie Layne, and Charles Davis; (fourth row) Mr. Hale, Reba May, George Ed ?, Leonard Frizzell, Billy ?, Patsy ?, and Mrs. Downey. (Courtesy of Ellis and Linda Sutherland.)

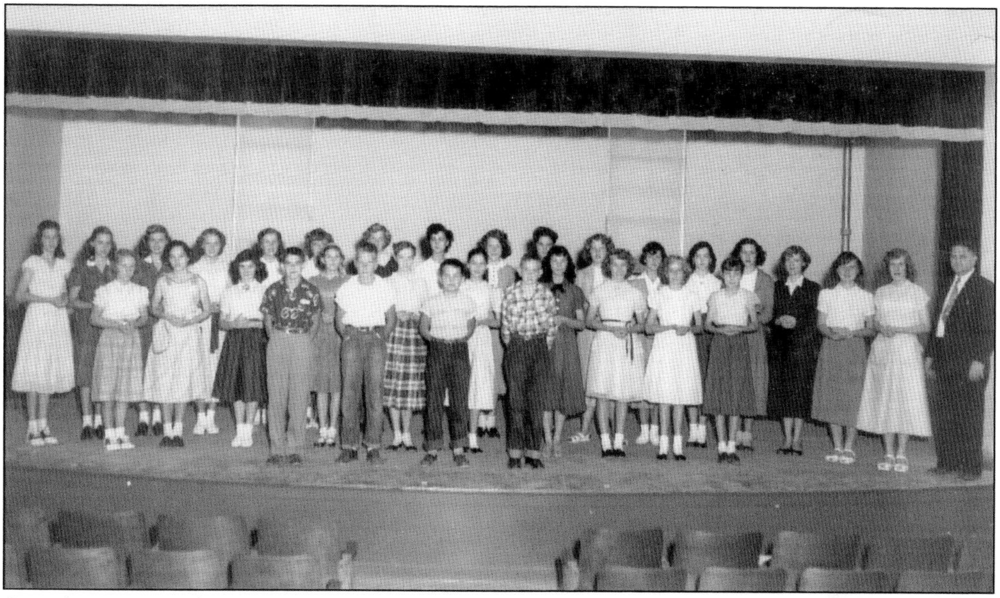

Specifications in the contract to build John H. Allen Elementary School called for a fireproof brick building with 12 classrooms, an auditorium, cafeteria, library, and an administrative unit. The dedication took place on October 12, 1952. The first principal was Clay Johnson, who had been transferred from the Falling Water district. Here students of the John H. Allen Elementary Glee Club pose for a photograph c. 1953. (Courtesy of Clara Bowman.)

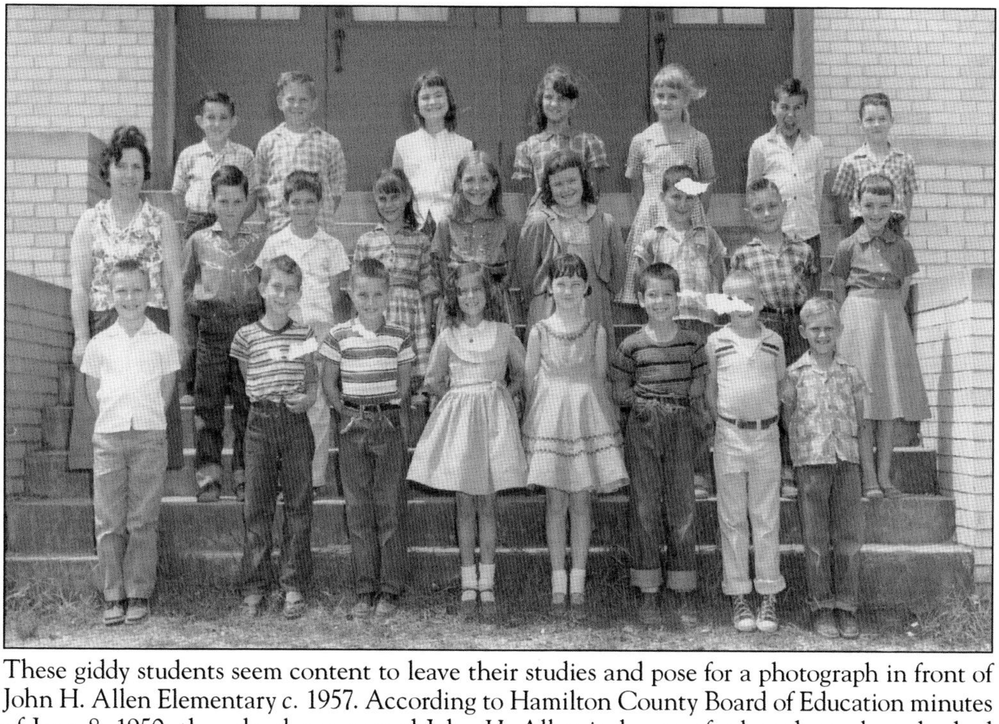

These giddy students seem content to leave their studies and pose for a photograph in front of John H. Allen Elementary c. 1957. According to Hamilton County Board of Education minutes of June 8, 1950, the school was named John H. Allen in honor of a board member who had been a "faithful and loyal" board member continuously for 48 years. (Courtesy of Ellis and Linda Sutherland.)

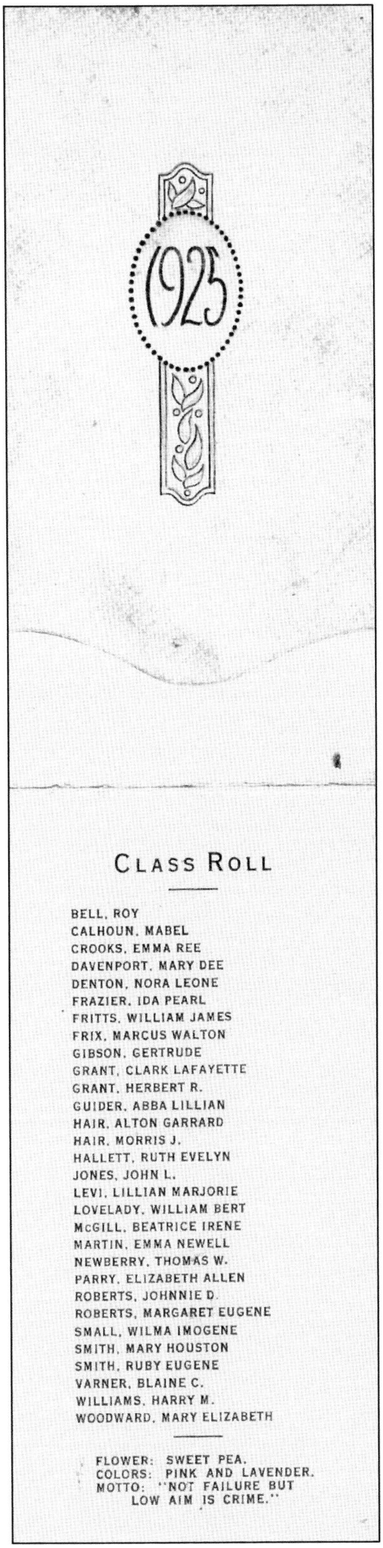

CLASS ROLL

BELL, ROY
CALHOUN, MABEL
CROOKS, EMMA REE
DAVENPORT, MARY DEE
DENTON, NORA LEONE
FRAZIER, IDA PEARL
FRITTS, WILLIAM JAMES
FRIX, MARCUS WALTON
GIBSON, GERTRUDE
GRANT, CLARK LAFAYETTE
GRANT, HERBERT R.
GUIDER, ABBA LILLIAN
HAIR, ALTON GARRARD
HAIR, MORRIS J.
HALLETT, RUTH EVELYN
JONES, JOHN L.
LEVI, LILLIAN MARJORIE
LOVELADY, WILLIAM BERT
McGILL, BEATRICE IRENE
MARTIN, EMMA NEWELL
NEWBERRY, THOMAS W.
PARRY, ELIZABETH ALLEN
ROBERTS, JOHNNIE D.
ROBERTS, MARGARET EUGENE
SMALL, WILMA IMOGENE
SMITH, MARY HOUSTON
SMITH, RUBY EUGENE
VARNER, BLAINE C.
WILLIAMS, HARRY M.
WOODWARD, MARY ELIZABETH

FLOWER: SWEET PEA.
COLORS: PINK AND LAVENDER.
MOTTO: "NOT FAILURE BUT LOW AIM IS CRIME."

This beautiful tri-fold invitation came from the Soddy High School senior class of 1925. Many familiar Soddy family names are recognizable among the graduates, including Denton, Grant, Frazier, Levi, McGill, Newberry, and Varner. Many of these families are descendants of the Welsh immigrants that settled the Soddy area to mine coal. (Courtesy of Tom and Barbara Levi.)

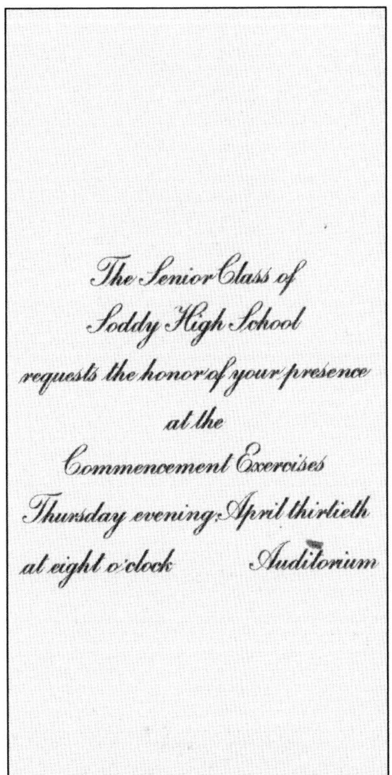

The Senior Class of
Soddy High School
requests the honor of your presence
at the
Commencement Exercises
Thursday evening, April thirtieth
at eight o'clock *Auditorium*

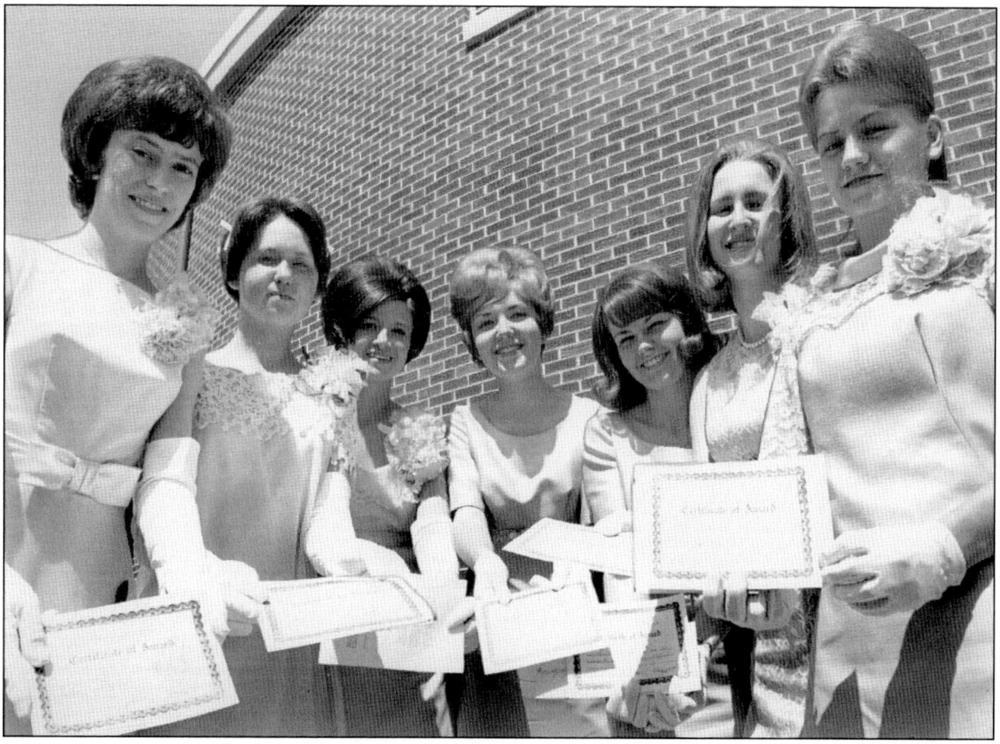

These lovely young ladies are, from left to right, Peggy Moore, Brenda Chauncey, Martha Tolbert, Janice Pendergrass, Sharon Johnson, Ann Hensley, and Janet Pickett. They were the four-year honor students at Soddy-Daisy High School for 1968. (Courtesy of Soddy-Daisy High School; photograph by Steve Wall.)

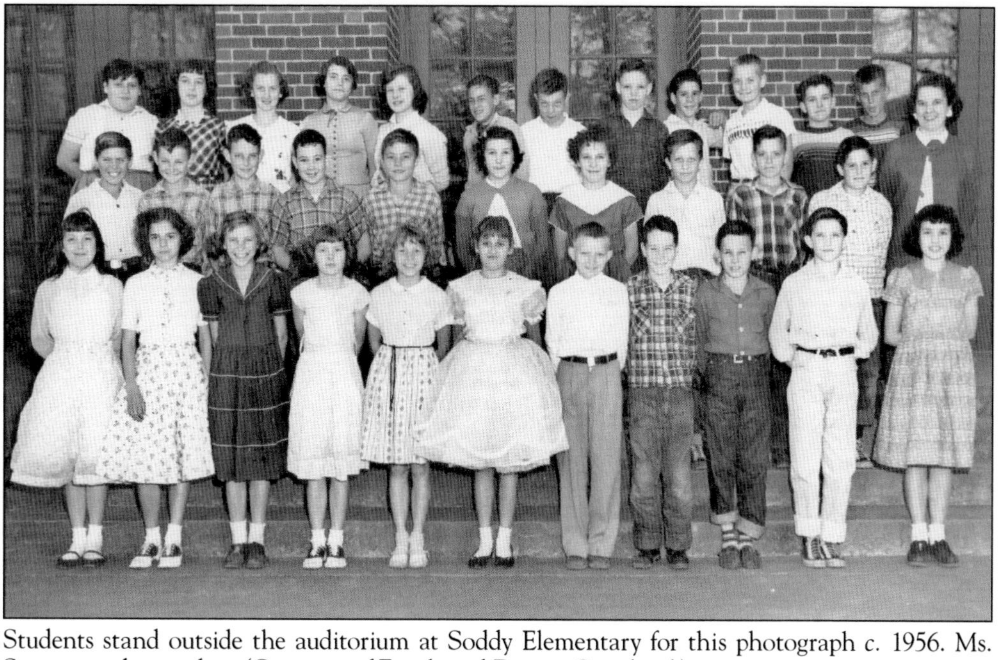

Students stand outside the auditorium at Soddy Elementary for this photograph c. 1956. Ms. Stone was the teacher. (Courtesy of Frank and Donna Copeland.)

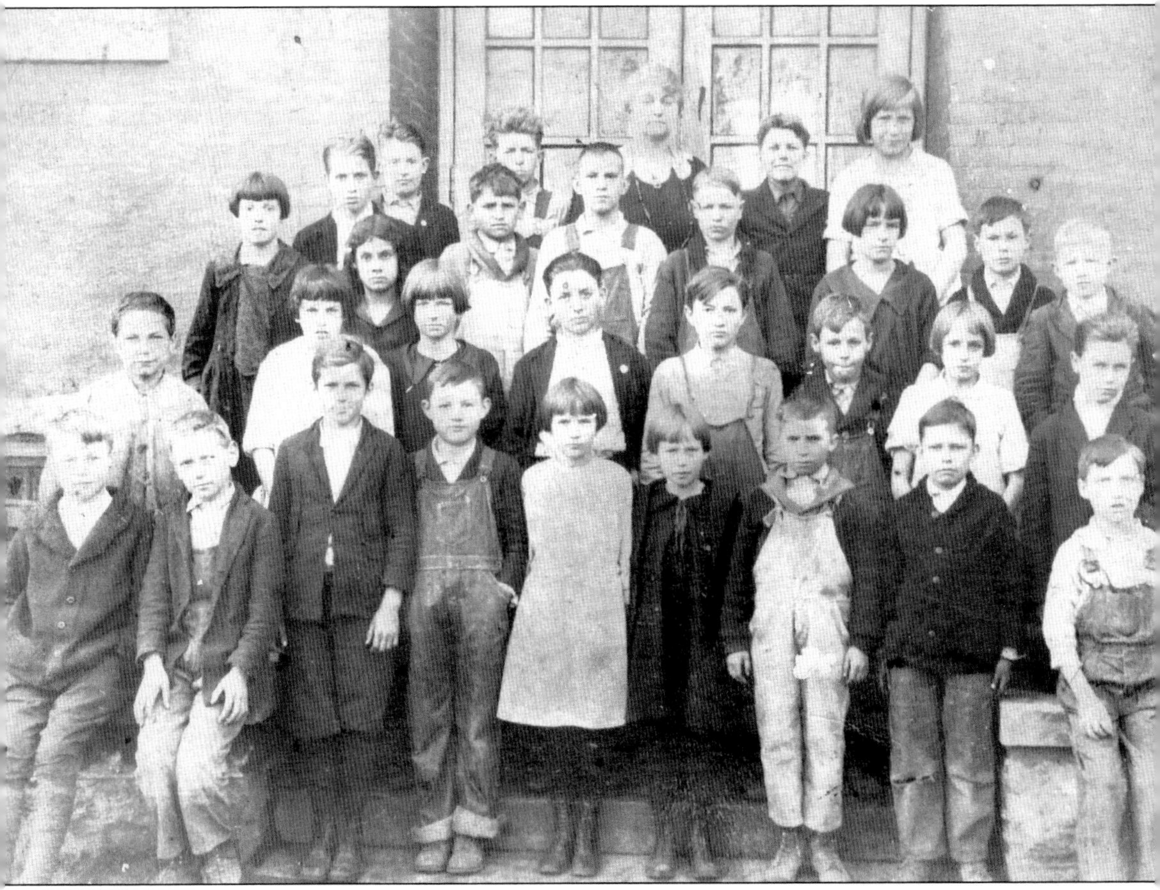

Though many children were taught reading, writing, and arithmetic skills at home, as well as homemaking and trade skills, young boys and girls such as these might have had little chance of a good education if not for public schools built in the early 20th century. It is certain that people were excited about the new schools. The students here were from Soddy Elementary c. 1922. (Courtesy of Tom and Barbara Levi.)

Four

CHURCHES

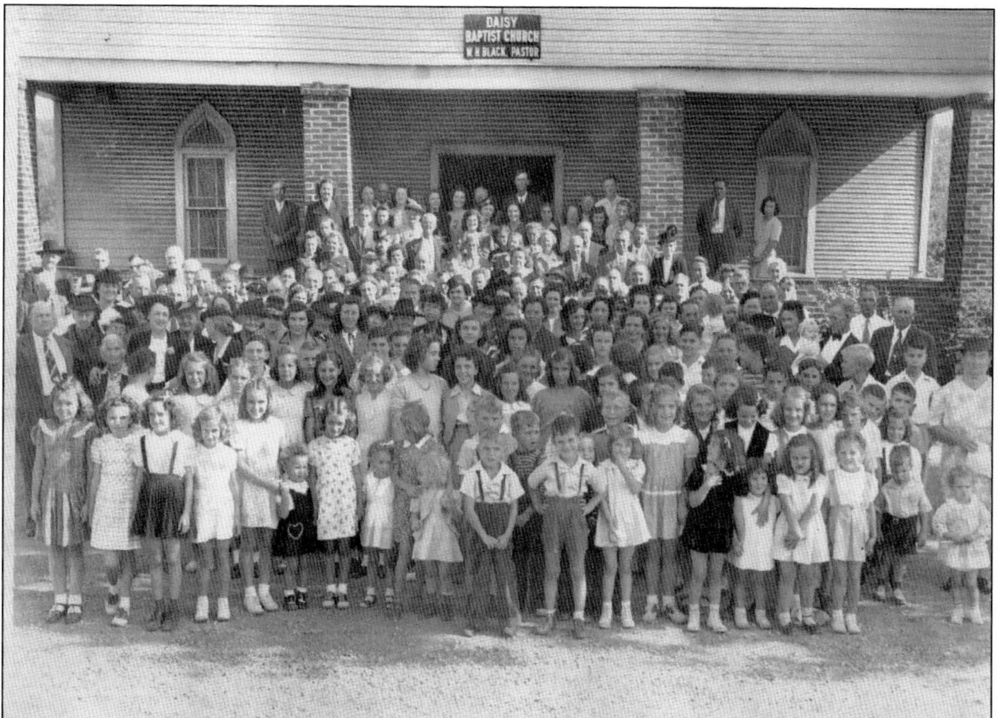

The Baptists worshipped in the Cumberland Presbyterian Church from October 1886 until the Baptist Church building was completed sufficiently for use. Rev. J. N. Millsaps delivered the first message in the new building on August 25, 1901. Members of the Daisy Baptist Church are shown here during homecoming on October 12, 1947. (Courtesy of First Baptist Church Soddy-Daisy; photograph made, developed, and enlarged by Hobart Millsaps.)

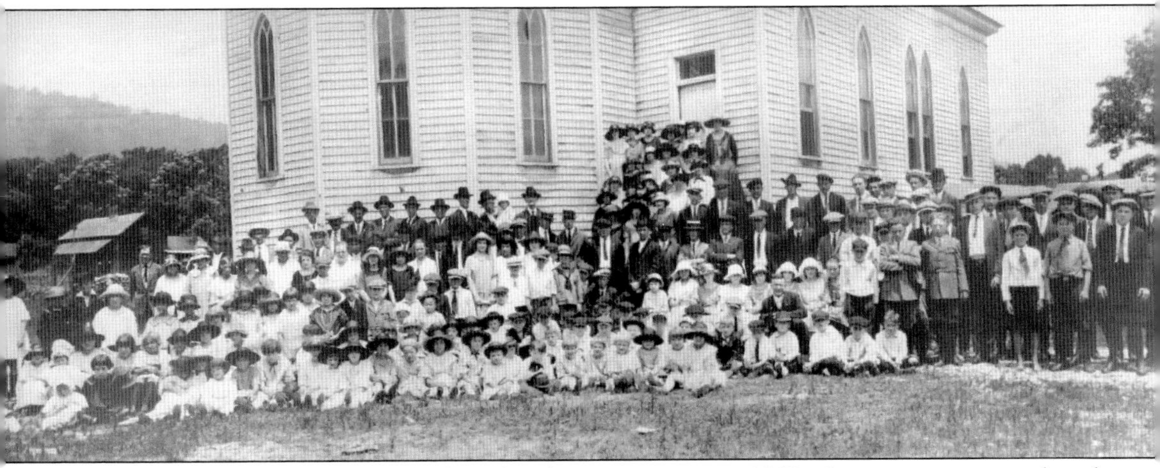

The Soddy-Daisy United Methodist Church traces its roots to 1860, when a woman remembered only as Miss Holland came into this small mining community and started a prayer meeting. These meetings were held regularly until finally a small log church was built near the corner of Hickman Road and Depot Street. The first preacher was Rev. J. B. Kenna, shown on page 36. The congregation is shown here c. 1921. (Courtesy of Buck Johnson.)

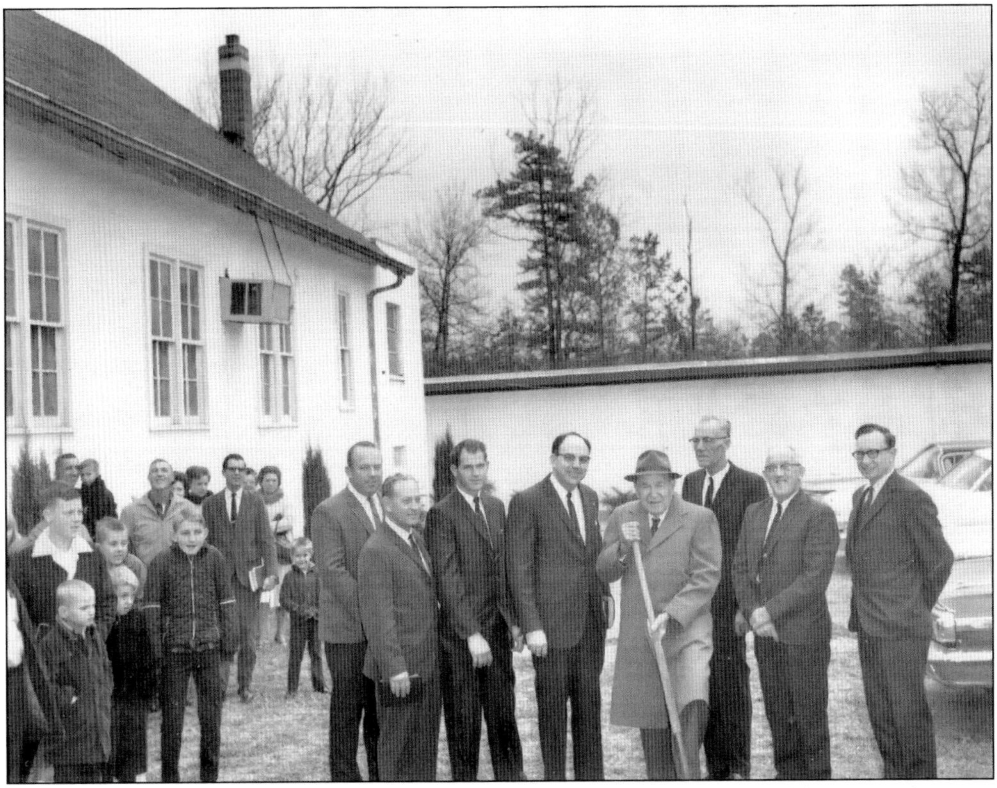

Among those present for the December 3, 1967, groundbreaking ceremony of the new auditorium of Mile Straight Baptist Church were Teddy Jenkins, Al Slater, Al Goss, Mr. Sutton, Walter Johnson, Tester Bunch, and Ralph Patterson. (Courtesy of Mile Straight Baptist Church.)

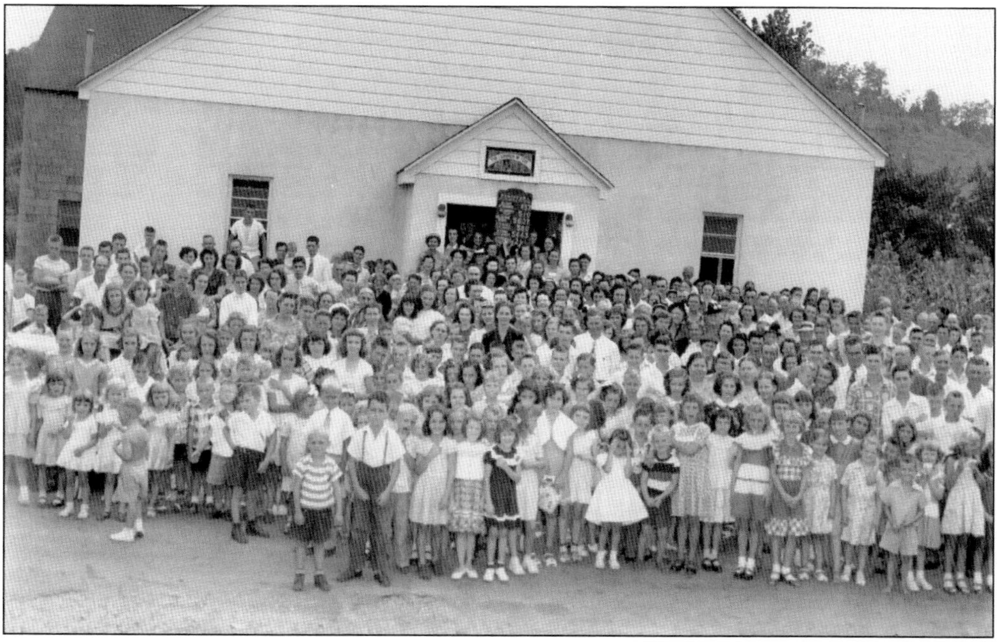

Members of the Daisy Church of God pose for this photograph in front of their building located on Church Street. The attendance register boasts a record attendance of 457 soon to be changed because, the day this photograph was taken, attendance was 510. Collection on this day was $56.07, and the offering the previous Sunday was $54.43. (Courtesy of Daisy Church of God.)

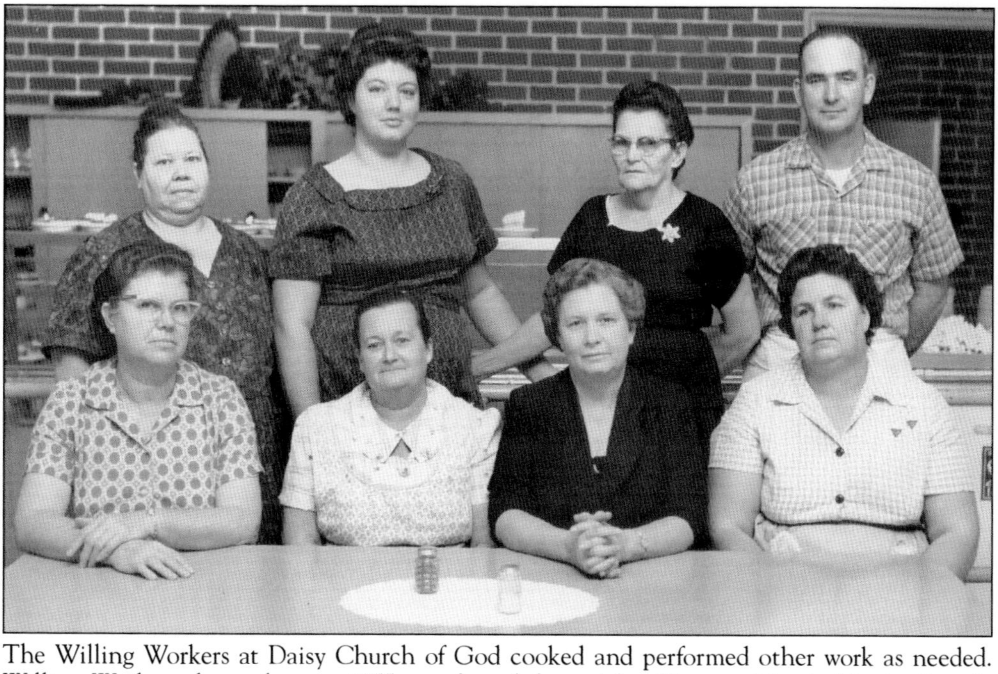

The Willing Workers at Daisy Church of God cooked and performed other work as needed. Willing Workers shown here *c.* 1955 are, from left to right, (first row) Jessie Manis, Evanda Qualls, Frances Phillips, and Frances Daughtrey; (second row) Gladys Delasmitte, Shirley Manis Lovelady, Ola Shannon, and James Daughtrey. The workers would cook and help do other things the church needed. (Courtesy of Daisy Church of God.)

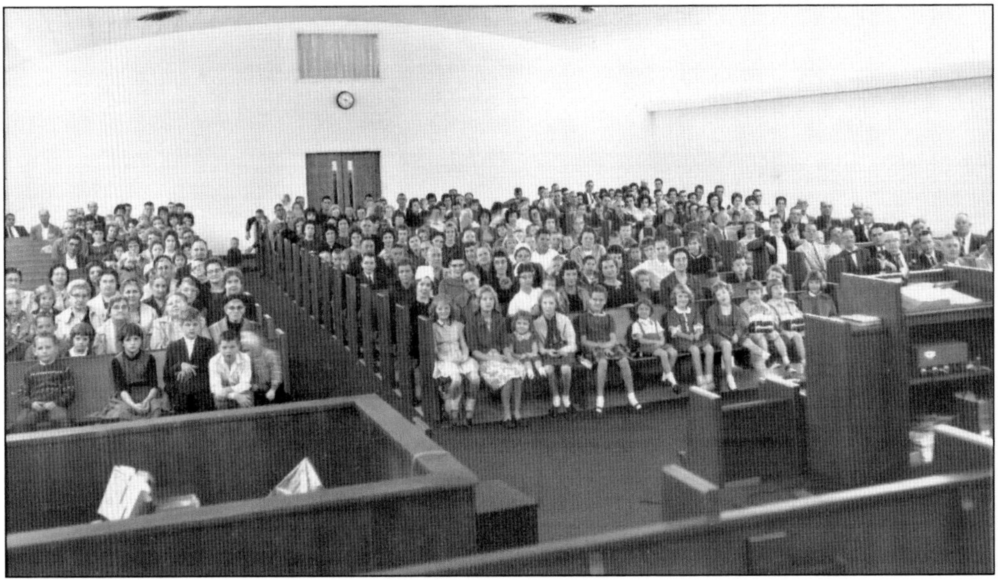

A postcard celebrating a new building for the Daisy Church of God boasts 32 Sunday school rooms, African mahogany furniture, and a completely air-conditioned facility. The building is located in downtown Daisy on land with two springs that formerly had furnished the city with drinking water. Shown here is one of the first photographs of members in the new sanctuary c. 1961. (Courtesy of Daisy Church of God.)

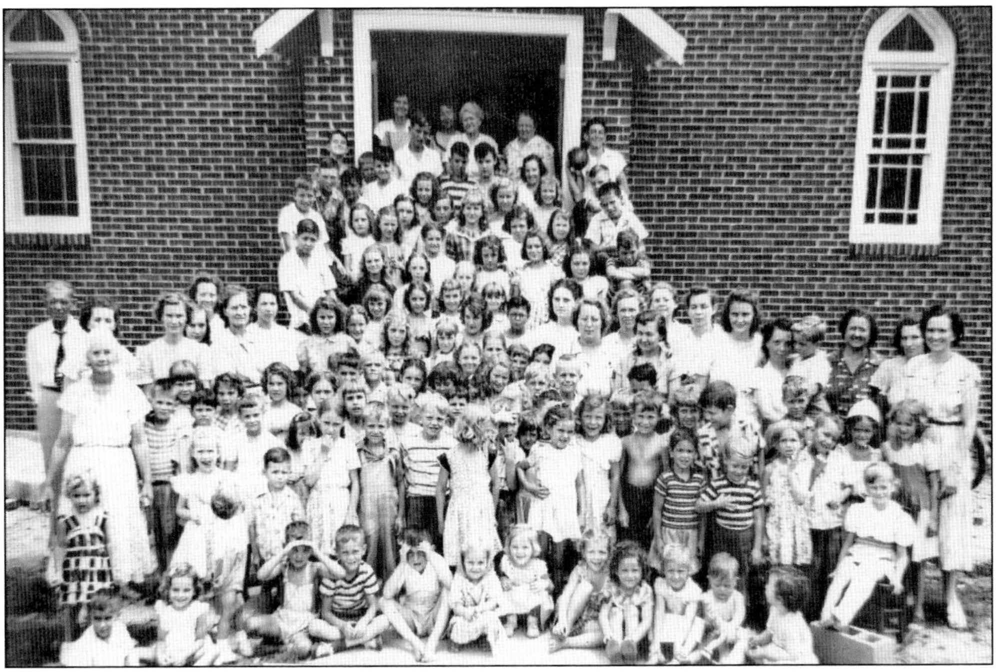

Vacation Bible school has always been a popular activity for young people in Soddy-Daisy during the summer. Children typically participate in arts and crafts activities, memorizing Bible verses and watching skits that help them remember stories from the Bible. Shown here are youngsters at the First Baptist Church Vacation Bible School in 1949. Rev. Welcome H. Black was the pastor. (Courtesy of First Baptist Church Soddy-Daisy.)

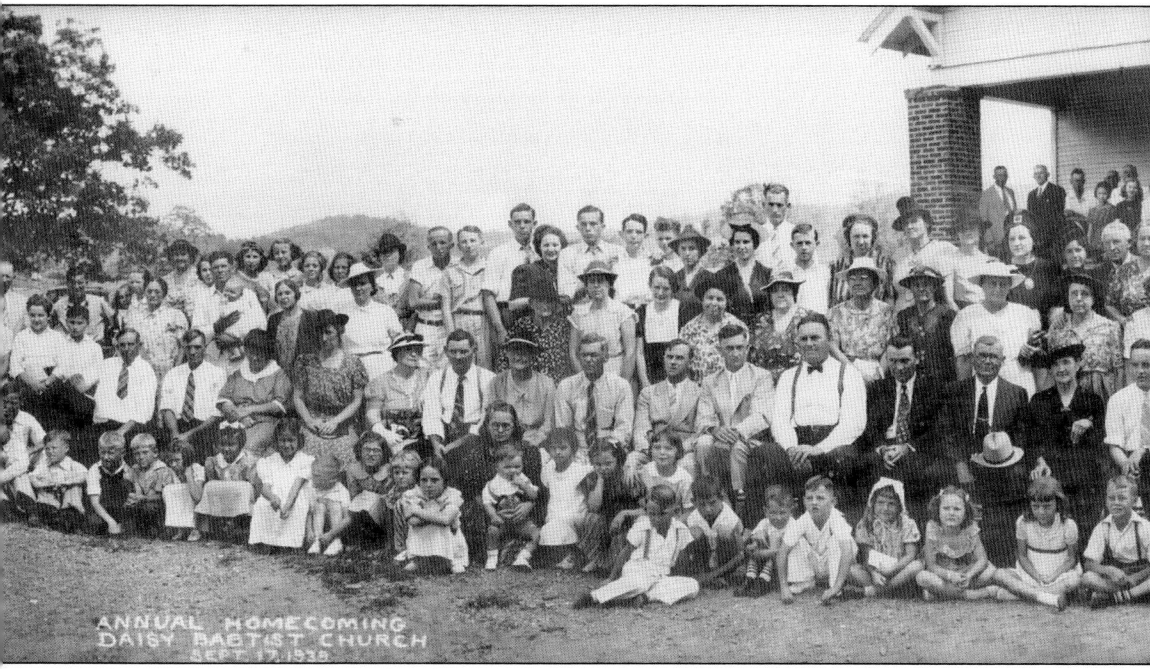

Members of the Daisy Baptist Church in Daisy gathered on September 17, 1939, for their annual homecoming celebration. Homecoming celebrations are a time when previous members who may have moved away and all current members come together to fellowship and reminisce. This split panoramic picture shows Baptists young and old and even one young man in a hospital bed who still made it a priority to attend. (Courtesy of the First Baptist Church Soddy-Daisy.)

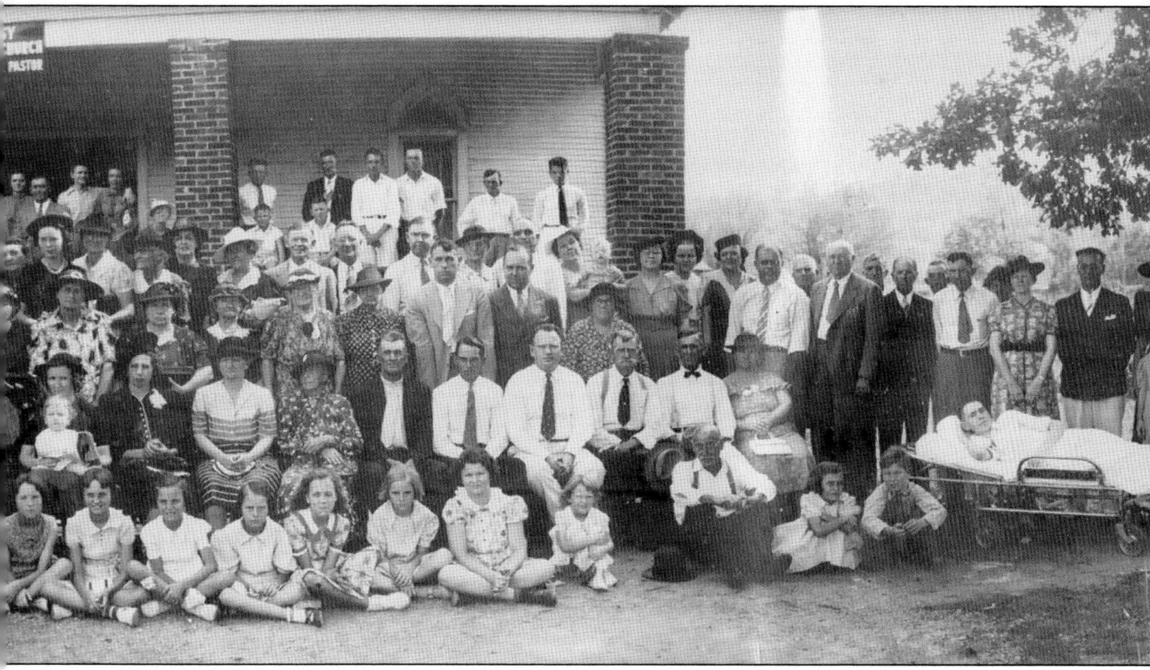

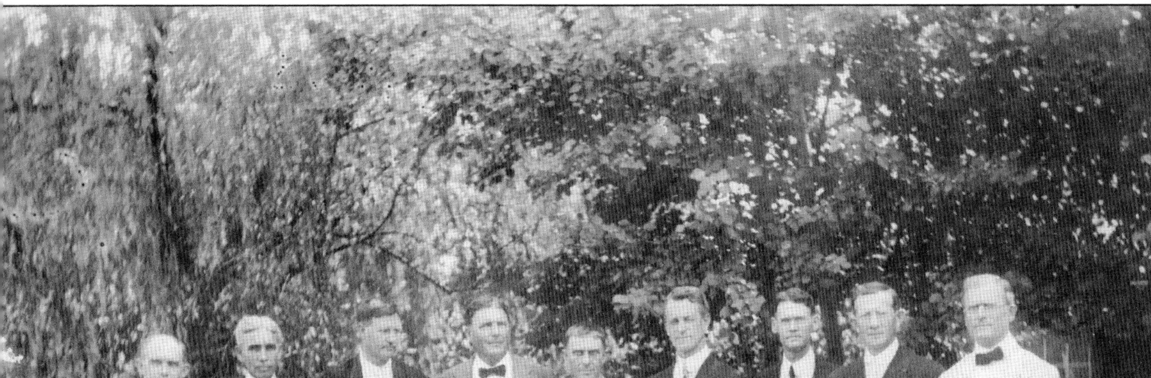

The Soddy Presbyterian Church was originally organized under the name Mount Bethel Presbyterian Church on December 1, 1828. Since that time, there have been a remarkable amount of religious leaders, including ministers, deacons, elders, and missionaries, sent out from the church. Ministers present for the 100th anniversary celebration from August 10 to 12, 1928, were the former pastor Dugald Monroe (front, left) and the present pastor Roy Bachman (front, right). Pastors who were sent out from the church also returned for the reunion. From left to right on the back row, with their congregations listed, are: James D. Wallace (Decatur, Alabama), Wallace Clift (Tampa, Florida), John R. Roberts (Carthage, North Carolina), Benjamin E. Wallace (Paris, Texas), Emmona Wallace (Seneca, South Carolina), J. R. McRee (Iva, South Carolina), Lewis Patterson (Savannah, Georgia), Quincy Wallace (Franklin, North Carolina), and Albert E. Wallace (Lancaster, Texas). Another notable minister sent out by Soddy Presbyterian Church was the Reverend Albert Wallace, who served as president of King College in Bristol, Tennessee. (Courtesy of Soddy Presbyterian Church.)

Five

WORK

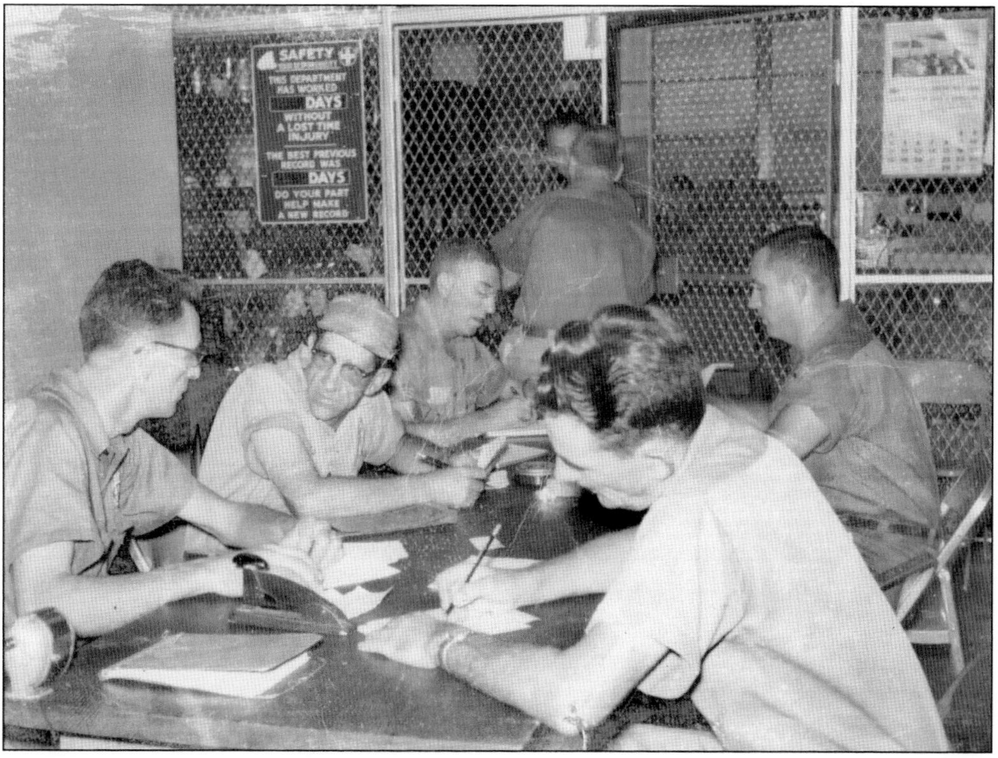

The Electric Power Board (EPB) in Chattanooga was created in 1935 by an act of the Tennessee Legislature. The EPB served its first customers, six homes in East Chattanooga, in 1939. In this image, Eugene Copeland (second from left) is preparing orders. The men were responsible for going to people's homes and repairing appliances, from water heaters to washers. Copeland worked at the EPB for about 30 years. (Courtesy of Frank Copeland.)

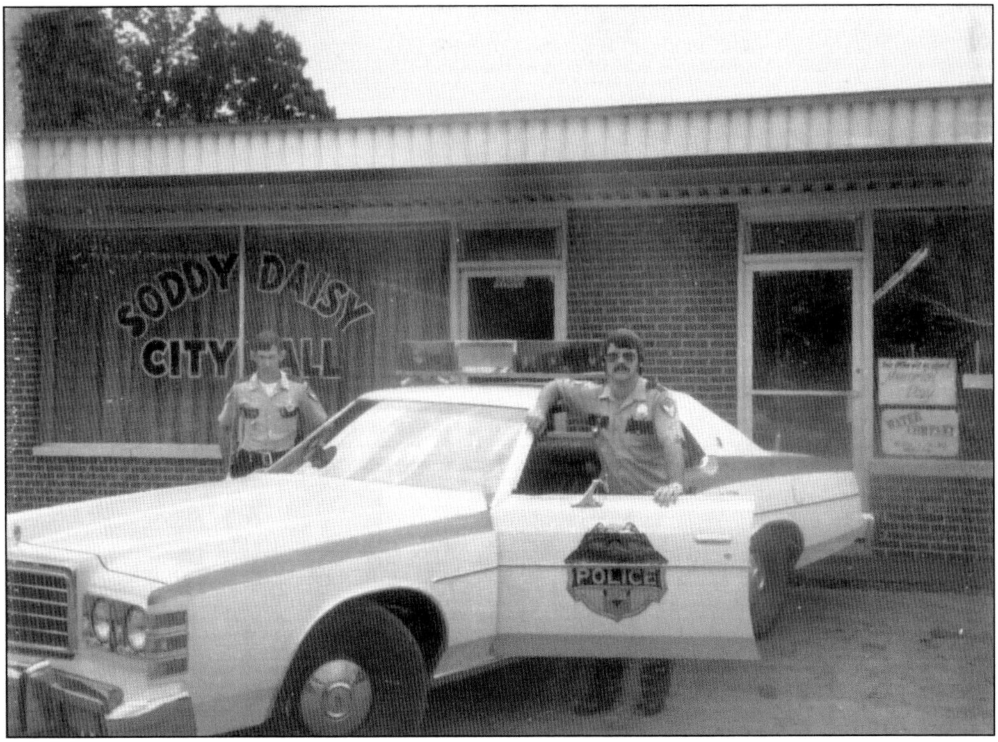

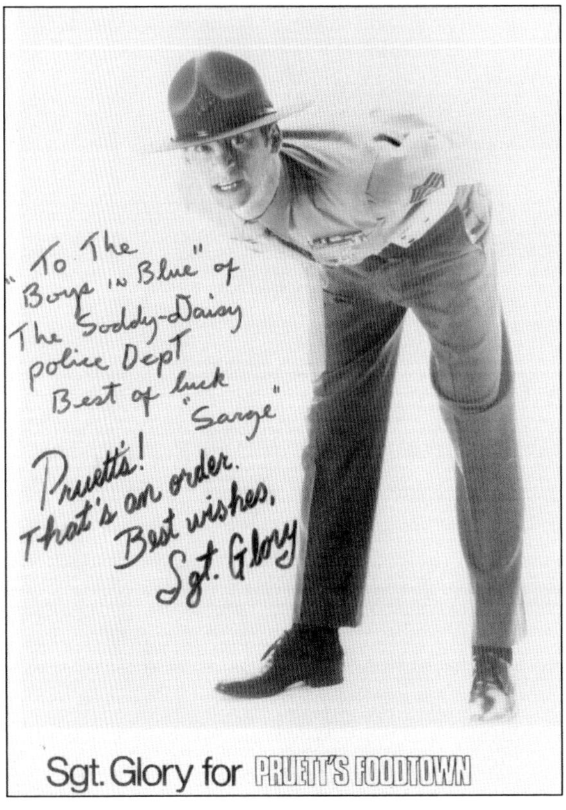

Bill Clendenon (left) and Allen Branum pause beside a new patrol car in front of Soddy-Daisy City Hall in 1977. The city obtained its first patrol cars in 1969, but additional resources are always welcome. Branum worked as a Soddy-Daisy policeman from 1977 to 1985 and then worked for the Sheriff's Department for a number of years. He returned to Soddy-Daisy as police chief in 1999. (Courtesy of Soddy-Daisy Police Department.)

Pruett's Food Town was located on Dayton Pike, where the Family Dollar now is. This was a convenient place to shop for many in and around Daisy. Sergeant Glory did television advertisements for the grocery store and often traveled around doing promotions. This picture was signed for the men of the Soddy-Daisy Police Department. (Courtesy of Soddy-Daisy Police Department.)

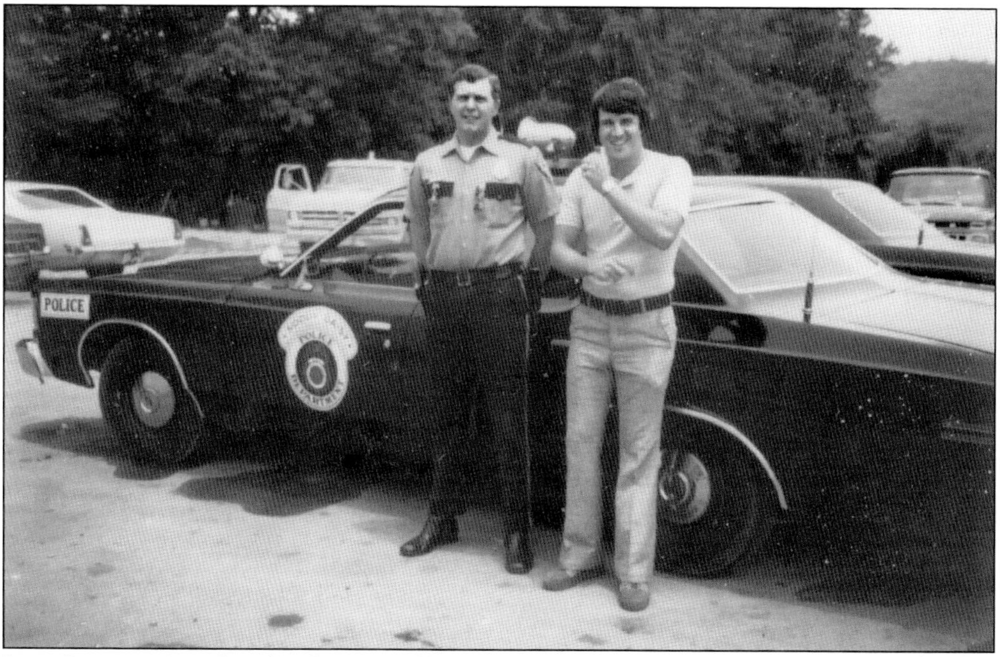

Larry Laverne Sneed and Robert McAllister pause from their duties to have this photograph taken in the early 1970s in front of a Soddy-Daisy police car. Sneed went on to serve as police chief at Red Bank. (Courtesy of Soddy-Daisy Police Department.)

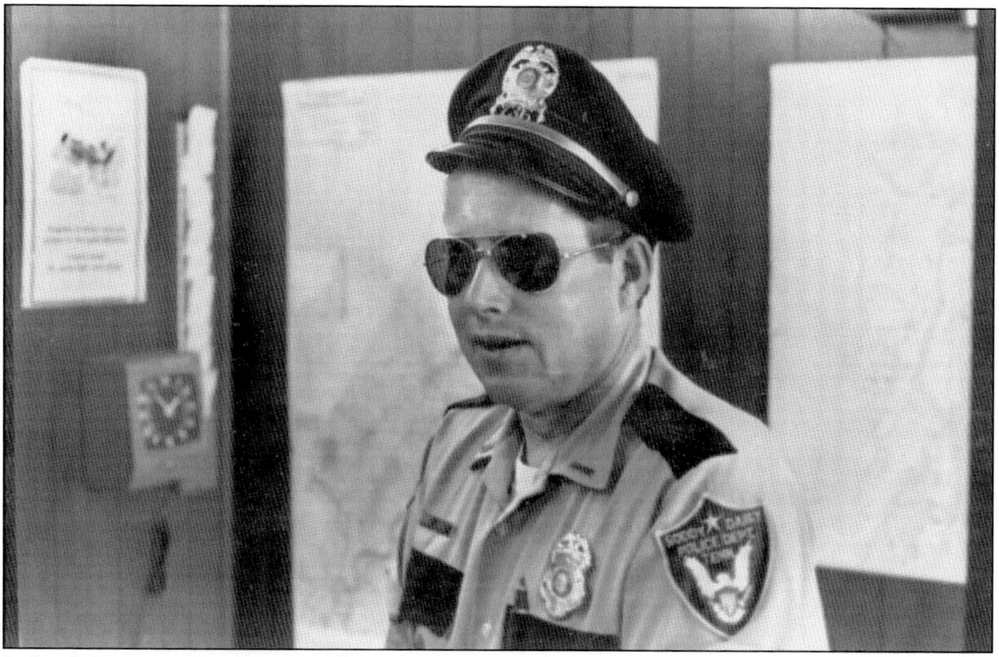

Roland Branum, known as "Shorty," was one of the first part-time officers hired in the early 1970s. Shorty performed traditional duties of a police officer, including patrolling the community, answering emergency calls, and tending to the needs of citizens. Flora Jett Branum, his wife, also worked for the Soddy-Daisy Police Department as a dispatcher and later retired as a communications sergeant. (Courtesy of Soddy-Daisy Police Department.)

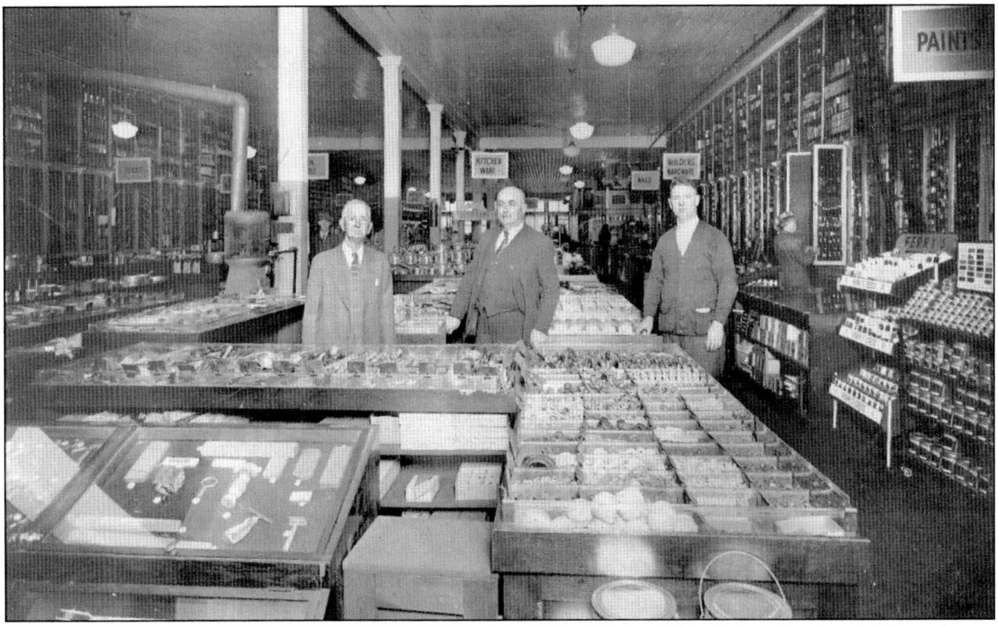

Chrisman Hardware was once the largest hardware store in Chattanooga. Typical hardware store items such as tools, nails, building supplies, and kitchenware can be seen advertised on signs throughout the store. Also pictured are two unidentified men and Robert S. Floyd (far right). Working for Chrisman inspired Floyd to start his own hardware company with his son, Malcolm, after Malcolm returned from World War II. (Courtesy of Rob Floyd.)

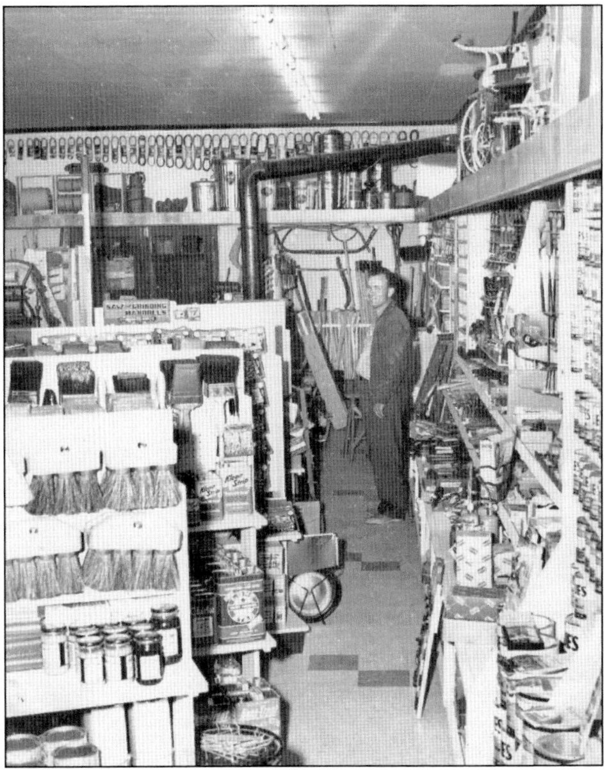

Malcolm Floyd, pictured here, started Floyd Hardware with his father, Robert S. Floyd (1898–1968), in 1947 in downtown Daisy, on Dayton Pike. Robert had worked for Chrisman Hardware, a large hardware store in Chattanooga, and he decided to open his own store in either Soddy-Daisy or St. Elmo. Obviously he ultimately chose Soddy-Daisy and went into business with his son, Malcolm. (Courtesy of Rob Floyd.)

Gene Clayton, pictured here, worked for Floyd Hardware for a number of years, performing duties from putting up stock to delivering general merchandise. Some of the items Floyd Hardware has carried over the years have included lamps and dishes, but you can also see the traditional items such as rakes, brooms, and baskets that are still sold at the store. (Courtesy of Rob Floyd.)

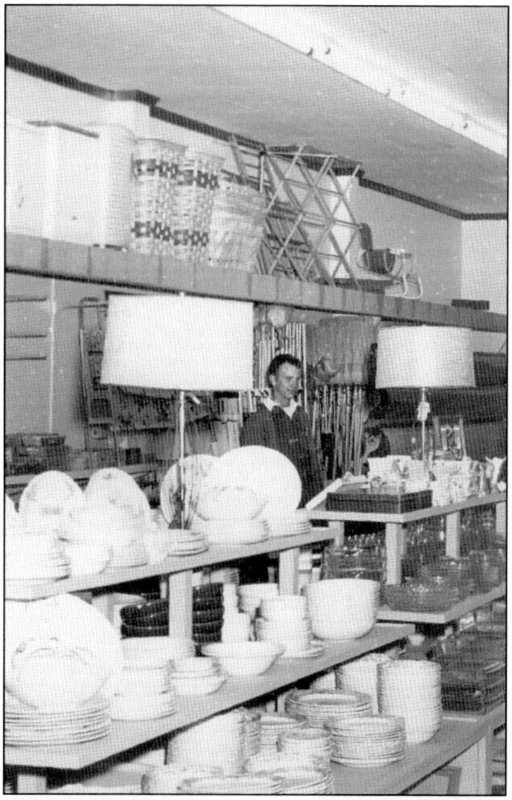

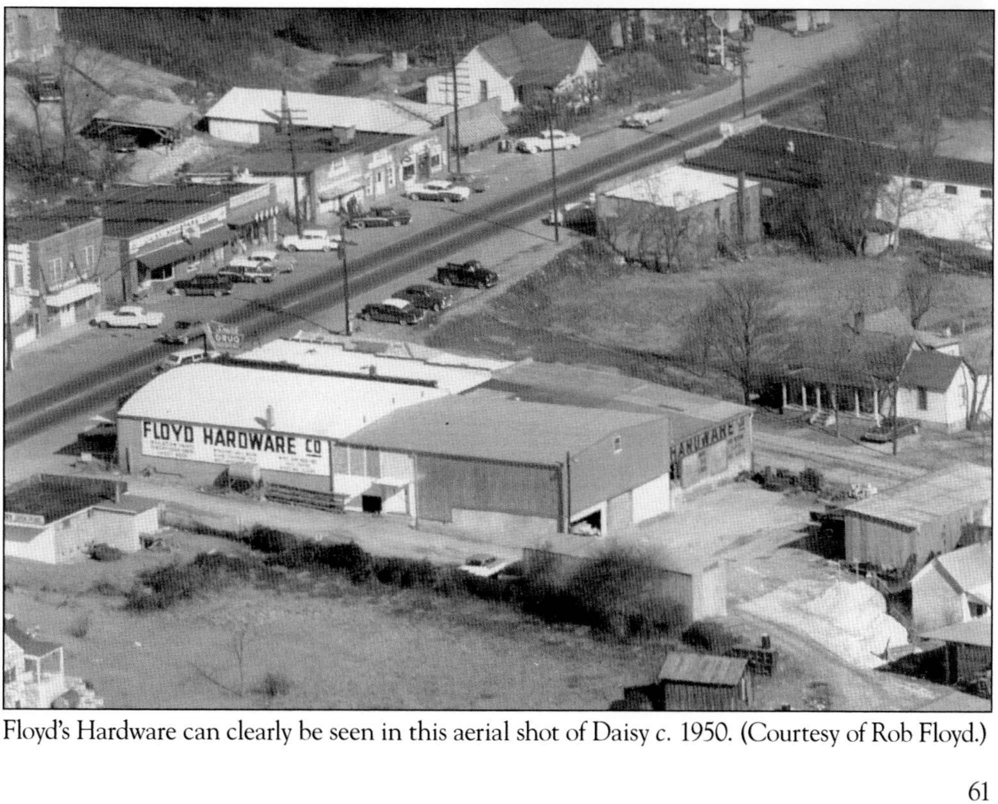

Floyd's Hardware can clearly be seen in this aerial shot of Daisy c. 1950. (Courtesy of Rob Floyd.)

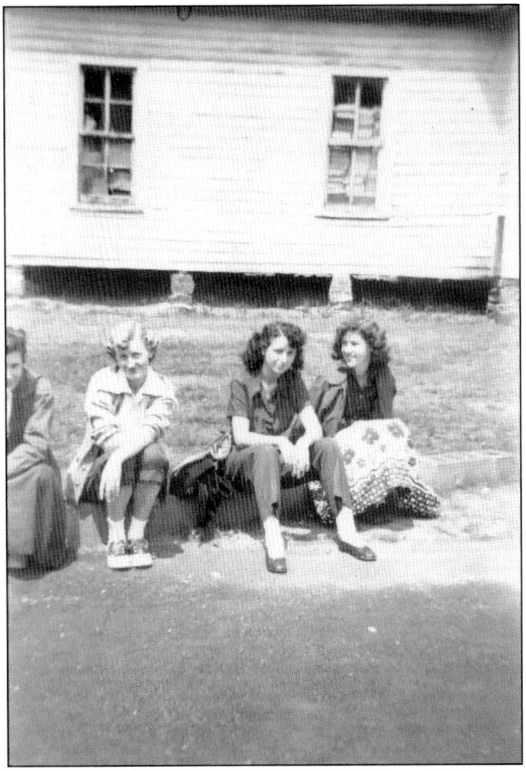

Janie Carney, Louise Ritchie, and Jean Wilson (left to right) pause for a lunch break at the Kingsboro Silk Mills c. 1950. There were various departments at the mill where the silk was processed, including a spinning room, dying room, and sewing room. There was also a shipping room where the lingerie made from the silk was shipped out. (Courtesy of Kay Williams.)

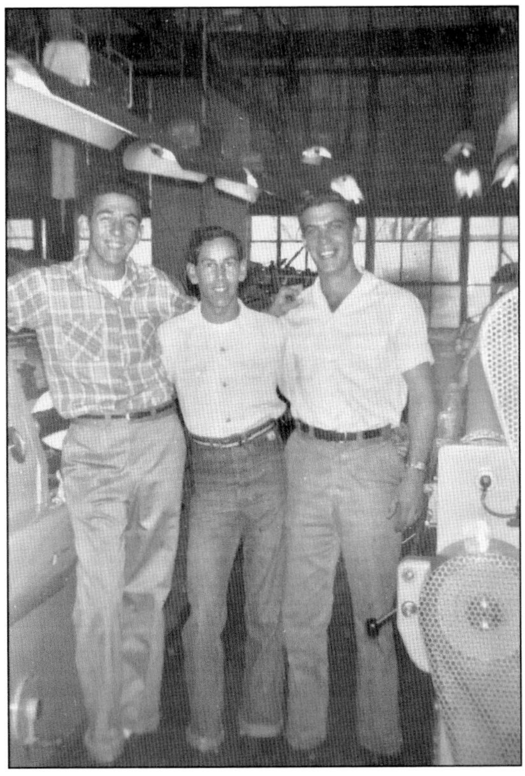

Employees of the Kingsboro Silk Mills pause for this 1954 photograph. From left to right are Bill Green, Dickie LeCroy, and Arlis Jones. Kingsboro was located on Bean Street in downtown Daisy, and the company made Rogers' Lingerie and other products. (Courtesy of Kay Williams.)

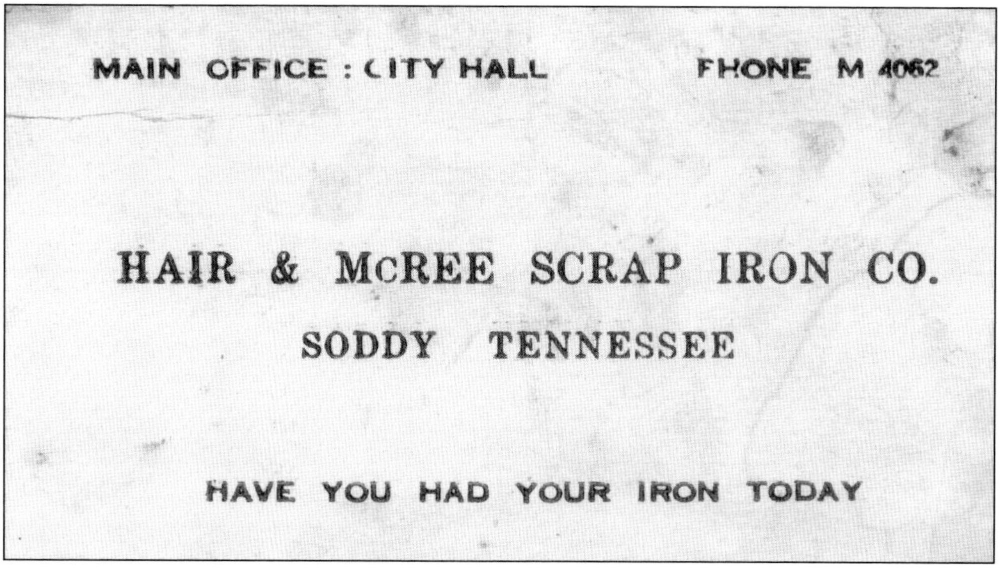

A business card for the Hair and McRee Scrap Iron Company in Soddy, Tennessee, advertises the office as being in city hall and the phone number as M 4062. (Courtesy of A. B. and Frankie McRee.)

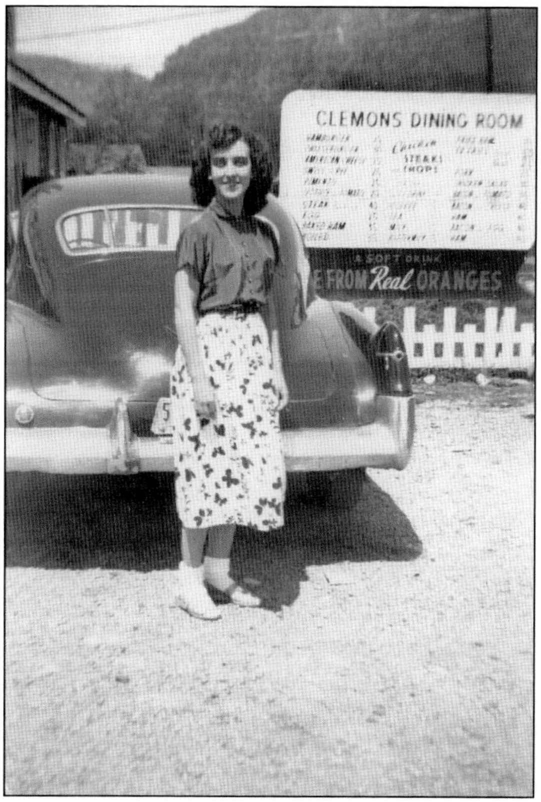

Anna Mae Jones stands in front of the Clemons Dining Room on Mile Straight, where she was taking her lunch break. One could buy a cheeseburger for 30¢, milk for a dime, and bacon and eggs for 40¢. Those were the good old days. (Courtesy of Kay Rogers Williams.)

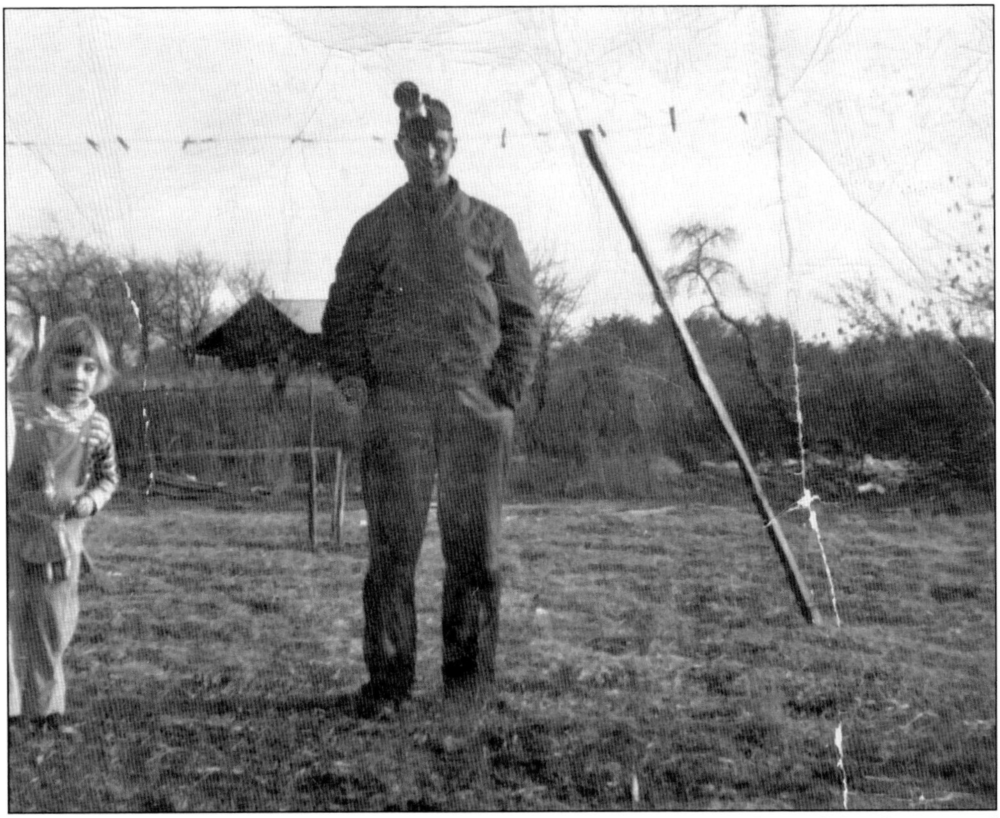

While the Native Americans and early settlers had little need for coal, need for the mineral increased dramatically following the Civil War. Industry was developing rapidly during this time, and coal was used as fuel for locomotives, coal stoves, and furnaces. Pictured here is an unidentified coal miner from Daisy in 1956. (From the authors' collection.)

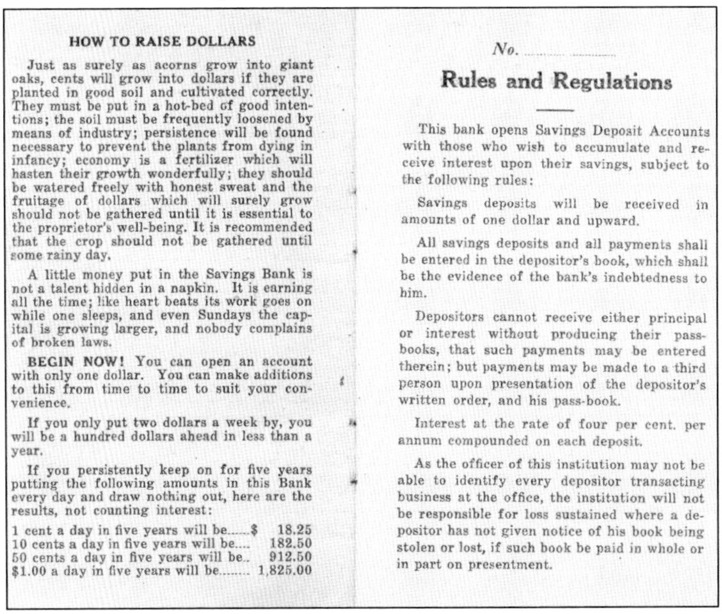

HOW TO RAISE DOLLARS

Just as surely as acorns grow into giant oaks, cents will grow into dollars if they are planted in good soil and cultivated correctly. They must be put in a hot-bed of good intentions; the soil must be frequently loosened by means of industry; persistence will be found necessary to prevent the plants from dying in infancy; economy is a fertilizer which will hasten their growth wonderfully; they should be watered freely with honest sweat and the fruitage of dollars which will surely grow should not be gathered until it is essential to the proprietor's well-being. It is recommended that the crop should not be gathered until some rainy day.

A little money put in the Savings Bank is not a talent hidden in a napkin. It is earning all the time; like heart beats its work goes on while one sleeps, and even Sundays the capital is growing larger, and nobody complains of broken laws.

BEGIN NOW! You can open an account with only one dollar. You can make additions to this from time to time to suit your convenience.

If you only put two dollars a week by, you will be a hundred dollars ahead in less than a year.

If you persistently keep on for five years putting the following amounts in this Bank every day and draw nothing out, here are the results, not counting interest:

1 cent a day in five years will be......$ 18.25
10 cents a day in five years will be.... 182.50
50 cents a day in five years will be.. 912.50
$1.00 a day in five years will be........ 1,825.00

No. ....

Rules and Regulations

This bank opens Savings Deposit Accounts with those who wish to accumulate and receive interest upon their savings, subject to the following rules:

Savings deposits will be received in amounts of one dollar and upward.

All savings deposits and all payments shall be entered in the depositor's book, which shall be the evidence of the bank's indebtedness to him.

Depositors cannot receive either principal or interest without producing their passbooks, that such payments may be entered therein; but payments may be made to a third person upon presentation of the depositor's written order, and his pass-book.

Interest at the rate of four per cent. per annum compounded on each deposit.

As the officer of this institution may not be able to identify every depositor transacting business at the office, the institution will not be responsible for loss sustained where a depositor has not given notice of his book being stolen or lost, if such book be paid in whole or in part on presentment.

The front of Elmer Bert Crites's bankbook from Soddy Banking Company asks patrons to "leave your book once a month for balancing." Also patrons are encouraged to put even small amounts of money away at a time because "just as surely as acorns grow into giant oaks, cents will grow into dollars if they are planted in good soil and cultivated correctly." (Courtesy of Scott Brogdon.)

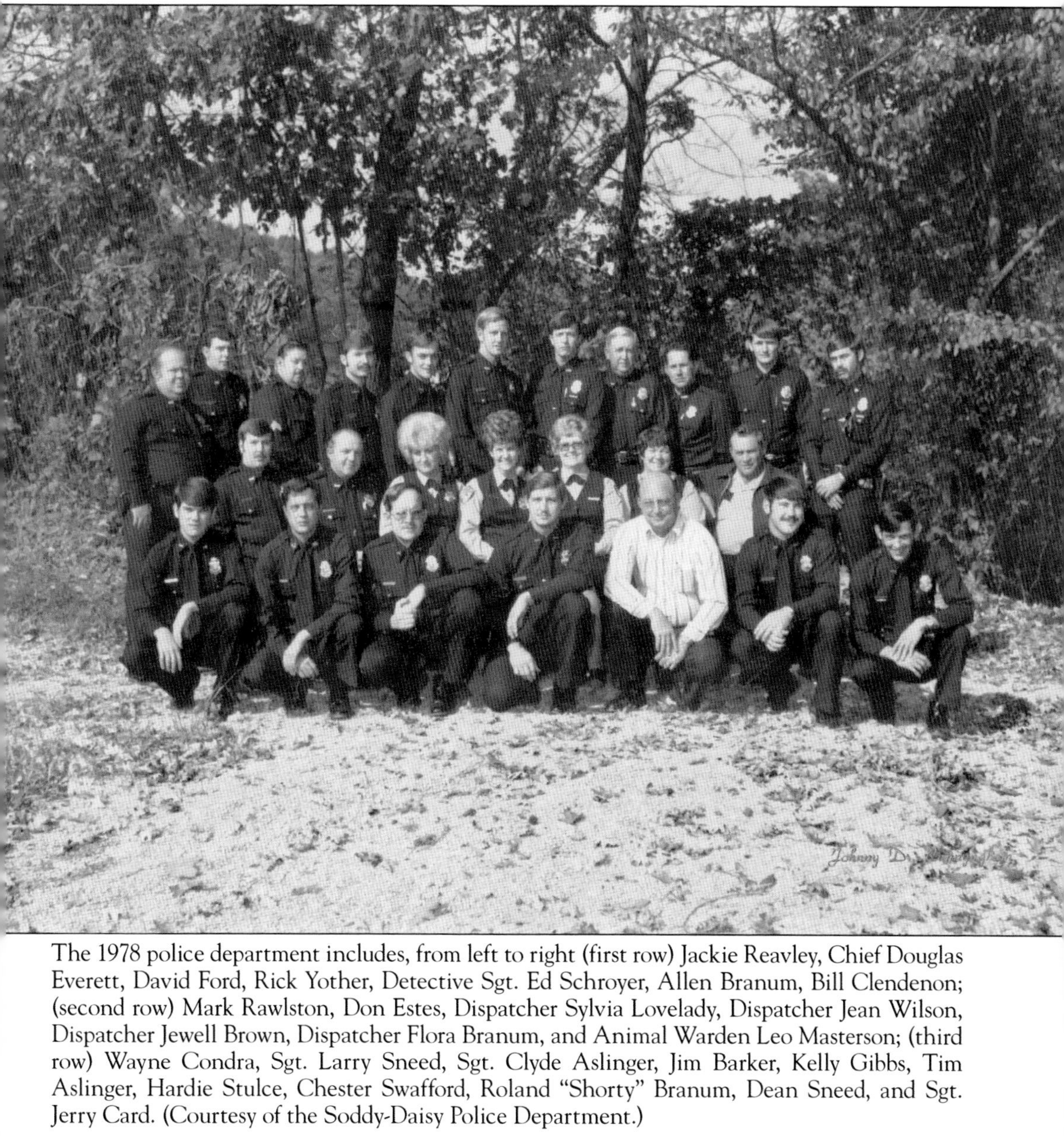

The 1978 police department includes, from left to right (first row) Jackie Reavley, Chief Douglas Everett, David Ford, Rick Yother, Detective Sgt. Ed Schroyer, Allen Branum, Bill Clendenon; (second row) Mark Rawlston, Don Estes, Dispatcher Sylvia Lovelady, Dispatcher Jean Wilson, Dispatcher Jewell Brown, Dispatcher Flora Branum, and Animal Warden Leo Masterson; (third row) Wayne Condra, Sgt. Larry Sneed, Sgt. Clyde Aslinger, Jim Barker, Kelly Gibbs, Tim Aslinger, Hardie Stulce, Chester Swafford, Roland "Shorty" Branum, Dean Sneed, and Sgt. Jerry Card. (Courtesy of the Soddy-Daisy Police Department.)

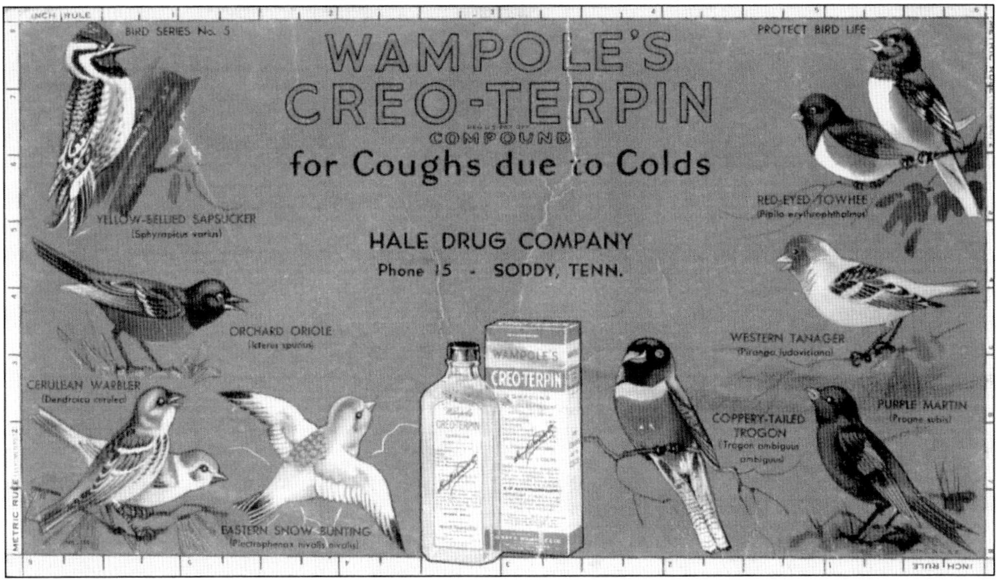

A card advertising Wampole's Creo-Terpin compound "for Coughs due to Colds" could also be used as a metric or inch ruler, and the back was used as an ink-blotter. The card could also be used to help identify birds. The cards were distributed by Hale Drug Company in Soddy. Notice the two-digit phone number (15) for Hale Drug Company. (Courtesy of Buck Johnson.)

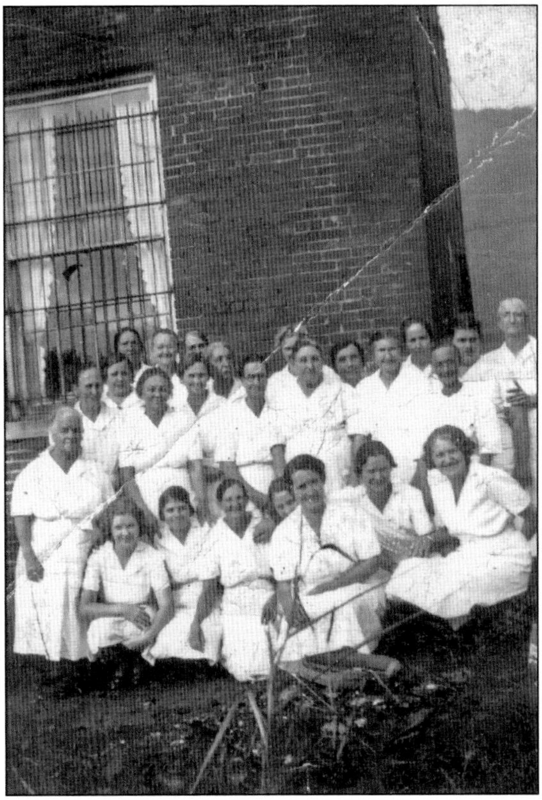

In the 1930s, during the Great Depression, Pres. Franklin D. Roosevelt initiated the Works Progress Administration (WPA) to put people back to work and boost the economy. Shown here are some of the women in the Soddy sewing unit of WPA in 1939. The women received a small salary, and the clothing they made would be distributed to local children. (Courtesy of Buck Johnson.)

Wesley Skiles, also known as "Mutt," stands in front of Rogers Grocery c. 1955. Earl Jonah Rogers opened the grocery store, which was located on Bean Street, in 1948, and he retired in 1972. Local people came in for groceries, animal feed, cloth, and other items of general interest and need. (Courtesy of Kay Williams.)

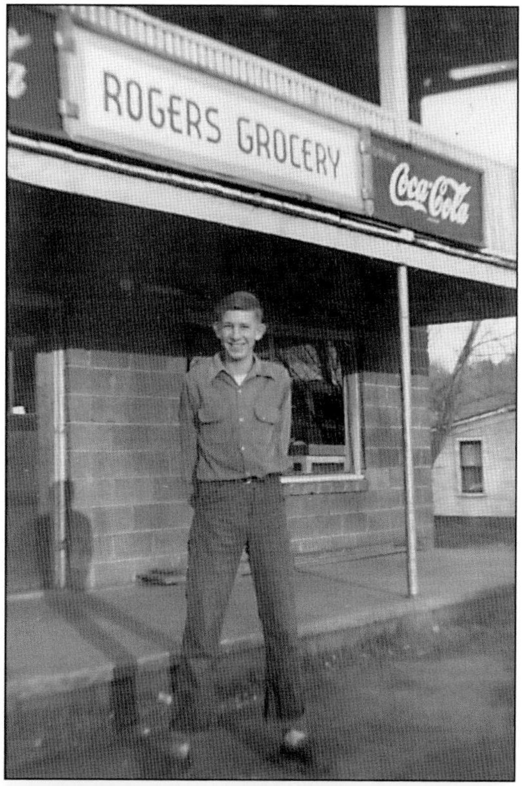

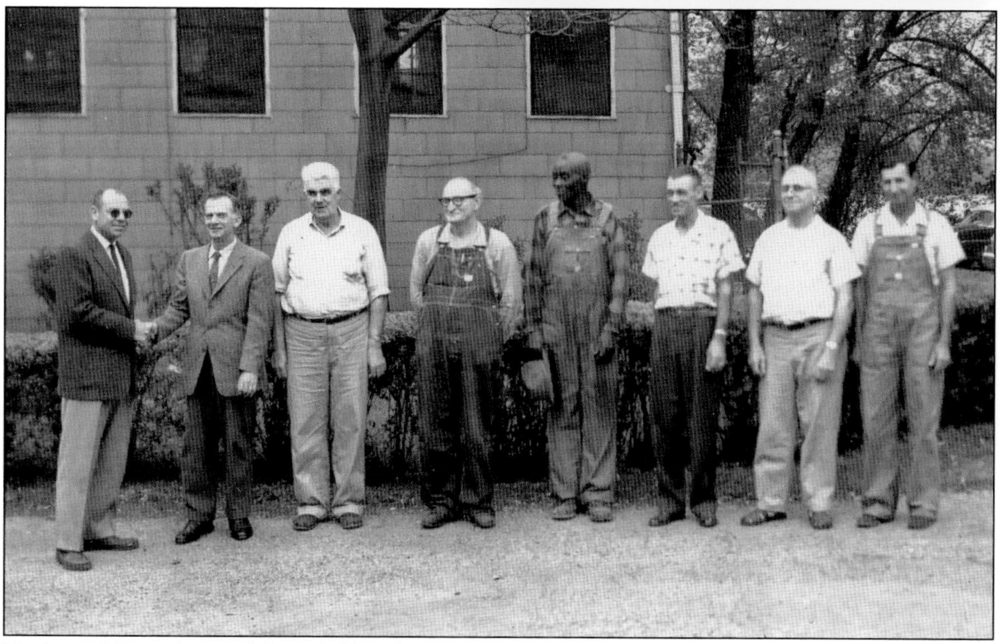

Nathaniel Levi (second from left) celebrates his retirement from the State of Tennessee with some fellow workers at the state garage c. 1960. Levi painted road signs. He was born on October 14, 1909, and died in June 1993. His wife was Francis Brown. (Courtesy of Tom and Barbara Levi.)

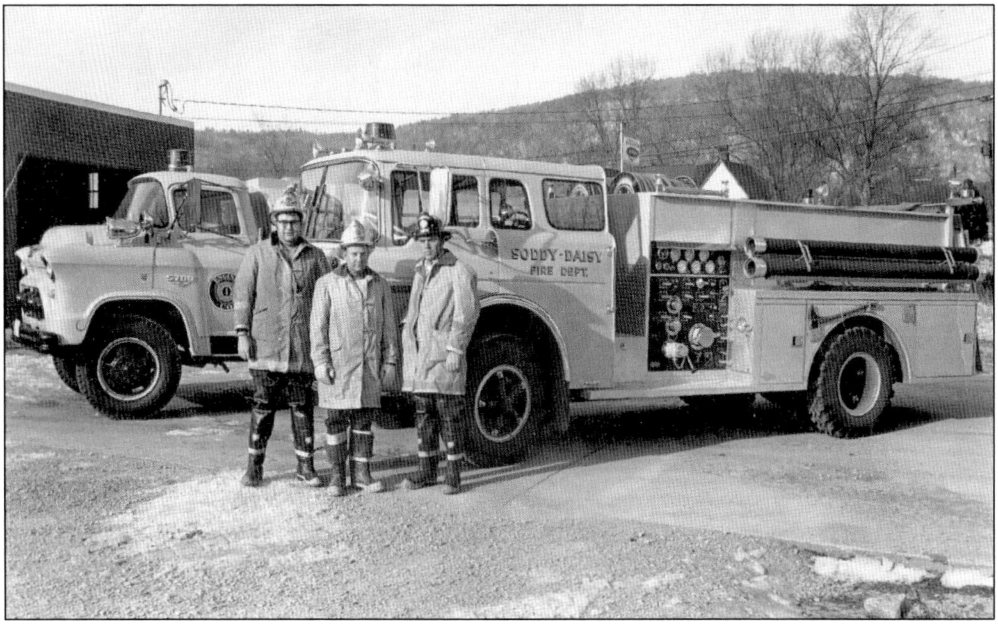

Before 1969, there was no fire protection available in this part of the county. Since the incorporation of Soddy-Daisy, the city has maintained volunteers. Shown here in 1971 is the first new fire engine, a pumper truck, purchased for the fire department. From left to right are Asst. Fire Chief Jerry Smith, Fire Chief Wayne Daniel, and Pump Operator Bill Blair. (Courtesy of Soddy-Daisy Fire Department.)

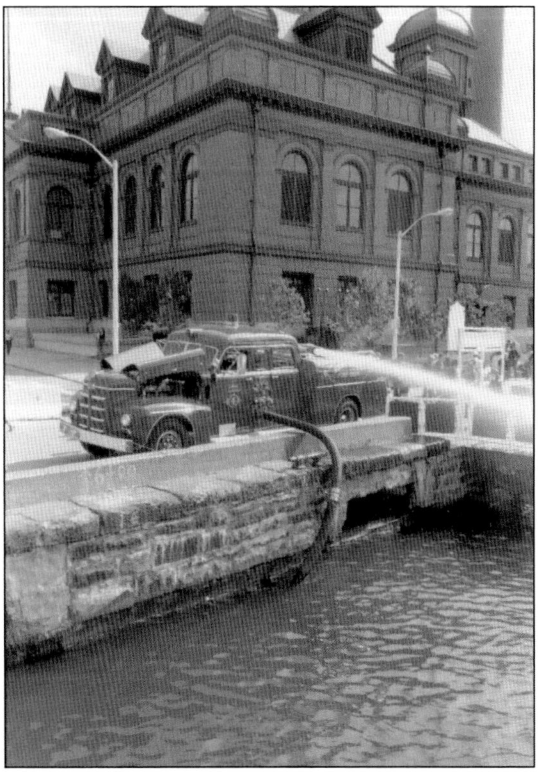

"Beulah," as this pumper truck is called, came to Soddy-Daisy from Friendship Royersford Fire Company in Pennsylvania. It is shown here at Boston Harbor. Beulah, a 1950 model Ahrens-Fox fire truck, was purchased for Soddy-Daisy in 1970. (Courtesy of Soddy-Daisy Fire Department.)

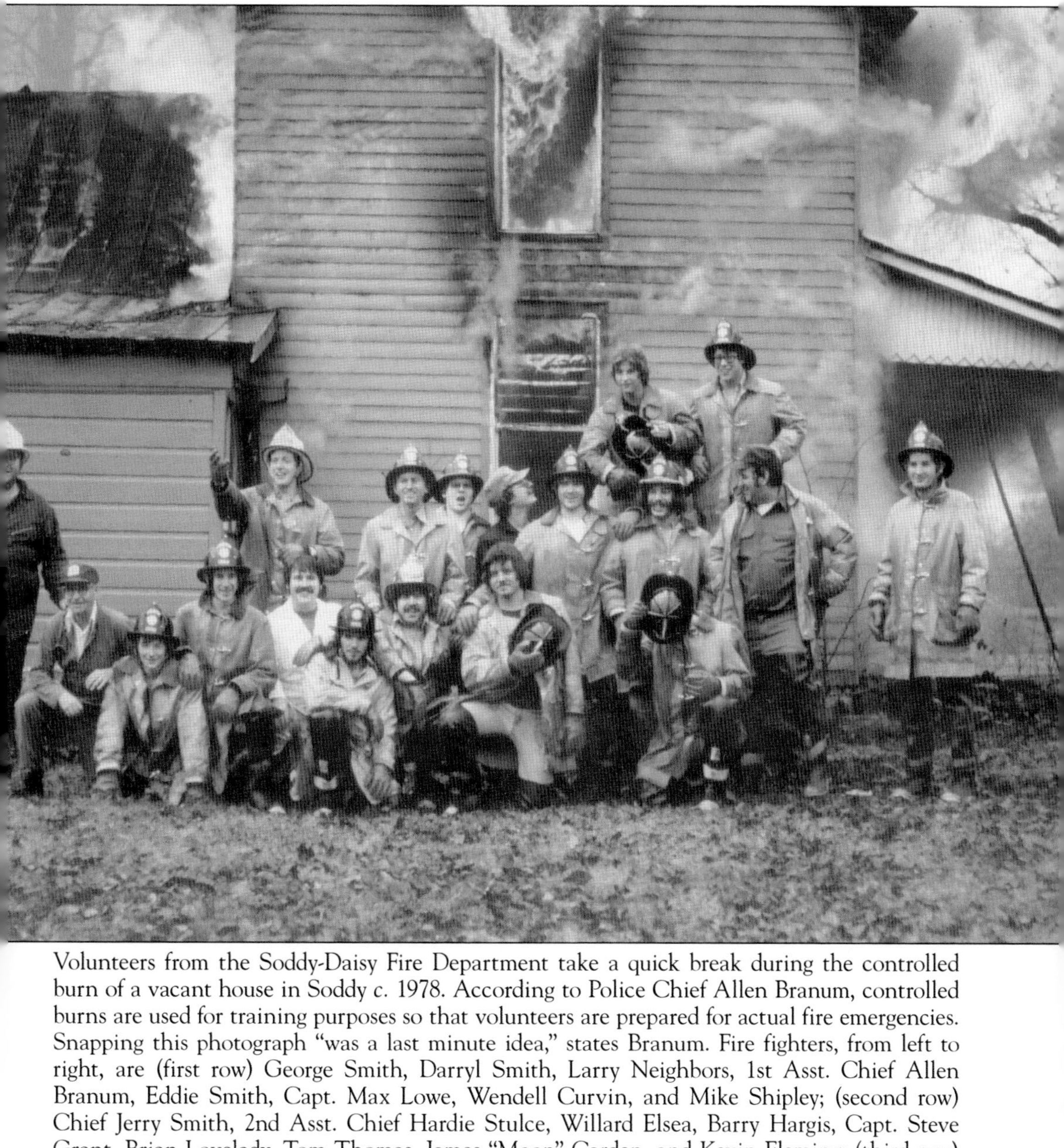

Volunteers from the Soddy-Daisy Fire Department take a quick break during the controlled burn of a vacant house in Soddy c. 1978. According to Police Chief Allen Branum, controlled burns are used for training purposes so that volunteers are prepared for actual fire emergencies. Snapping this photograph "was a last minute idea," states Branum. Fire fighters, from left to right, are (first row) George Smith, Darryl Smith, Larry Neighbors, 1st Asst. Chief Allen Branum, Eddie Smith, Capt. Max Lowe, Wendell Curvin, and Mike Shipley; (second row) Chief Jerry Smith, 2nd Asst. Chief Hardie Stulce, Willard Elsea, Barry Hargis, Capt. Steve Grant, Brian Lovelady, Tom Thomas, James "Moon" Carden, and Kevin Fleming; (third row) Jimmy Carden and David Johnston. (Courtesy of Soddy-Daisy Fire Department; photograph used by permission from *Chattanooga Times*.)

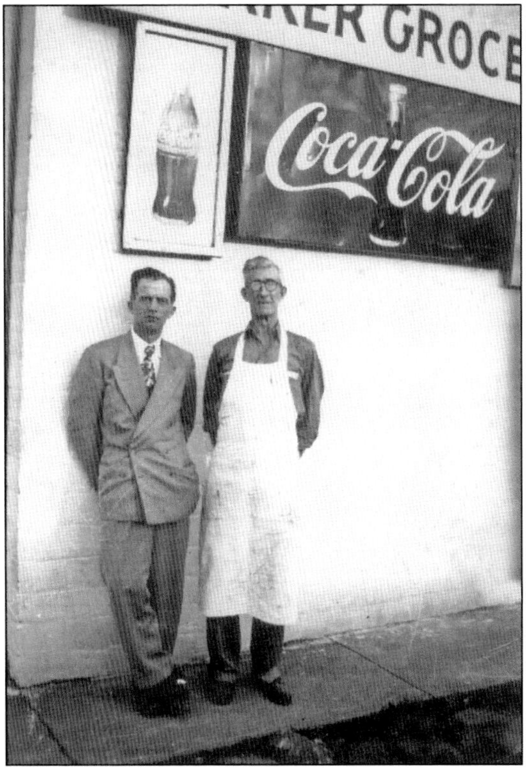

Mandriel Levi (left) and Joe Ottinger stand outside Barker Grocery in 1955. In the mid-20th century, many local farmers still grew their own produce, but grocery stores were appreciated for supplying items that weren't typically grown at home, such as salt, sugar, and cereals, or paper goods like toilet paper. Barker's grocery store was located on Depot Street. (Courtesy of Tom and Barbara Levi.)

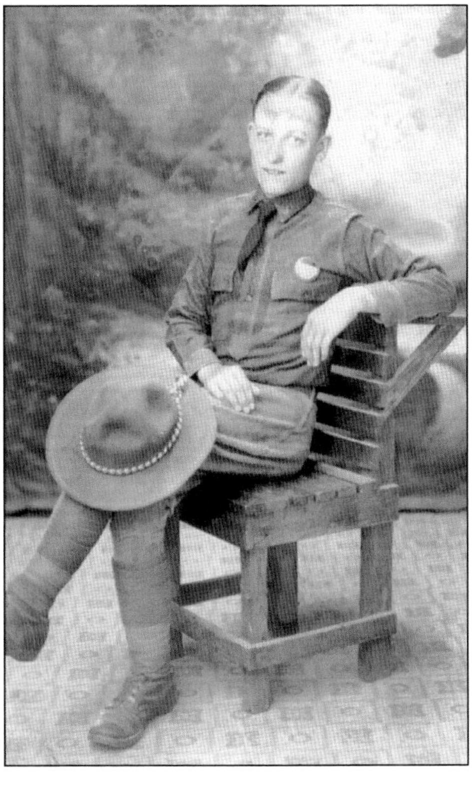

Elmer Bert Crites is dressed in a Civilian Conservation Corp (CCC) uniform c. 1935. The CCC was set up by Franklin D. Roosevelt as part of the New Deal program in 1933. The agency's goal was to put unemployed young men back to work following the Great Depression. The men planted trees, fought forest fires, built dams, and participated in other activities that conserved natural resources. (Courtesy of Scott Brogdon.)

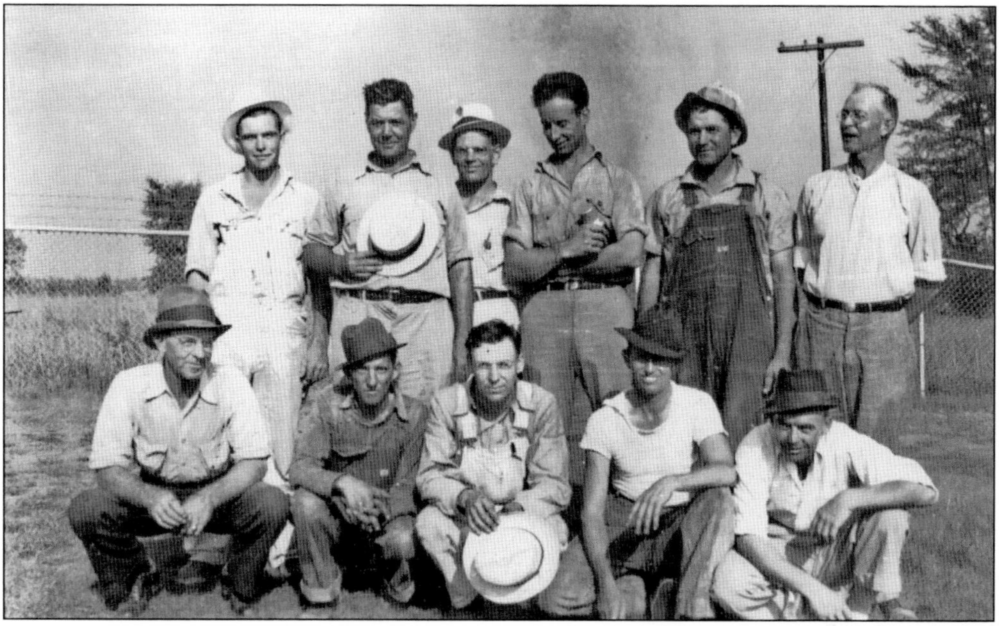

Construction started on the Tennessee Valley Authority's (TVA) Chickamauga Dam on January 13, 1936, at an initial cost of $39.8 million. The dam began to back up water on January 15, 1940, and the first hydroelectric turbine unit was put into power March 4, 1940. Dam construction workers are pictured here. For more information on the dam, consult the TVA Web site at www.tva.com. (Courtesy of Tom and Barbara Levi.)

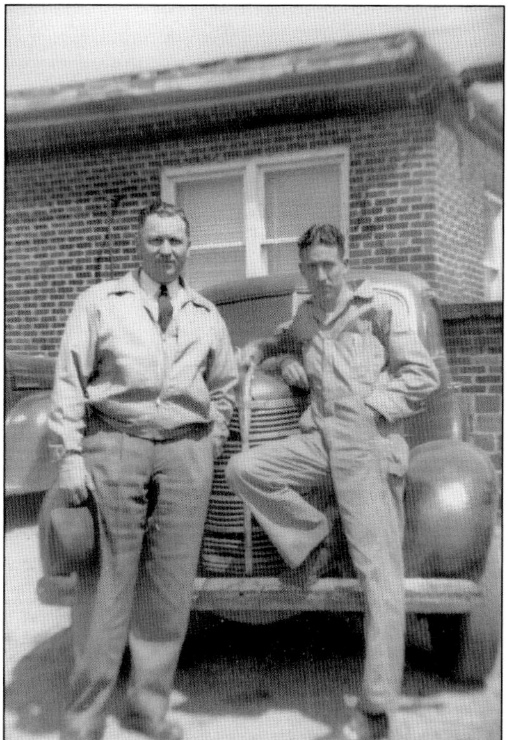

Kenneth Griswald (left) and Ray Shoemate pose in front of an office building at the Kingsboro Silk Mills. Both Griswald and Shoemate were in management at Kingsboro. (Courtesy of Kay Williams.)

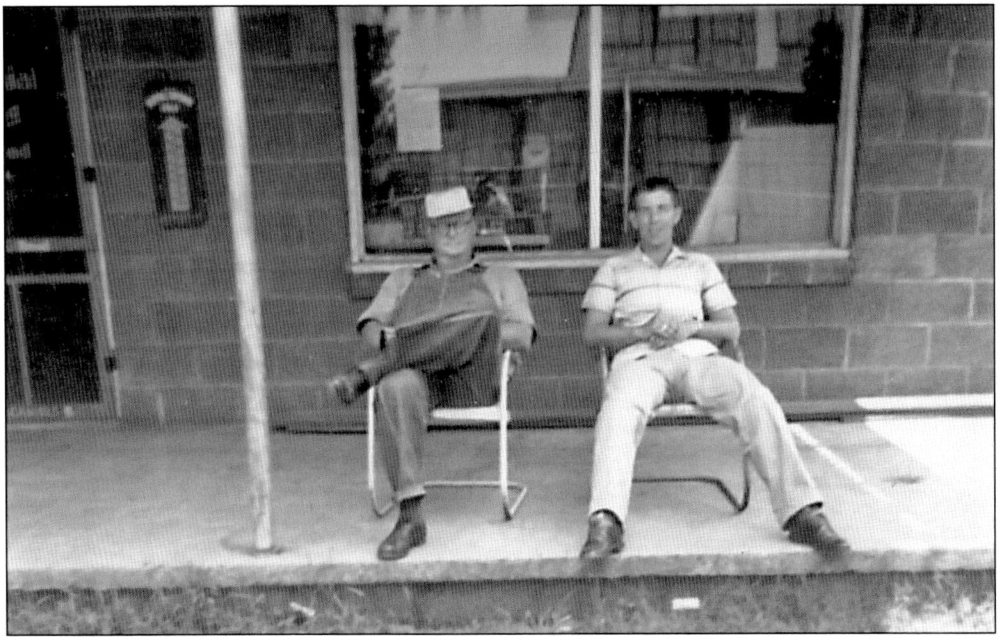

Jonah Rogers (left) and Duke Berry sit on the porch of Rogers' Grocery. Rogers was the owner of the store and not only enjoyed serving customers, but visiting with them as well. Young and old alike had the tradition of sitting on rocking chairs or barrels on the porch of the general store where they would "swap tales." Typical discussions would include history, news, and family information. (Courtesy of Kay Williams.)

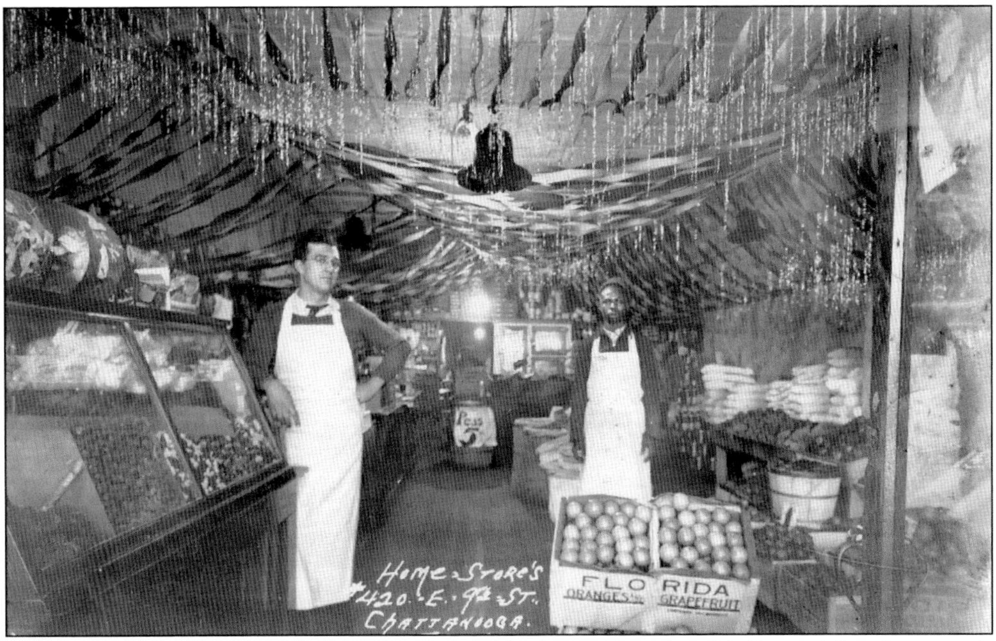

Clarence H. Elliott managed Home Stores in Chattanooga and Soddy-Daisy. The photograph was actually taken at the 420 E. Ninth Street, Chattanooga, location. Based on the decorations, this was around Christmas time. The Home Stores were owned by the McDonald family, who also owned the *Chattanooga Free Press*. (Courtesy of Tom and Barbara Levi.)

Joe Neal Sr. (left) and Walter Cothran owned the only barrel and drum company in Soddy-Daisy. The men traveled around the United States buying and selling used drums. They would frequently clean up drums from one location just to go sell them to another company. This photograph of the men was taken around 1956. (Courtesy of David and Clara Bowman.)

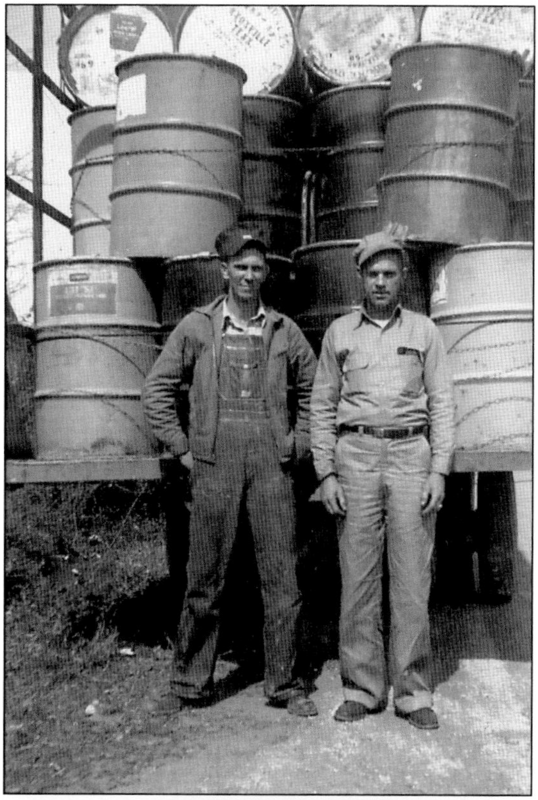

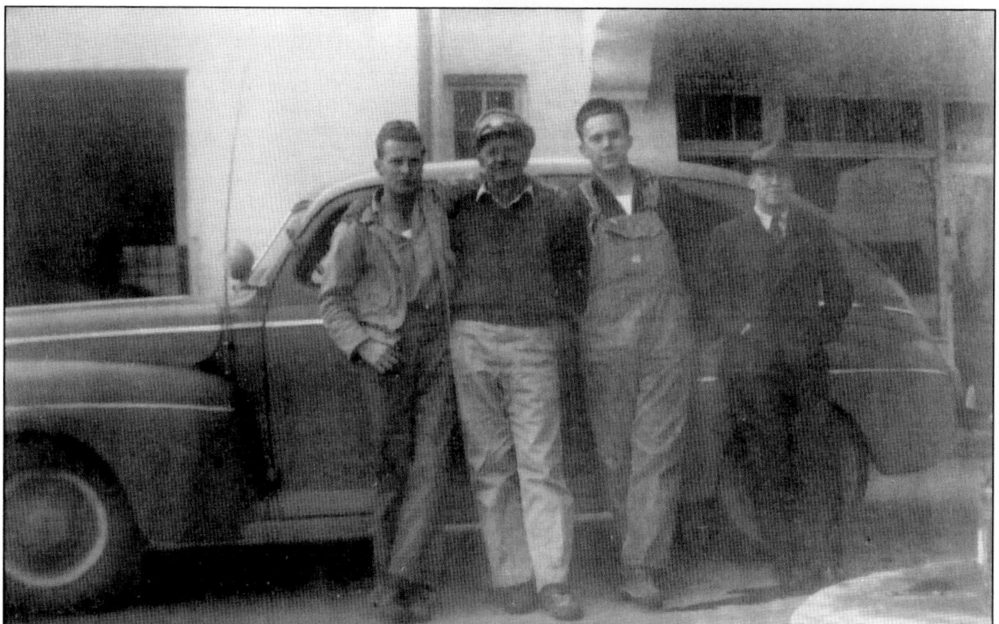

Sam Varner, Ernest Layne, Jim Longmire, and E. M. Glover (left to right) pause to pose for a photograph in front of the Daisy Gulf Station. Ernest Layne opened the station in the early 1930s and worked there until the mid-1960s. (Courtesy of Virgil Loftis.)

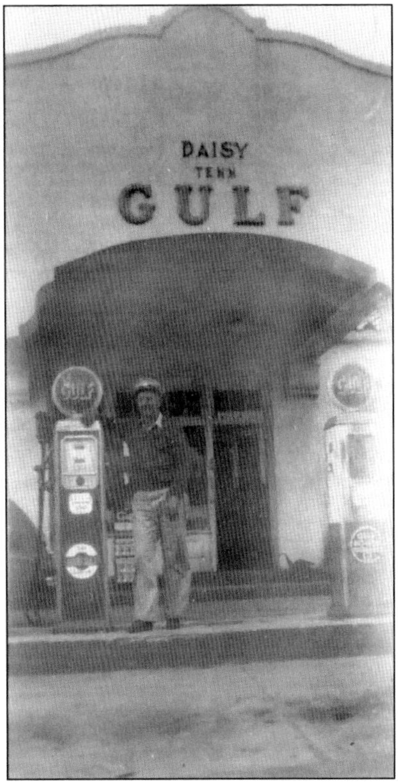

Ernest Layne opened the Daisy Gulf Station c. 1933. His son-in-law, Virgil Loftis, joined Layne in the business around 1945, after he returned from World War II. Layne sold the station to Brown Thurman about 1964. Thurman continued it as a gas station until his retirement. The building then stood empty for numerous years, but has recently been put to use again. (Courtesy of Virgil Loftis.)

Prior to 1969, when Soddy and Daisy incorporated, the Hamilton County Sheriff's Department was responsible for law enforcement in the area. After incorporation, the city formed its own police department. Since then, the Soddy-Daisy Police Department has used several different uniform patches, beginning with the patch on the left in 1969. The patch on the right has been worn since 1998. (Courtesy of Soddy-Daisy Police Department.)

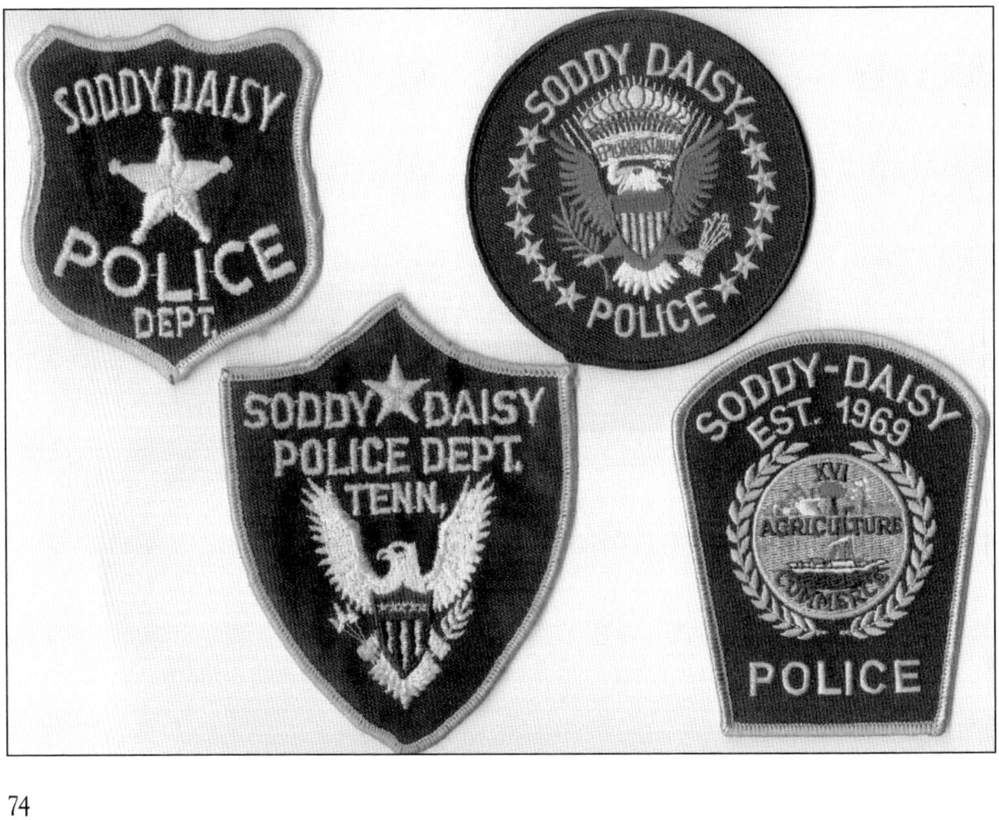

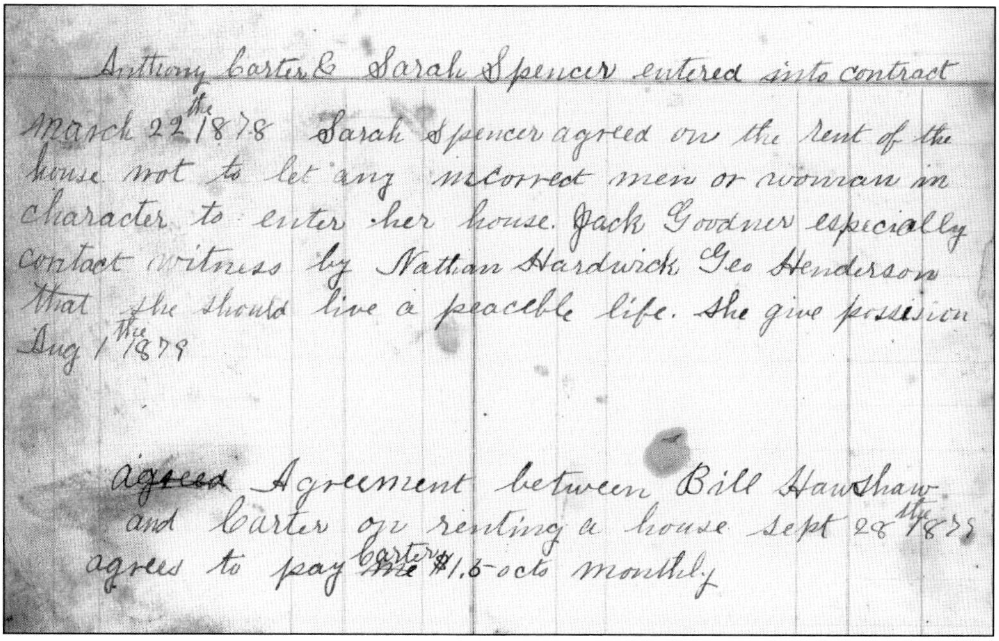

Anthony Carter & Sarah Spencer entered into contract March 22the 1878 Sarah Spencer agreed on the rent of the house not to let any incorrect men or woman in character to enter her house. Jack Goodner especially contact witness by Nathan Hardwick Geo Henderson that she should live a peacble life. She give possession Aug 1the 1879

~~agreed~~ Agreement between Bill Hawshaw and Carter on renting a house Sept 28the 187[illegible] agrees to pay Carter ~~the~~ $1.50cts monthly

Isaac and Paul Crites sold general merchandise at their I. Crites and Brother stores in Soddy (run by Isaac) and Cleveland, Tennessee (run by Paul). Items receipted in the ledger include eggs, beans, salt, and "sirup." Obviously, from the entry shown here, the ledgers were also used to keep track of various contractual agreements as well. (Courtesy of Scott Brogdon.)

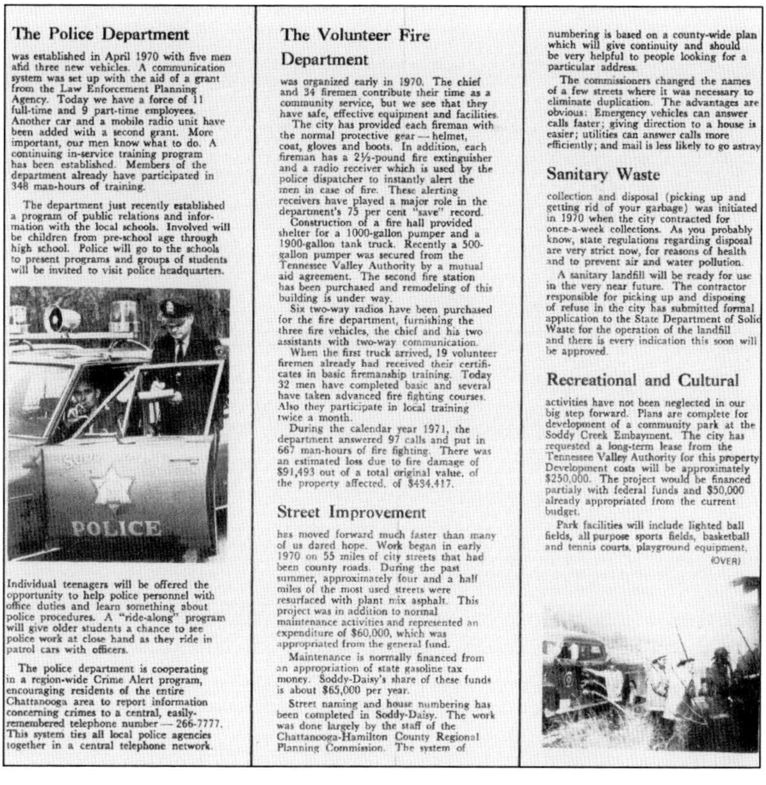

The Police Department

was established in April 1970 with five men afid three new vehicles. A communication system was set up with the aid of a grant from the Law Enforcement Planning Agency. Today we have a force of 11 full-time and 9 part-time employees. Another car and a mobile radio unit have been added with a second grant. More important, our men know what to do. A continuing in-service training program has been established. Members of the department already have participated in 348 man-hours of training.

The department just recently established a program of public relations and information with the local schools. Involved will be children from pre-school age through high school. Police will go to the schools to present programs and groups of students will be invited to visit police headquarters.

Individual teenagers will be offered the opportunity to help police personnel with office duties and learn something about police procedures. A "ride-along" program will give older students a chance to see police work at close hand as they ride in patrol cars with officers.

The police department is cooperating in a region-wide Crime Alert program, encouraging residents of the entire Chattanooga area to report information concerning crimes to a central, easily-remembered telephone number — 266-7777. This system ties all local police agencies together in a central telephone network.

The Volunteer Fire Department

was organized early in 1970. The chief and 34 firemen contribute their time as a community service, but we see that they have safe, effective equipment and facilities.

The city has provided each fireman with the normal protective gear — helmet, coat, gloves and boots. In addition, each fireman has a 2½-pound fire extinguisher and a radio receiver which is used by the police dispatcher to instantly alert the men in case of fire. These alerting receivers have played a major role in the department's 75 per cent "save" record.

Construction of a fire hall provided shelter for a 1000-gallon pumper and a 1900-gallon tank truck. Recently a 500-gallon pumper was secured from the Tennessee Valley Authority by a mutual aid agreement. The second fire station has been purchased and remodeling of this building is under way.

Six two-way radios have been purchased for the fire department, furnishing the three fire vehicles, the chief and his two assistants with two-way communication.

When the first truck arrived, 19 volunteer firemen already had received their certificates in basic firemanship training. Today 32 men have completed basic and several have taken advanced fire fighting courses. Also they participate in local training twice a month.

During the calendar year 1971, the department answered 97 calls and put in 667 man-hours of fire fighting. There was an estimated loss due to fire damage of $91,493 out of a total original value, of the property affected, of $434,417.

Street Improvement

has moved forward much faster than many of us dared hope. Work began in early 1970 on 55 miles of city streets that had been county roads. During the past summer, approximately four and a half miles of the most used streets were resurfaced with plant mix asphalt. This project was in addition to normal maintenance activities and represented an expenditure of $60,000, which was appropriated from the general fund.

Maintenance is normally financed from an appropriation of state gasoline tax money. Soddy-Daisy's share of these funds is about $65,000 per year.

Street naming and house numbering has been completed in Soddy-Daisy. The work was done largely by the staff of the Chattanooga-Hamilton County Regional Planning Commission. The system of numbering is based on a county-wide plan which will give continuity and should be very helpful to people looking for a particular address.

The commissioners changed the names of a few streets where it was necessary to eliminate duplication. The advantages are obvious: Emergency vehicles can answer calls faster; giving direction to a house is easier; utilities can answer calls more efficiently; and mail is less likely to go astray

Sanitary Waste

collection and disposal (picking up and getting rid of your garbage) was initiated in 1970 when the city contracted for once-a-week collections. As you probably know, state regulations regarding disposal are very strict now, for reasons of health and to prevent air and water pollution.

A sanitary landfill will be ready for use in the very near future. The contractor responsible for picking up and disposing of refuse in the city has submitted formal application to the State Department of Solid Waste for the operation of the landfill and there is every indication this soon will be approved.

Recreational and Cultural

activities have not been neglected in our big step forward. Plans are complete for development of a community park at the Soddy Creek Embayment. The city has requested a long-term lease from the Tennessee Valley Authority for this property Development costs will be approximately $250,000. The project would be financed partialy with federal funds and $50,000 already appropriated from the current budget.

Park facilities will include lighted ball fields, all purpose sports fields, basketball and tennis courts, playground equipment.

(OVER)

An early brochure for the newly incorporated city of Soddy-Daisy reveals some interesting details. (Courtesy of the Soddy-Daisy Police Department.)

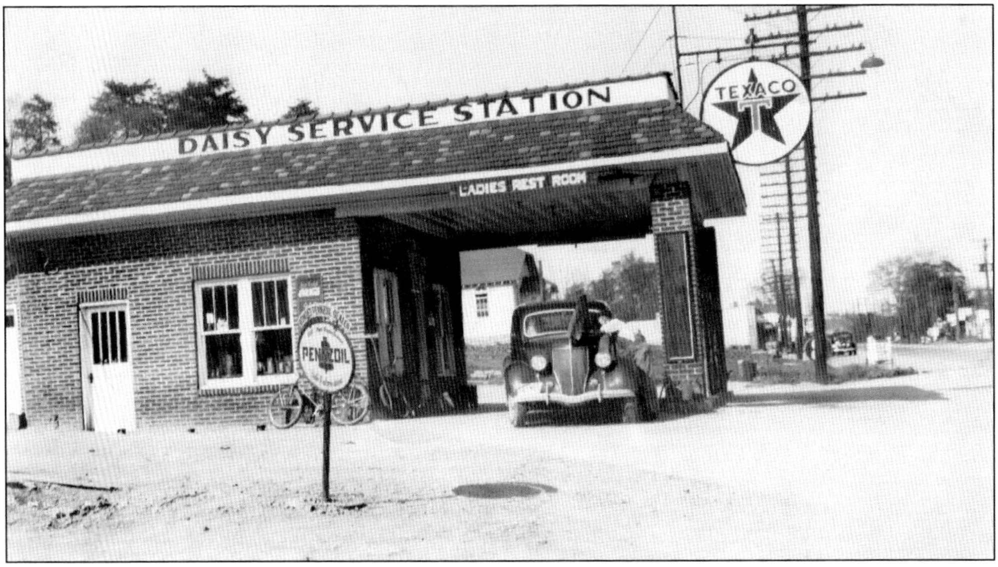

Pictured here c. 1936 is the Daisy Service Station started by George C. Hensley in 1926. Hensley ran the station until he was 96 years old in 1996. The station had provided service for customers for 70 years. (Courtesy of Bill and Patsy Hensley.)

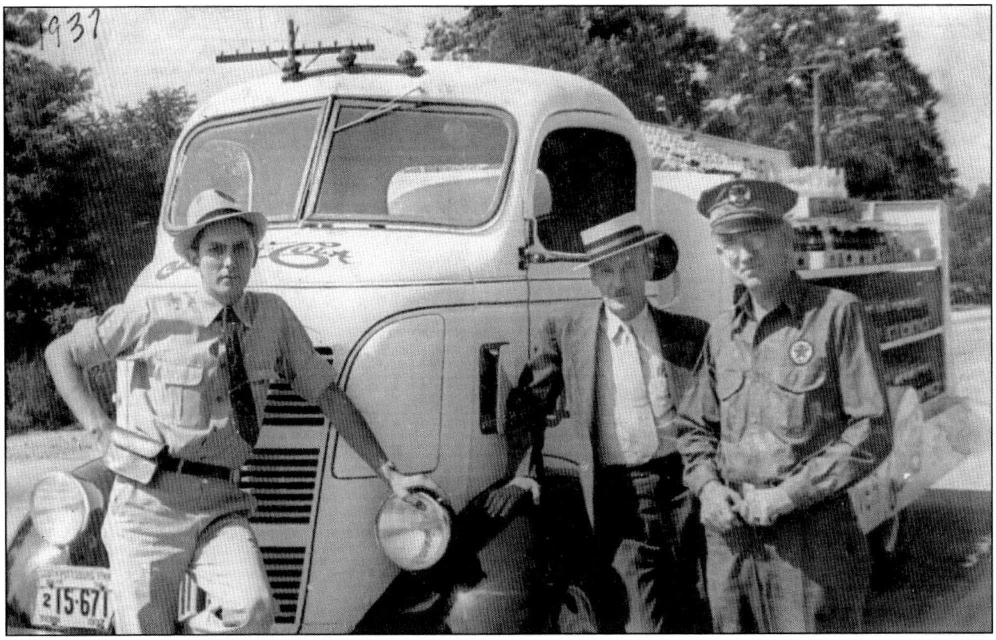

Representatives from the Coca-Cola Bottling Company would deliver bottles of Coke throughout the region. Shown here is a Coca-Cola delivery truck in 1937. George Hensley, accepting the order for his Daisy Service Station, is standing on the far right. (Courtesy of Bill and Patsy Hensley.)

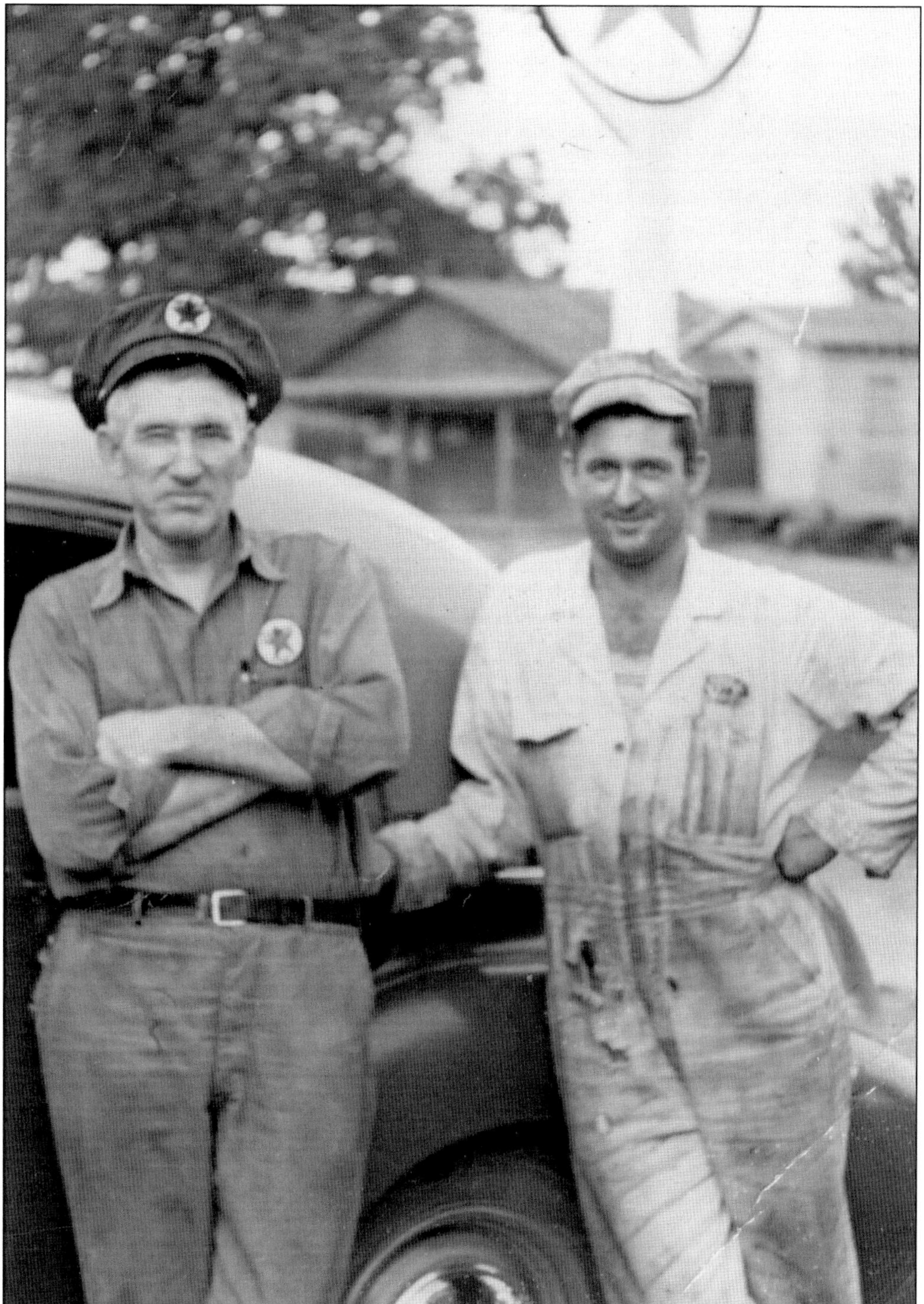

George Hensley (left) and Ernest Sluder pause to have their photograph taken outside the Daisy Service Station. Hensley owned the station and Sluder was a local mechanic. (Courtesy of Bill and Patsy Hensley.)

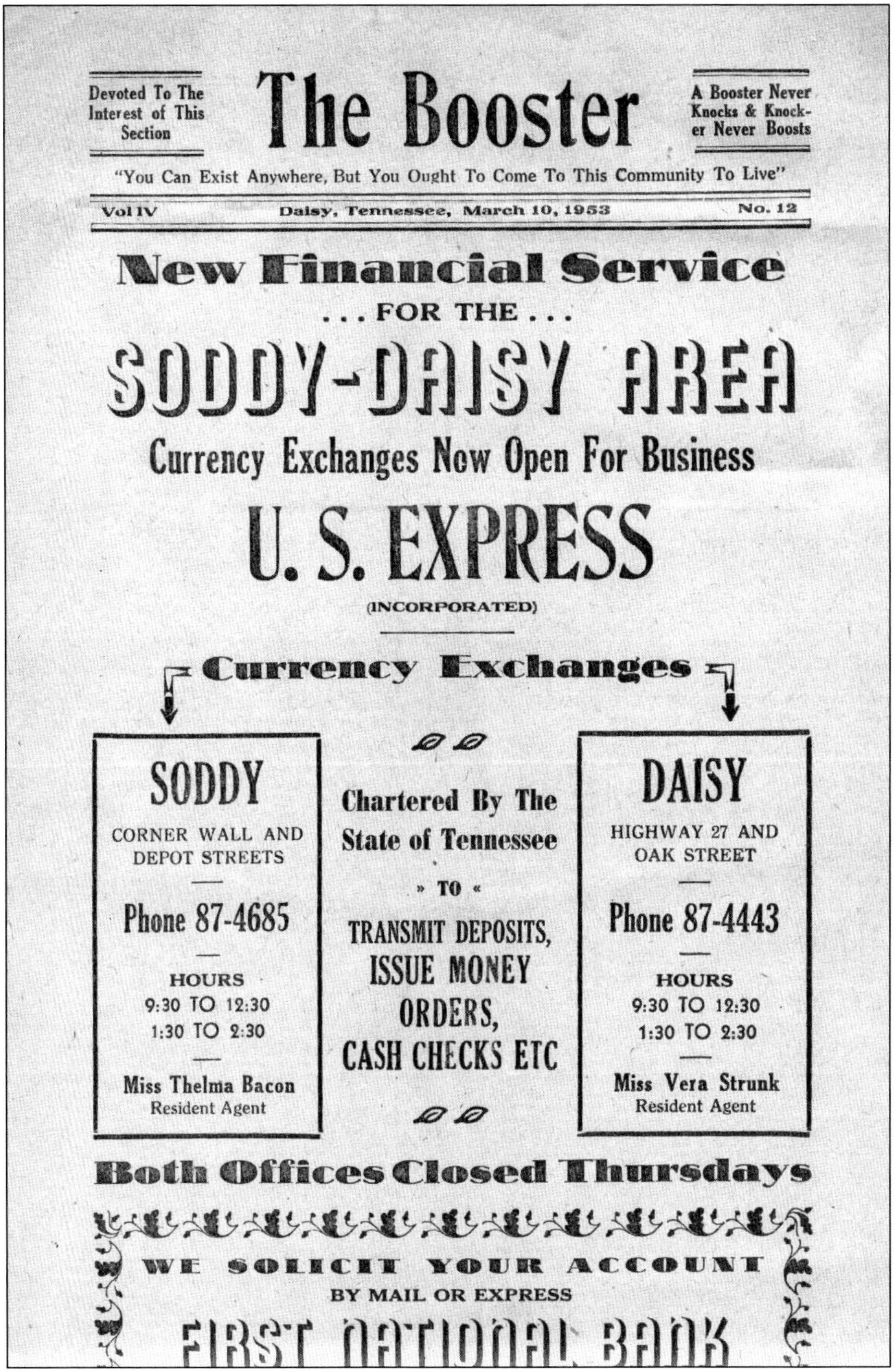

Devoted To The Interest of This Section

The Booster

A Booster Never Knocks & Knocker Never Boosts

"You Can Exist Anywhere, But You Ought To Come To This Community To Live"

Vol IV — Daisy, Tennessee, March 10, 1953 — No. 12

New Financial Service

. . . FOR THE . . .

SODDY-DAISY AREA

Currency Exchanges Now Open For Business

U. S. EXPRESS

(INCORPORATED)

Currency Exchanges

SODDY

CORNER WALL AND DEPOT STREETS

Phone 87-4685

HOURS

9:30 TO 12:30

1:30 TO 2:30

Miss Thelma Bacon

Resident Agent

Chartered By The State of Tennessee

» TO «

TRANSMIT DEPOSITS, ISSUE MONEY ORDERS, CASH CHECKS ETC

DAISY

HIGHWAY 27 AND OAK STREET

Phone 87-4443

HOURS

9:30 TO 12:30

1:30 TO 2:30

Miss Vera Strunk

Resident Agent

Both Offices Closed Thursdays

WE SOLICIT YOUR ACCOUNT

BY MAIL OR EXPRESS

FIRST NATIONAL BANK

A flyer soliciting business for First National Bank shows the hyphenated name of Soddy-Daisy already being used as early as March 1953. Notice interesting aspects of the flyer, such as the bank being closed on Thursdays, the six-digit phone number with a hyphen, and the shortened bank hours. (Courtesy of Scott Brogdon.)

Six

Military

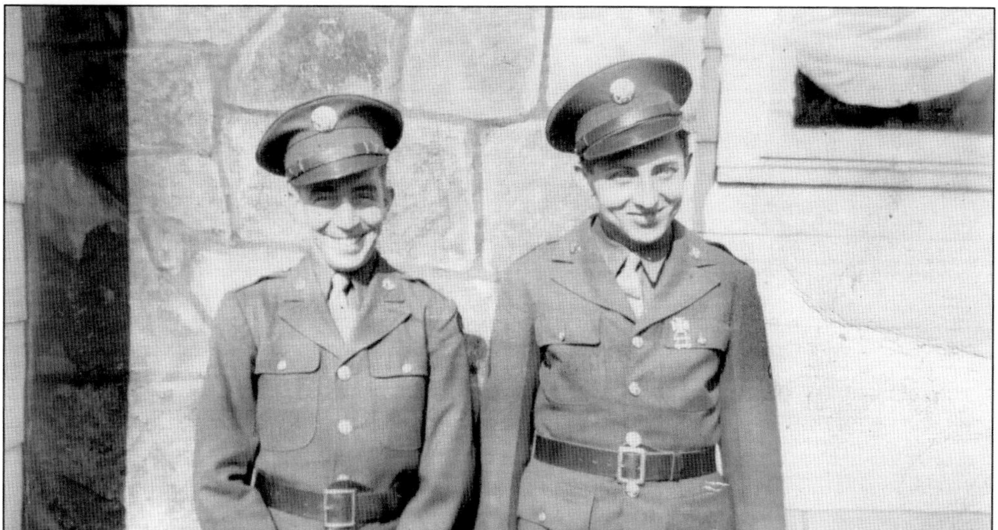

Norris Eugene Clift (right) graduated from Soddy High School in 1936. He graduated from MacKenzie Business School in 1937 and was drafted into the U.S. Army Air Force in 1942. During World War II, Clift served as a motor sergeant in various parts of England and Europe as part of the European theater of operations (ETO). He served until 1945. (Courtesy of Norris and Mary Clift.)

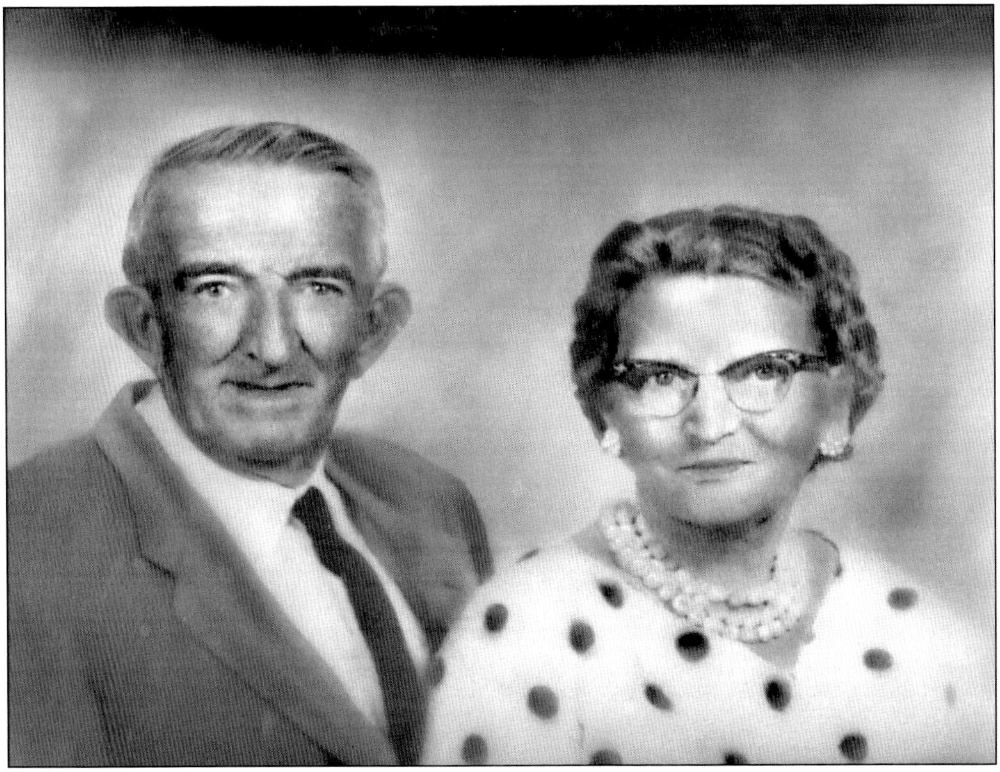

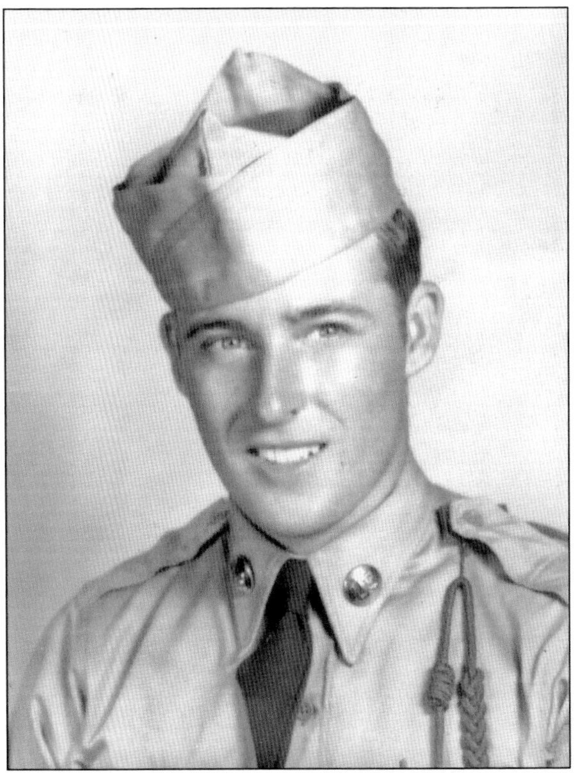

As a young man, F. Thomas McClure served in the army during World War I in Europe, where he was gassed. After the war, Thomas was a police detective at the Read House. He is shown here with his wife, Flossie Eustice McClure. The couple had nine children: Ovalene, James R., J. C., Thomas L., Lamar, Martha Jo, Correne, and two children who died as infants. (Courtesy of Correne Poe.)

Lloyd Herbert Lively lied about his age to join the Air Force in 1951. Nine months later, he was discharged, but joined the army in 1953 when he was 17. After training, Lively spent most of his duty in Korea. Lively married Virginia, and they had four children. He worked for Chattanooga Glass Company and made Coca-Cola bottles for 21 years. (Courtesy of Rosa Lee Hambrick.)

Amos Sutherland (born in February 11, 1922) and Lucille Bowman (born in November 1923) were married September 14, 1943, probably while Amos was on a short military leave. Amos served in the army from 1941 to 1945, mostly in the Philippine Islands after the infamous Bataan Death March. The couple had nine children who survived and three children who died as infants. (From the authors' collection.)

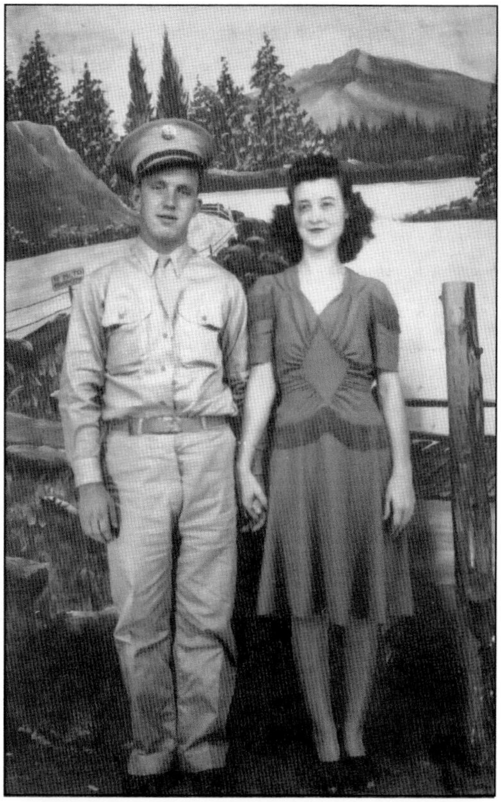

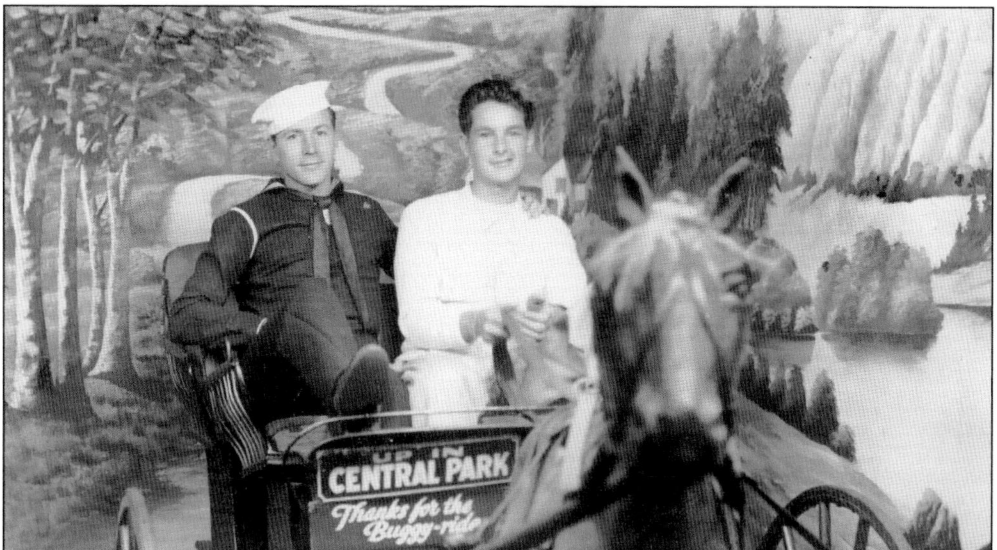

Ralph Franklin Penney (left) served in the navy during World War II. He retired as navigator of a submarine. Penney, one of six siblings, married Alma Ray Underwood, and the couple has three sons. (Courtesy of A. B. and Frankie McRee.)

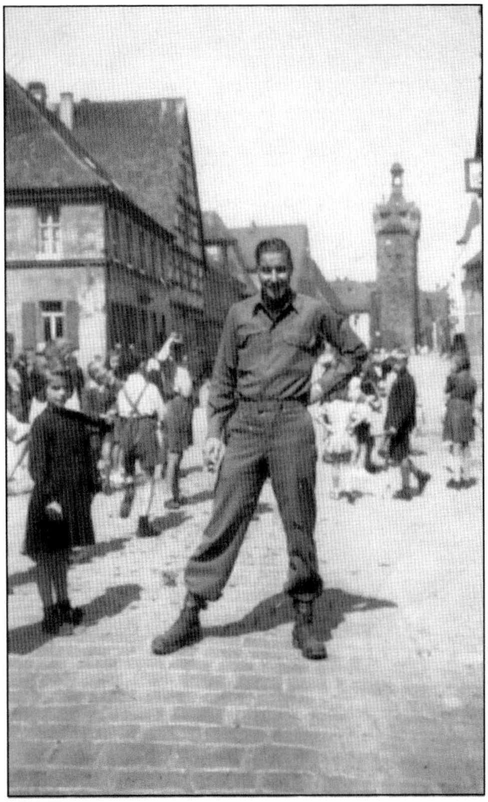

Hodley Osborne (September 27, 1917–September 30, 2001) wrote a letter to his sister, Mrs. E. B. Crites of Soddy, during World War II. Shown here are a picture of Osborne in Europe and the envelope that contained his letter about a German concentration camp. "I can't put it in words and tell you how bad it was," he states. After describing some of the horrid details, Hodley states that "people won't believe me when I tell them, so I have pictures of it that I took." (Courtesy of Scott Brogdon.)

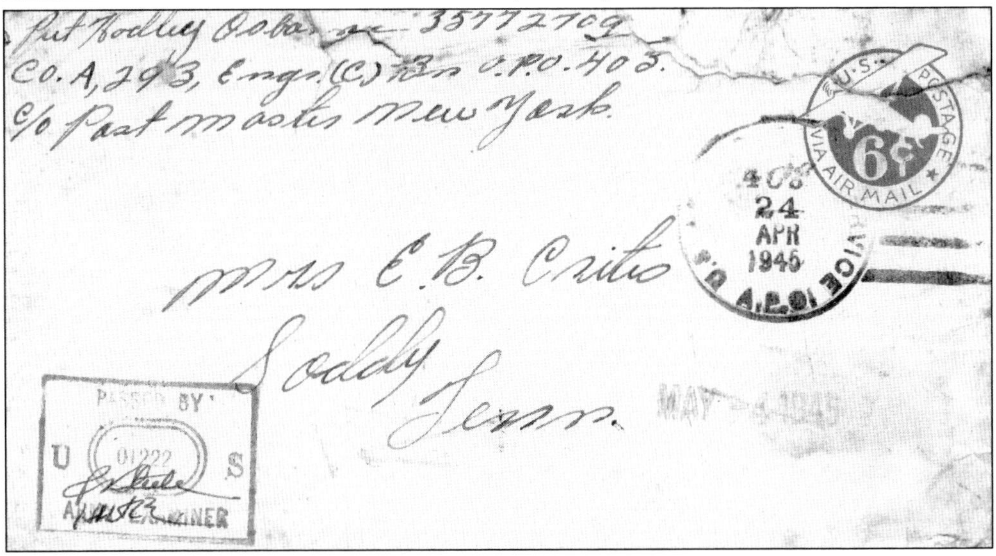

Malcolm Floyd (August 30, 1924–April 4, 1997) was a first lieutenant in the U.S. Air Force during World War II, responsible for piloting a B-26 bomber. Following the war, in 1947, Malcolm helped start Floyd Hardware in Daisy with his father, Rob Floyd. Malcolm was married to Laura McCullough, and the couple raised four children. (Courtesy of Rob Floyd.)

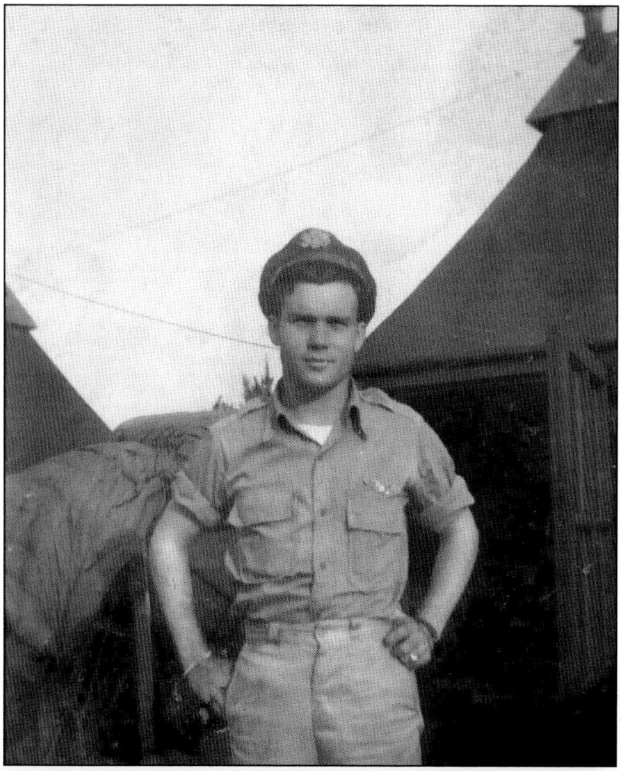

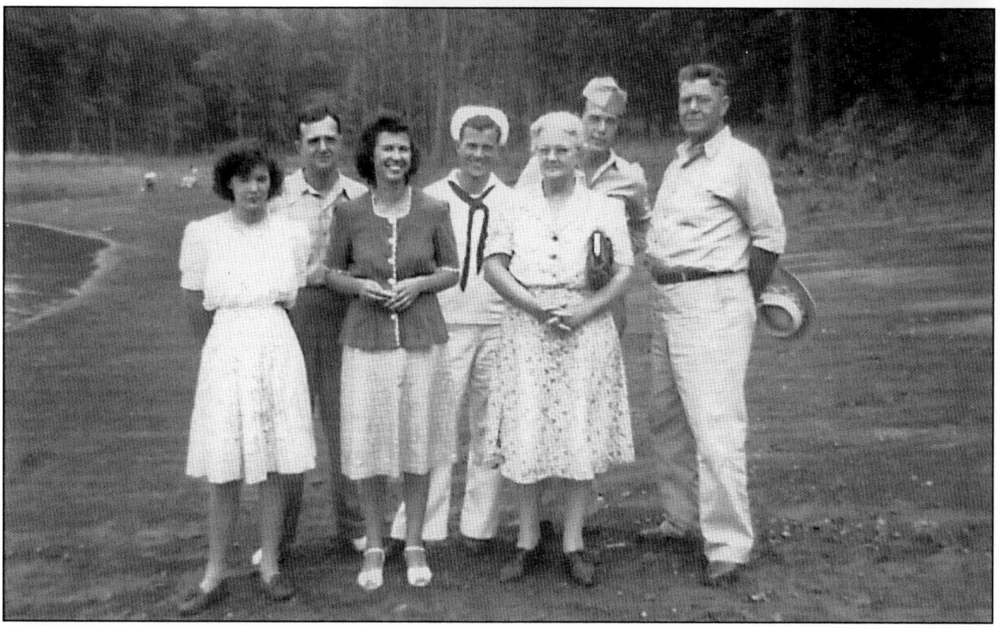

Families are always happy to have their sons, brothers, and husbands home for a visit, particularly when they are in the military and our country may be involved in war. Pictured here *c.* 1940, from left to right, are: (front row) Ruth Etta Elliott, Rita McRee, Gussie Elliott, and Joe B. Elliott; (back row) Clarence Elliott, Robert Elliott, and Joe Ed Elliott. (Courtesy of A. B. and Frankie McRee.)

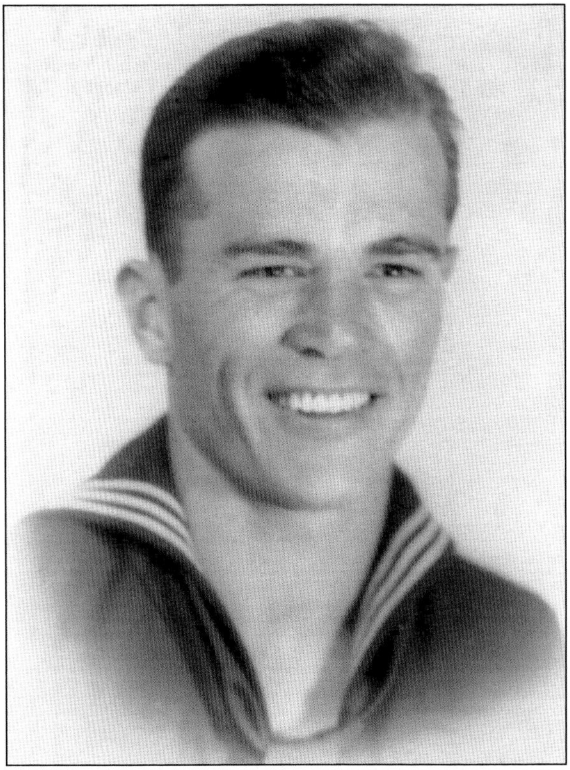

Robert A. Elliott (1912–1995) attended Soddy High School and then married his high school sweetheart, Mildred Price (1916–1998), in June 1934. The couple had four children: Barbara, Dr. Robert Price, Carlos Don, and William Morris. Elliott, shown at left in his military uniform, volunteered for the navy the day after Pearl Harbor and served in World War II. Mildred, also pictured here, was a homemaker. (Courtesy of Tom and Barbara Levi.)

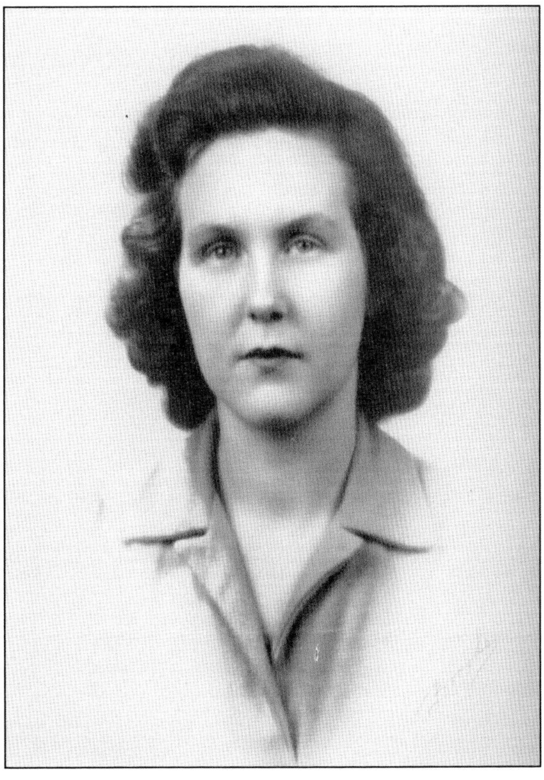

Oscar Bowman, shown here *c.* 1944 in Fort Bliss, Texas, left a pregnant wife and two sons at home when he was drafted into the Army Air Corps. During the war, Oscar's wife and infant son died during childbirth. The Red Cross brought him home for a short period of time to arrange care for David, six, and Luther, five, until the war was over. (Courtesy of David and Clara Bowman.)

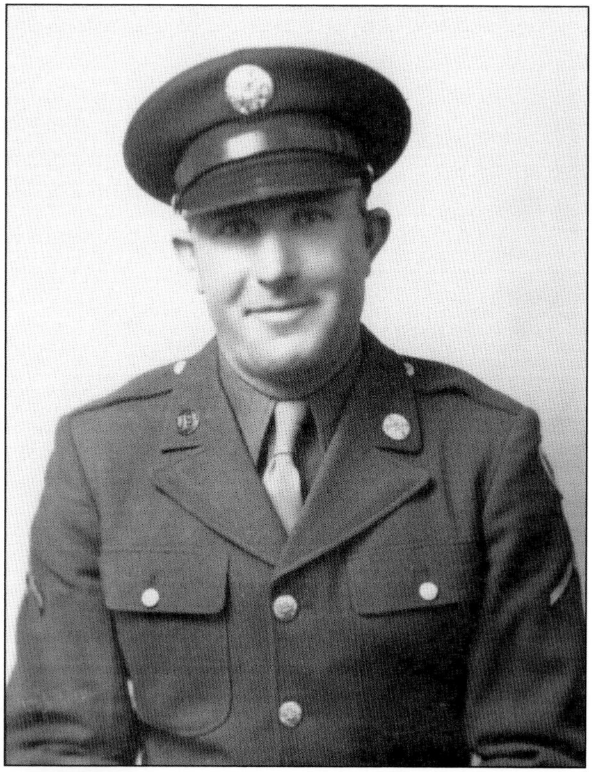

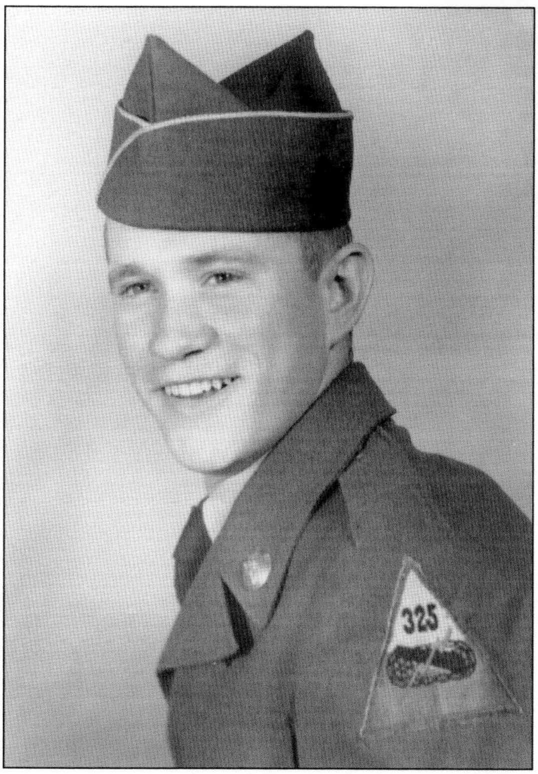

Harold Laymon Penney, the son of Mosie and Goldie Penney, served in the army in World War II. After the war, Harold became a long-distance truck driver. (Courtesy of A. B. and Frankie McRee.)

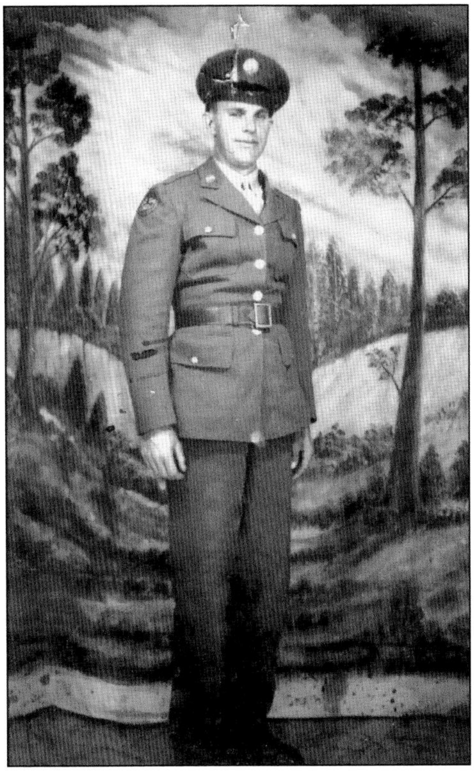

Walter E. Cothran (1910–1981) poses in his army uniform. Cothran served in World War II, which killed more people, damaged more property, and cost more money than any other war in history. The United States came into World War II when Japan attacked Pearl Harbor on December 7, 1941. The war ended September 2, 1945, only a few weeks after the Allies dropped atomic bombs on Japan. (Courtesy of Clara Bowman.)

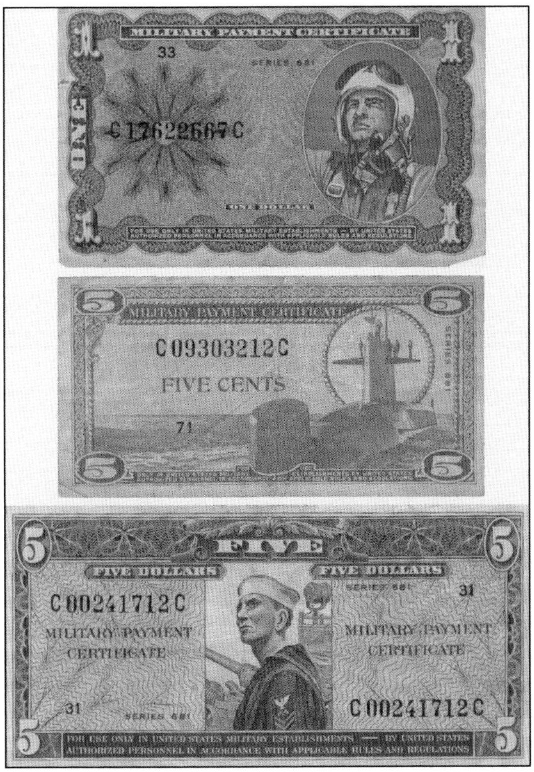

James Conner joined the Marines *c.* 1969 and was sent overseas to fight in the Vietnam War. Though the Vietnam War began in the late 1950s, the United States had combat troops in Vietnam from 1965 to 1973. Money certificates, shown here, were used by Conner and other military personnel in the commissary to purchase items such as soap, stamps, clothing, an so forth. (Courtesy of Lucille Conner and Marlene Hudson.)

Seven

CHILDREN

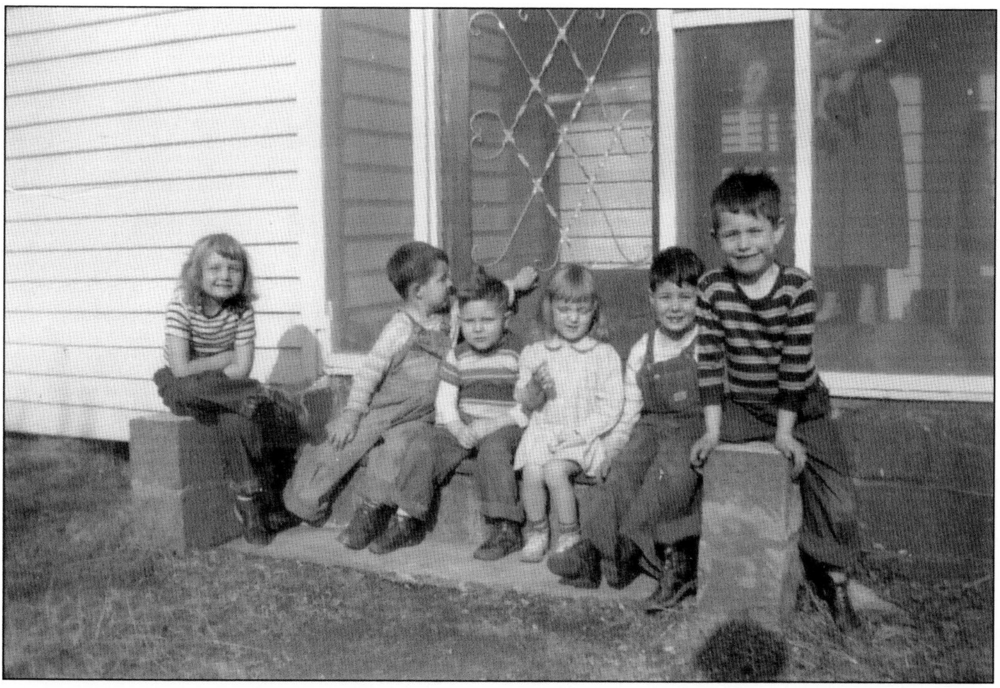

First cousins (left to right) Ann Rigsby, Gene Clift, Layne Rigsby, Carolyn Rigney, Jim Clift, and Jerry Sanders gather for a photograph on concrete steps. Gene Clift and Jim Clift are descendants of Col. William Clift, who was instrumental in organizing the Mount Bethel Presbyterian Church (later Soddy Presbyterian Church) and the Soddy community in the early 19th century. (Courtesy of Norris and Mary Clift.)

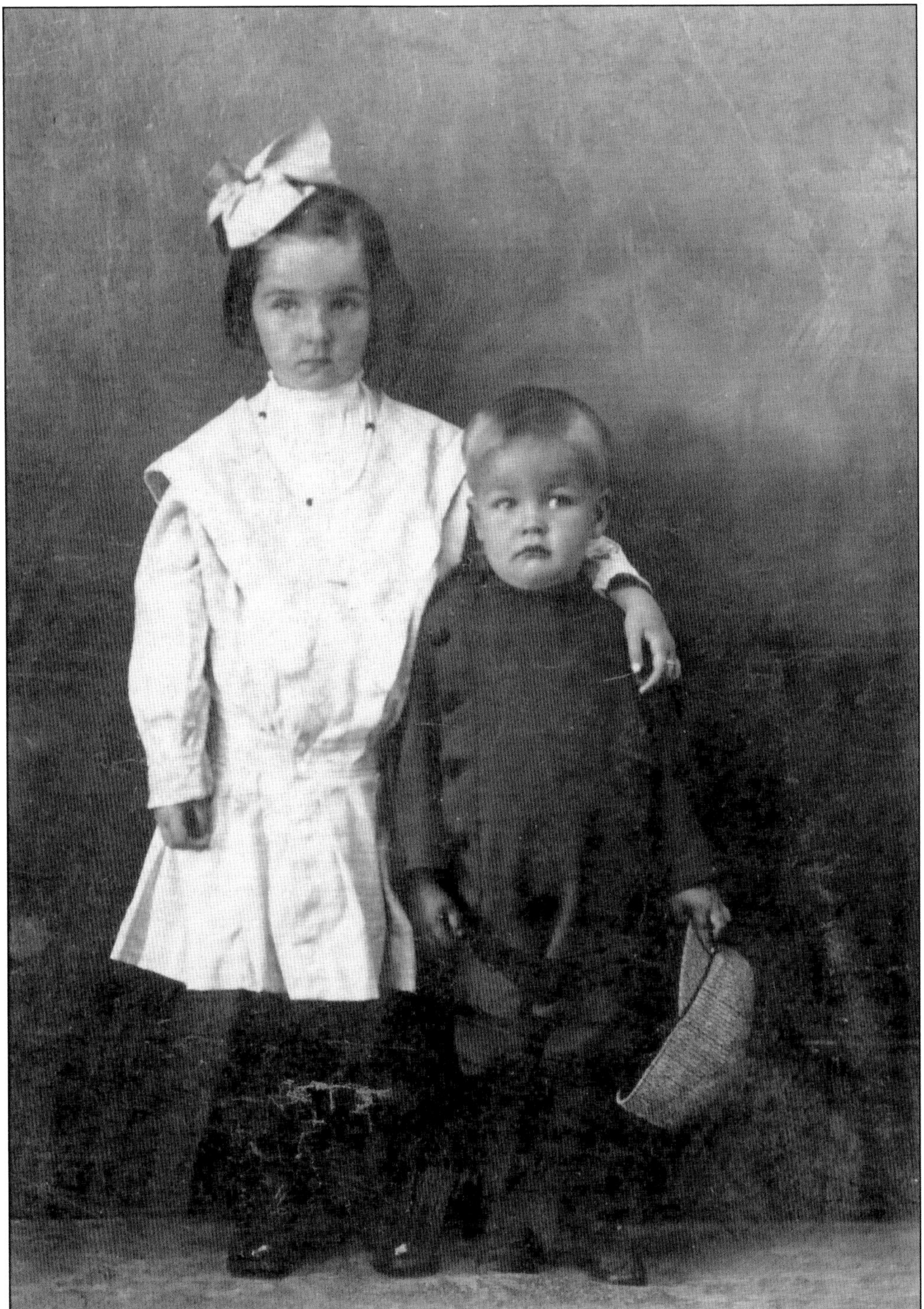

Lelah Gladys Rudd, age five, and James William Rudd, two years and 10 months old, appear bashful in this November 22, 1912, photograph. Their parents, Miriam and Fred Rudd, were from Soddy, but had lived in Chicago following the great fire of 1871. (Courtesy of Madge Lockhart.)

Jossette (left) and Patricia Crites are the daughters of Elmer Bert and Mayme Crites. Patricia Crites married Joe Brogdon and had four sons, Joe Bert (a dentist), Patrick Scott (a photographer), David Grant (a chiropractor), and Timothy Andrew (a landscaper). Jossette married Manuel Abello and had five children, Patty Lynn (who died when she was two), Nora, Manuel Jr., Monica, and Mary Beth. (Courtesy of Scott Brogdon.)

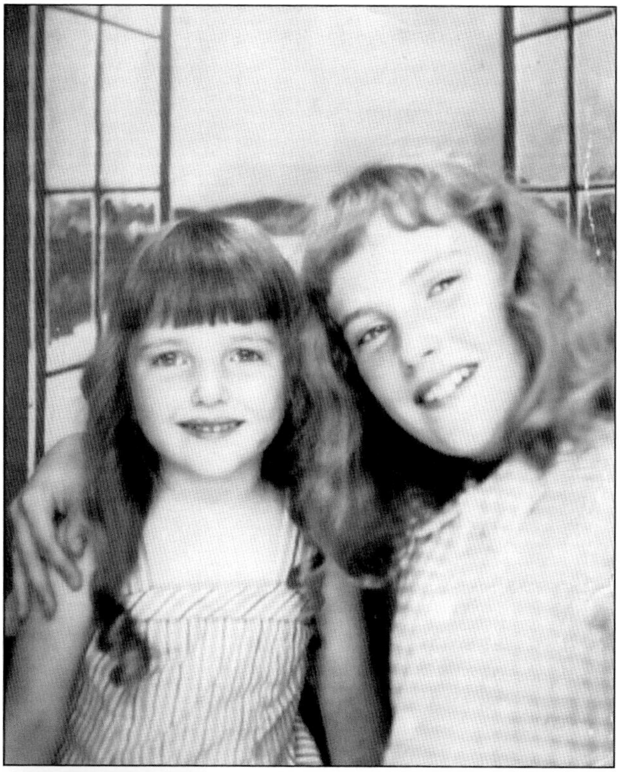

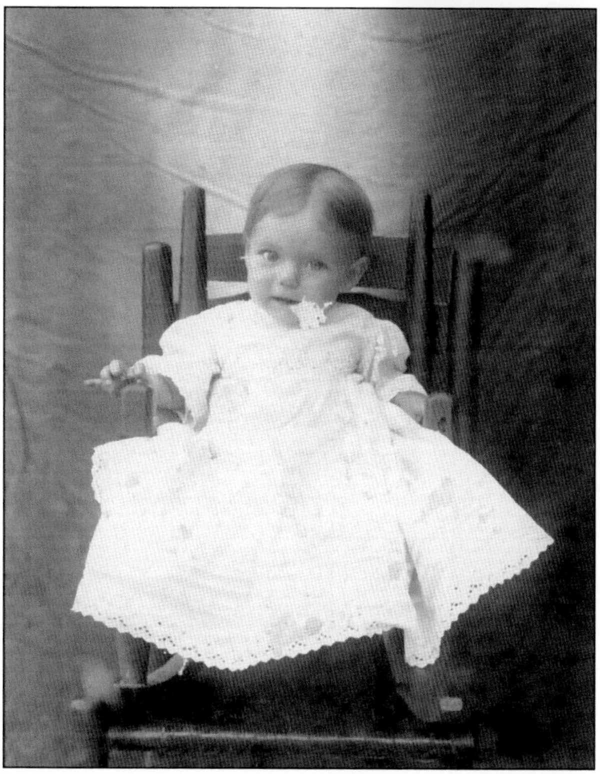

The Stephenson family immigrated from England in the late 19th century searching for a better life. The family first lived in Pennsylvania and then came to Daisy mountain to mine coal when Mary Stephenson was about two years old. This delightful portrait of Mary sitting in a rocker placed up on a chair was most likely taken while the family was still in Pennsylvania. Mary married J. R. Reynolds. (Courtesy of Norris and Mary Clift.)

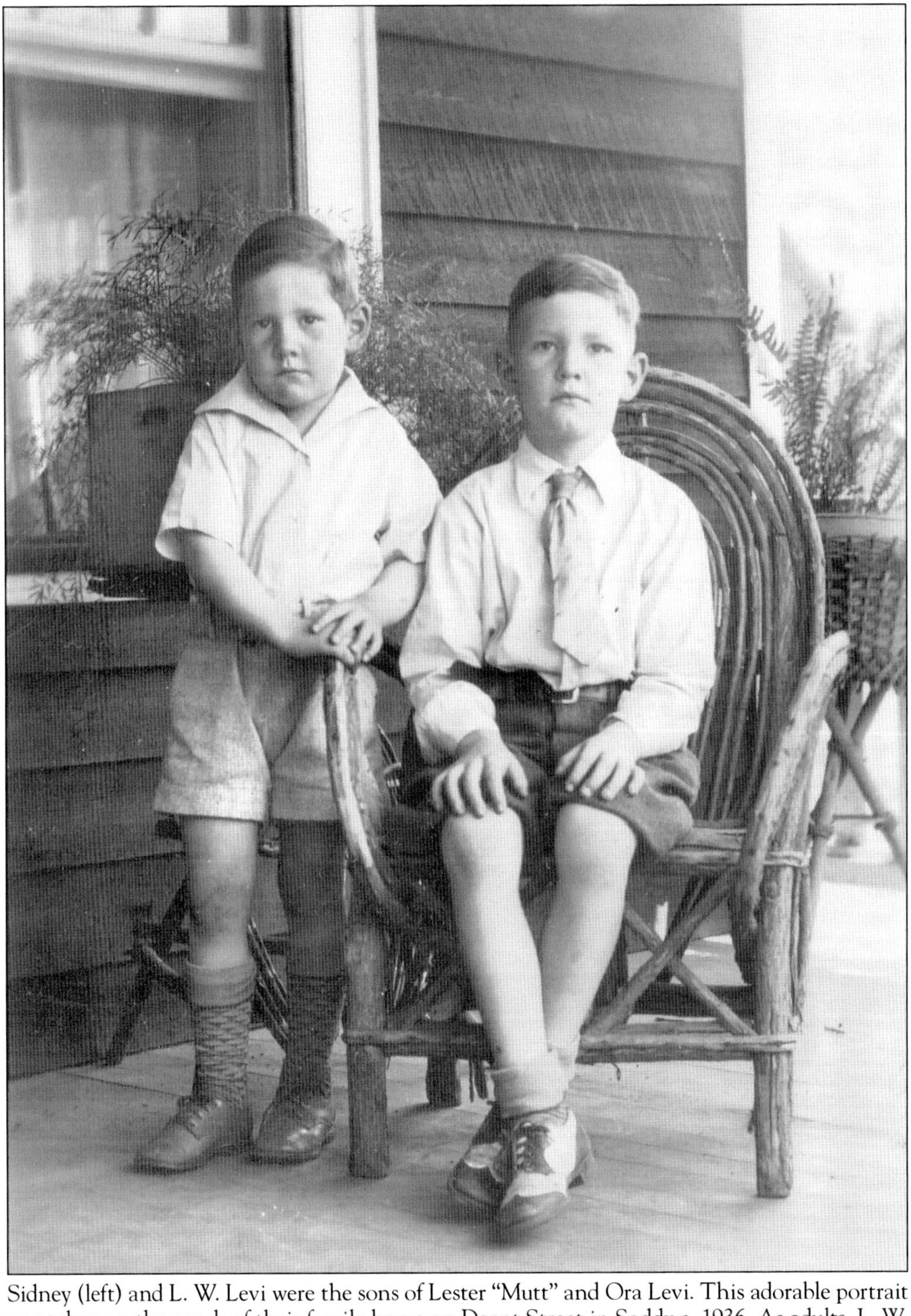

Sidney (left) and L. W. Levi were the sons of Lester "Mutt" and Ora Levi. This adorable portrait was taken on the porch of their family home on Depot Street in Soddy c. 1936. As adults, L. W. retired as a professor from Middle Tennessee State University. Sidney was a teacher, assistant principal, and coach at Soddy-Daisy High School and Red Bank Junior High School. (Courtesy of Tom and Barbara Levi.)

When Ollie Sparks Clements died in June 1988, she and her husband, James Arlie Clements, had a total of 134 direct descendents. Among the grandchildren, from left to right, are (first row) Barbara Crawley, Philip Crawley, Clyde Crawley, and Steve Matherly; (second row) David Yasko, Valerie Martin, and Sherry Yasko; (third row) Fran Matherly and Polly Clements. Note the washboard and butter churn on the porch. (Courtesy of Madge Lockhart.)

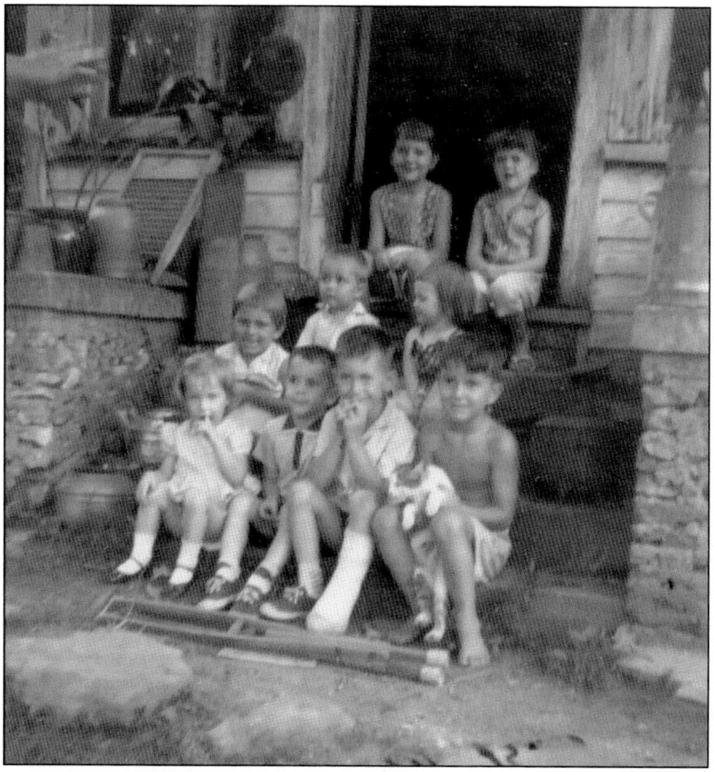

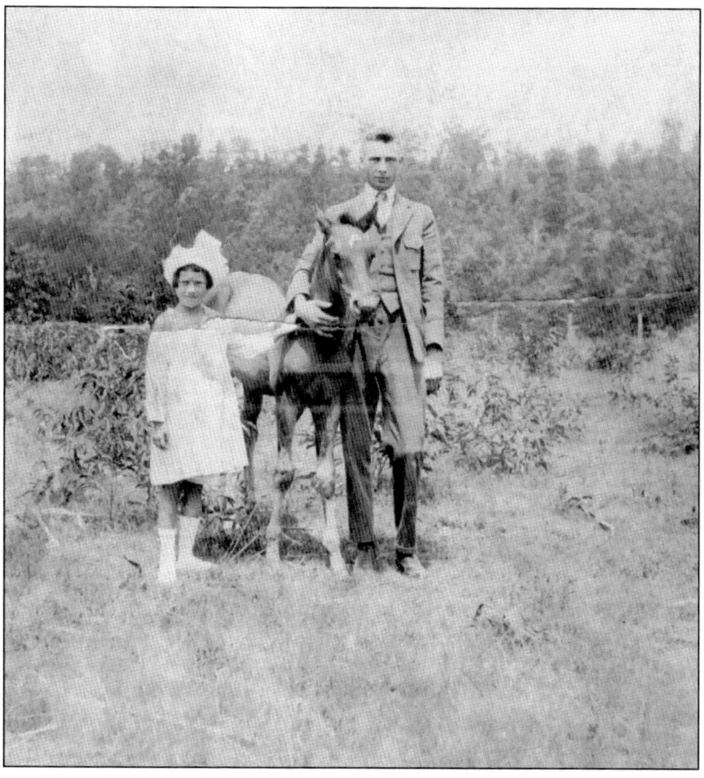

Dorothy Card, the daughter of Matt and Laura Card, stands with her brother, Earl Card, and a young foal in the early 20th century. Dorothy married Mandriel Levi and passed away in 2000 at the age of 90. (Courtesy of Tom and Barbara Levi.)

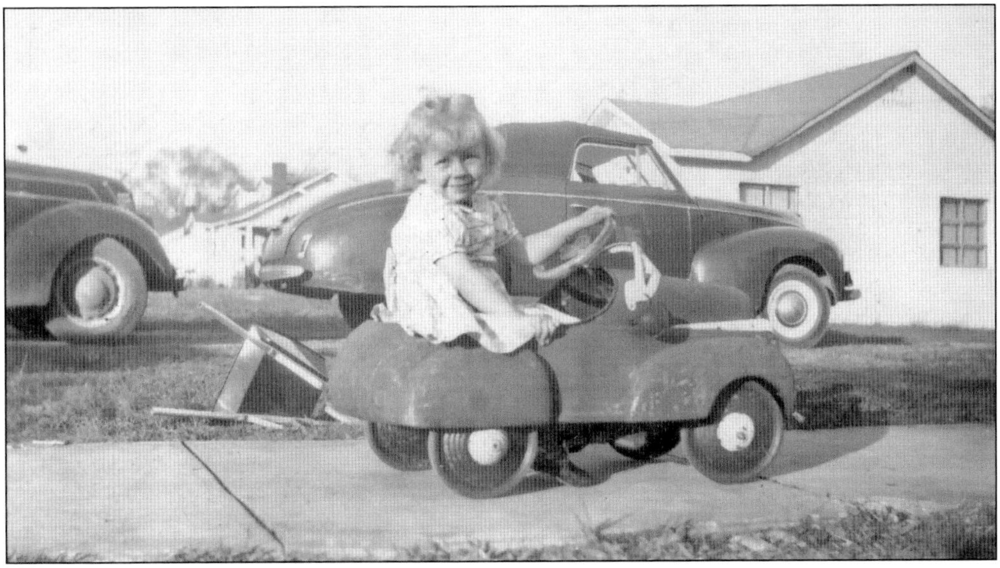

Catherine Copeland was probably visiting her cousin Diana's house in Red Bank when this photograph was taken *c.* 1946. Catherine was about three years old. Catherine graduated from Soddy-Daisy High School in 1961 and married Jimmy Coffman shortly thereafter. The couple had two children, Melinda and Allen. For a while, Catherine was a bank teller, and then she worked for an insurance company for numerous years. Both she and her husband were killed in an automobile accident in Georgia in March 1990. (Courtesy of Frank and Donna Copeland.)

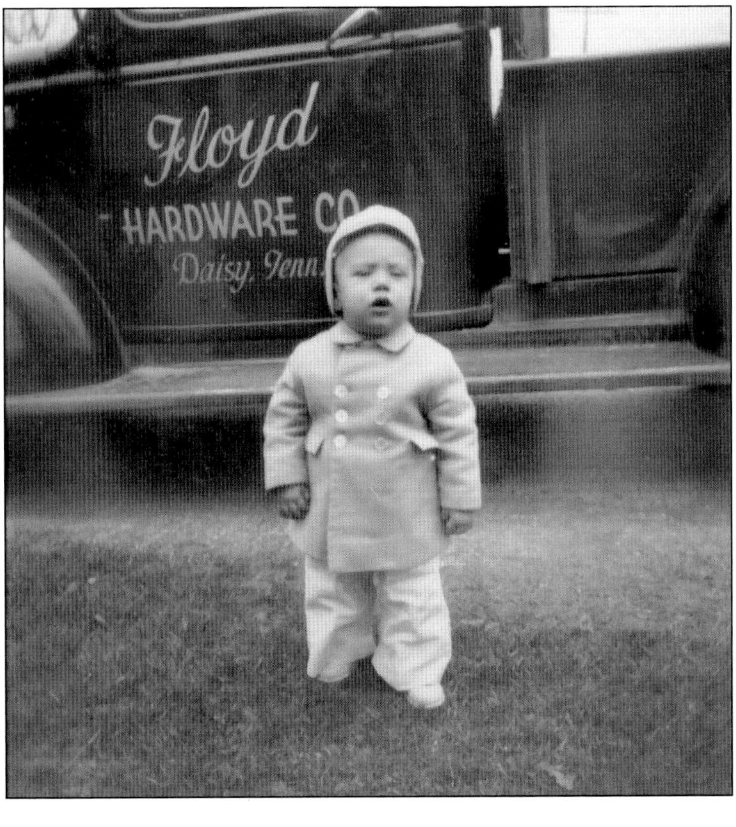

Robert Malcolm Floyd, who was named after his dad and granddad, stands in front of the Floyd Hardware delivery truck *c.* 1949. When Robert grew up, he married Candice Morgan and had two children, Melissa and Brent. He also carries on the family business as owner of Floyd Hardware. His daughter Melissa and her husband, Eddie Nelson, manage the business. (Courtesy of Rob Floyd.)

Larry Copeland sits in his grandpa's boat *c.* 1943. Ed Copeland would put trotlines, strong fishing lines with smaller lines attached across them with hooks, across the Tennessee River. This enables the fisherman to catch several fish at once. Notice the wash tub on the outside wall of the house. This would have been used for washing laundry and also taking baths. (Courtesy of Frank and Donna Copeland.)

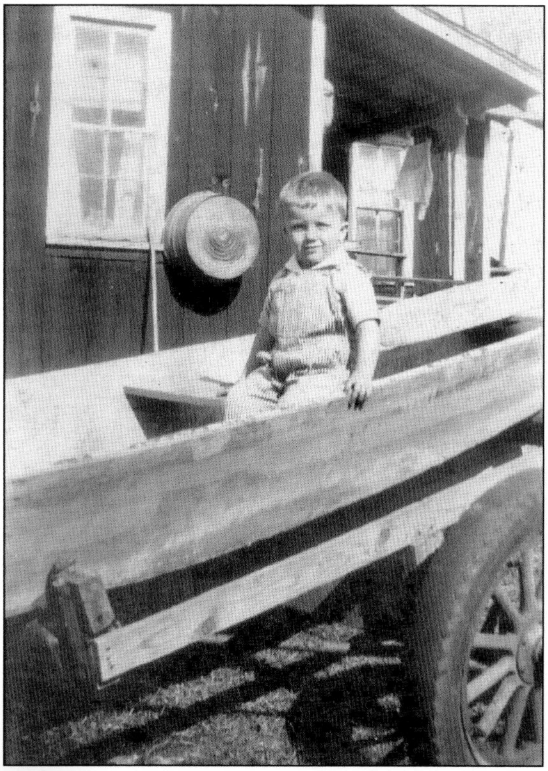

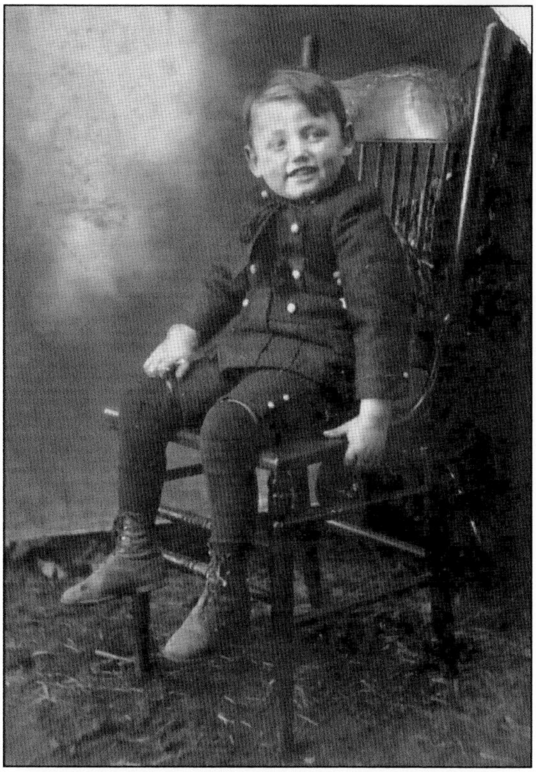

Leland Crites, shown here *c.* 1895, was the son of Bert and Susie Crites. As an adult, Leland had a son named Franklin who was the last male living to carry on the family name. Though this exempted the young man from going to Vietnam, he volunteered anyway. Sadly Franklin was killed there, and the Crites name has now practically vanished from the area. (Courtesy of Scott Brogdon.)

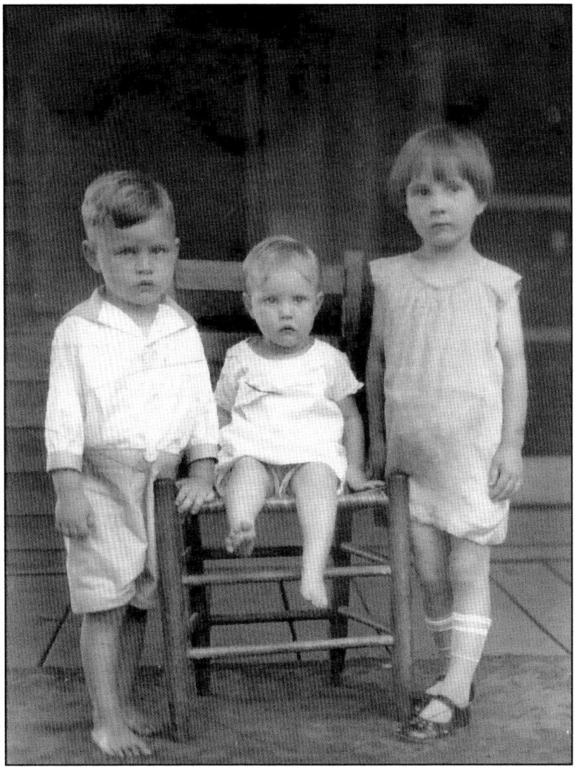

These adorable children, photographed c. 1926, are, from left to right, Lloyd, Frances, and Vernon Lasley. These are the oldest children of Richard Eliga and Rosa Mae Hackney Lasley, who later added Freida Sue to the family. (Courtesy of Freida Sutherland.)

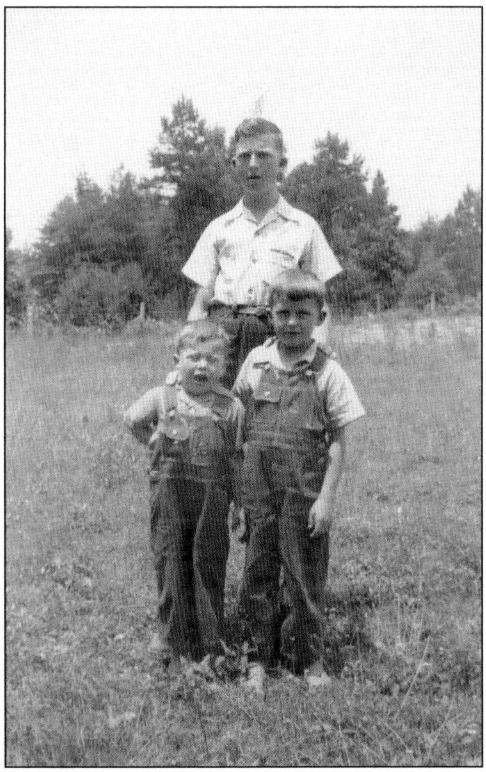

The three sons of Luther and Winnie Sutherland pose for a photograph c. 1950. From left to right are Ivan (September 3, 1946–January 14, 1951), Wallace (July 16, 1935–August 25, 2002) and Ellis Sutherland. If you look closely, you will notice that the two younger boys are without shoes, as was common then. Ivan died of pneumonia a few months after this photograph was taken. (Courtesy of Freida Sutherland.)

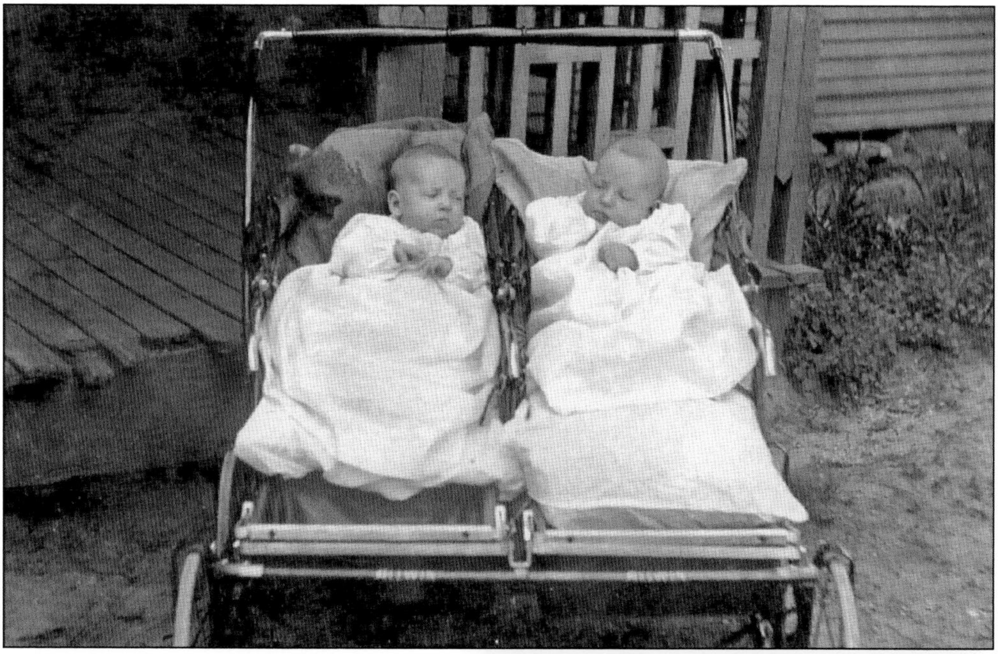

Identical twins Ray and Roy Crites were born on March 2, 1916. The boys had an undiagnosed kidney disease that killed them both within a year. Ray died on January 22, 1938, and Roy died on December 25, 1938. The boys are pictured here in a very early unique double stroller and about four years later in sailor outfits. (Courtesy of Scott Brogdon.)

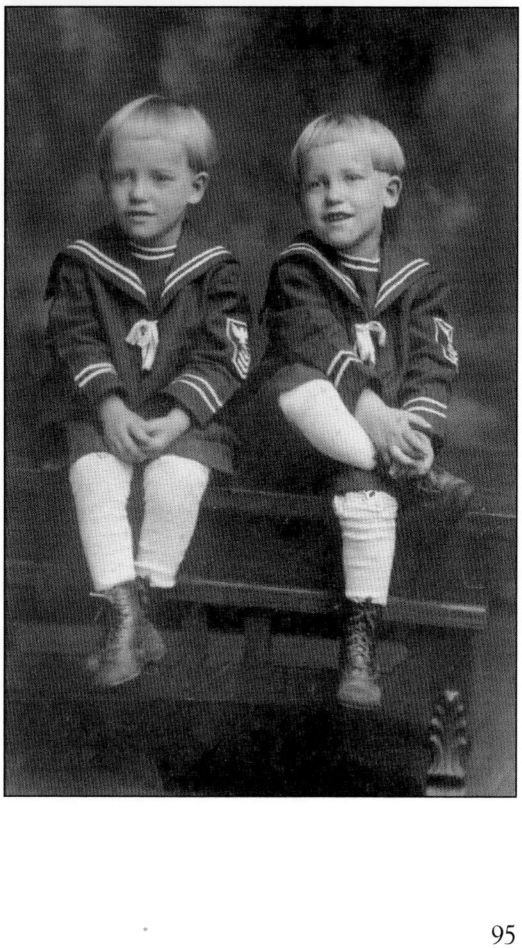

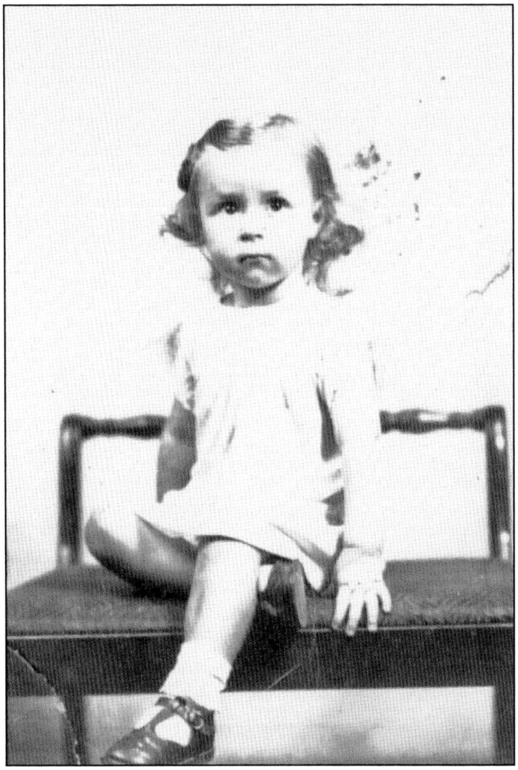

Judy Dianna Sunderland was 17 months old when this photograph was taken. Judy lived with her parents, Howard and Marie Sunderland, in the Mowbray community. (Courtesy of Lucille Conner and Marlene Hudson.)

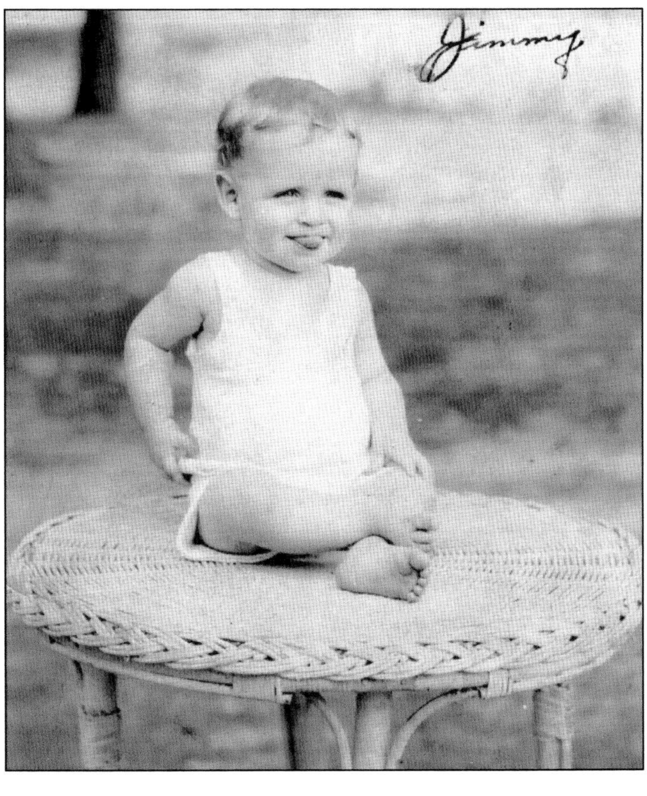

Jimmy Copeland is the son of Edmund and Lena Copeland. He was born in 1924. Jimmy attended Soddy Elementary School and Soddy-Daisy High School, graduating in 1941. Jimmy says his father was a great gardener and kept the children quite busy in the winter and summer with chores such as gardening, chopping firewood, and helping around the house. Jimmy married Sue Bowman and had one child, David. (Courtesy of Frank Copeland.)

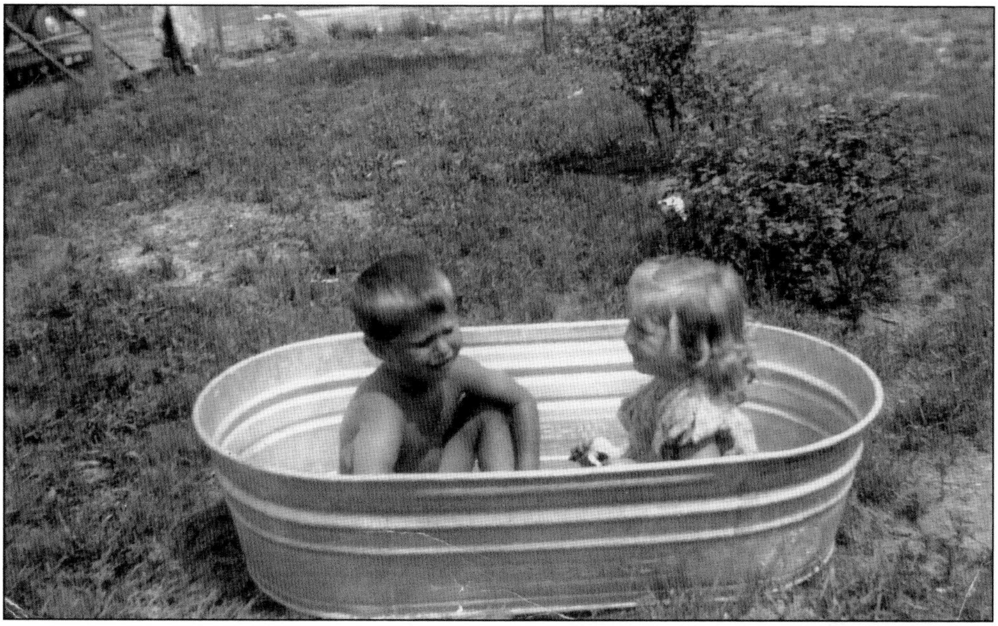

Siblings Johnnie Lee and Cathy Ann Johnson use a washtub for a swimming pool. The children's parents were visiting Curtis Winn on Melville Hill around 1956, when they received permission to cool off in the water. After graduation, Johnnie joined the Marines. He married Lila Garner, and they had one daughter, Amanda Lynn. Johnnie died of small-cell carcinoma in 2001. Cathy is coauthor of this book. (From authors' collection.)

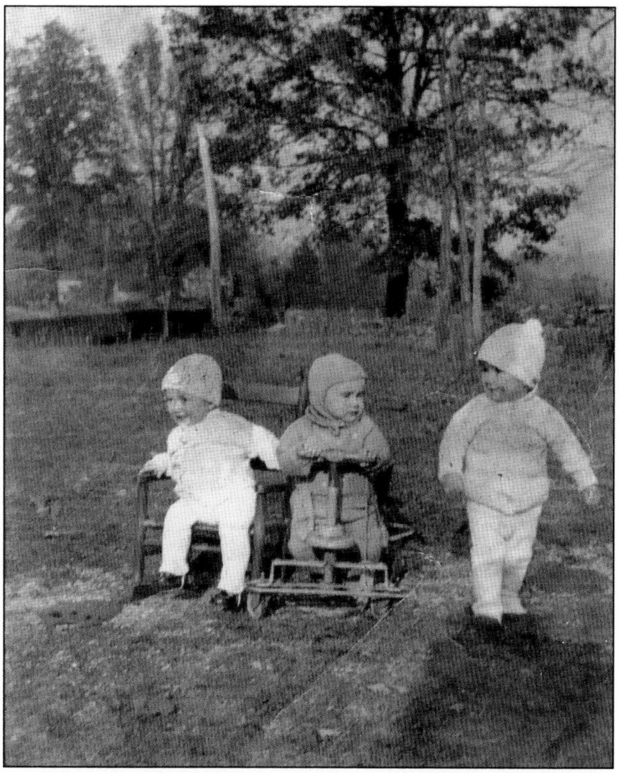

Three toddlers enjoy a moment outdoors in the winter of 1933. Mary Ann Priddy (left) sits in a child's rocking chair; Betty Gray (middle) sits on a sort of riding toy; and A. B. McRee III is ready for a walk. The children are cousins. (Courtesy of A. B. and Frankie McRee.)

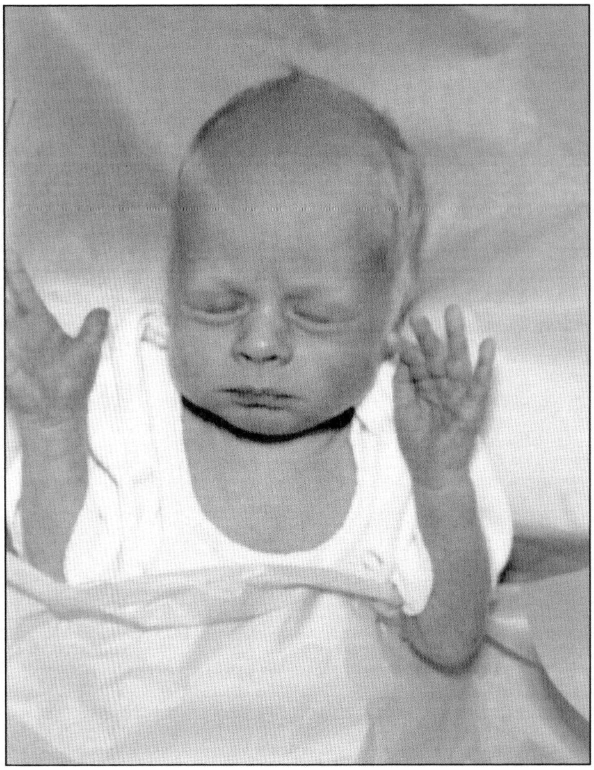

Mobley Joe Brown was born February 19, 1974, at 11:19 p.m. to Johnny Mack and Cathy Brown. At three weeks of age, the tiny infant weighed only three pounds, eight and a half ounces, but he survived despite a grim prognosis for viability. Joe was born early due to his mother's umbilical hernia, and the surgery to correct the condition caused her to go into labor three months early. (From the authors' collection.)

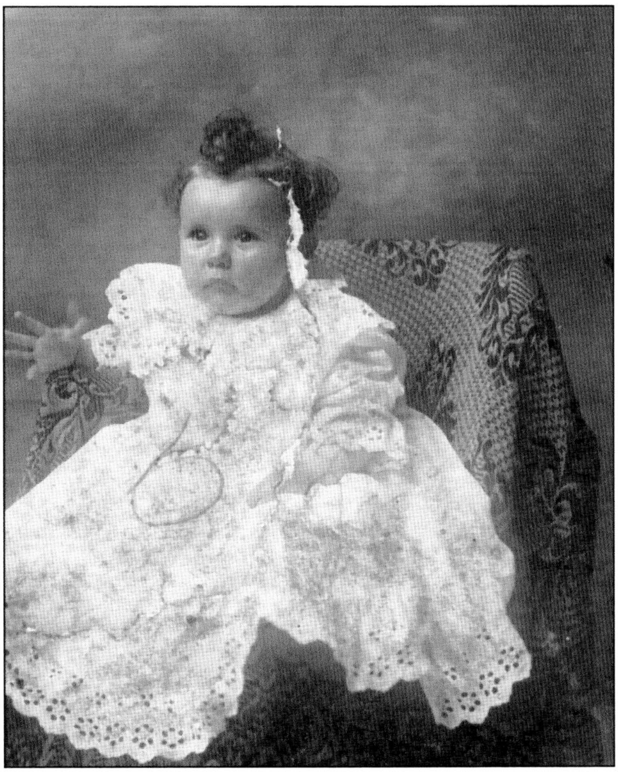

Though time has taken its toll on this photograph, it is still a relatively well-preserved and treasured memento of a family member who lived long ago. The little girl in this beautiful eyelet-trimmed dress is Goldie Melissa Lee, who married Mosie Laymon Penney when she grew up. Preserve your photographs by keeping them away from sunlight, moisture, or heat and storing them in a protective cover such as a manila envelope. Keeping photographs safe and negatives in a separate collection will ensure that your own family history is preserved for future generations to cherish. (Courtesy of A. B. and Frankie McRee.)

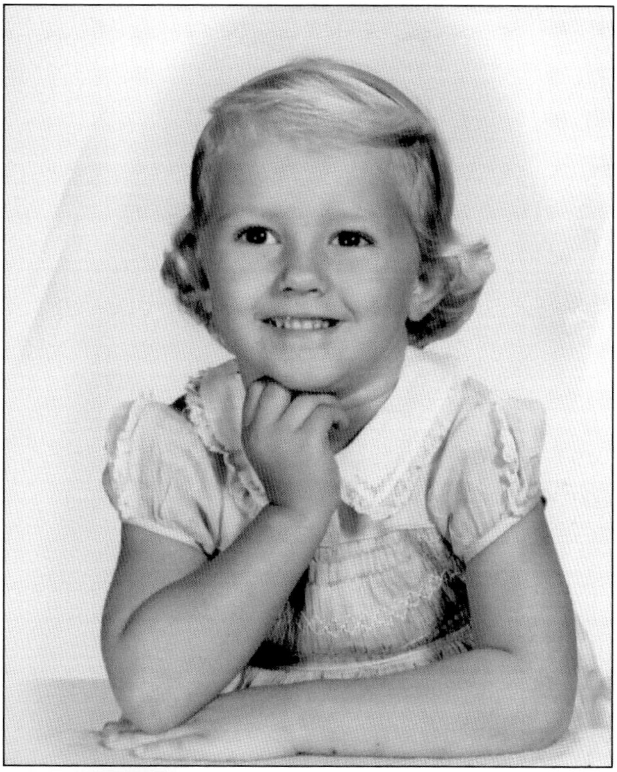

Karen and Joan McRee are the adorable daughters of A. B. and Frankie McRee. Karen, pictured at right, was four years of age when this photograph was taken. She is now a nurse and is married to Richard Mathis. Joan, shown below, was 19 months of age when this picture was made. (Courtesy of A. B. and Frankie McRee.)

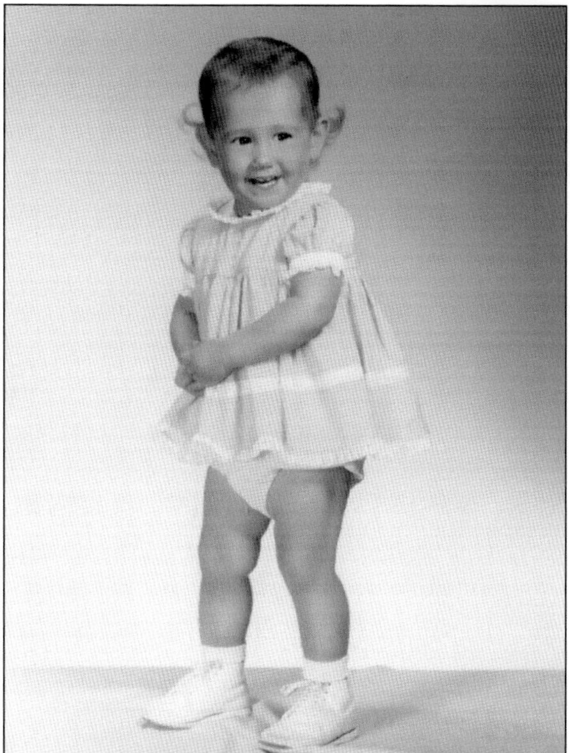

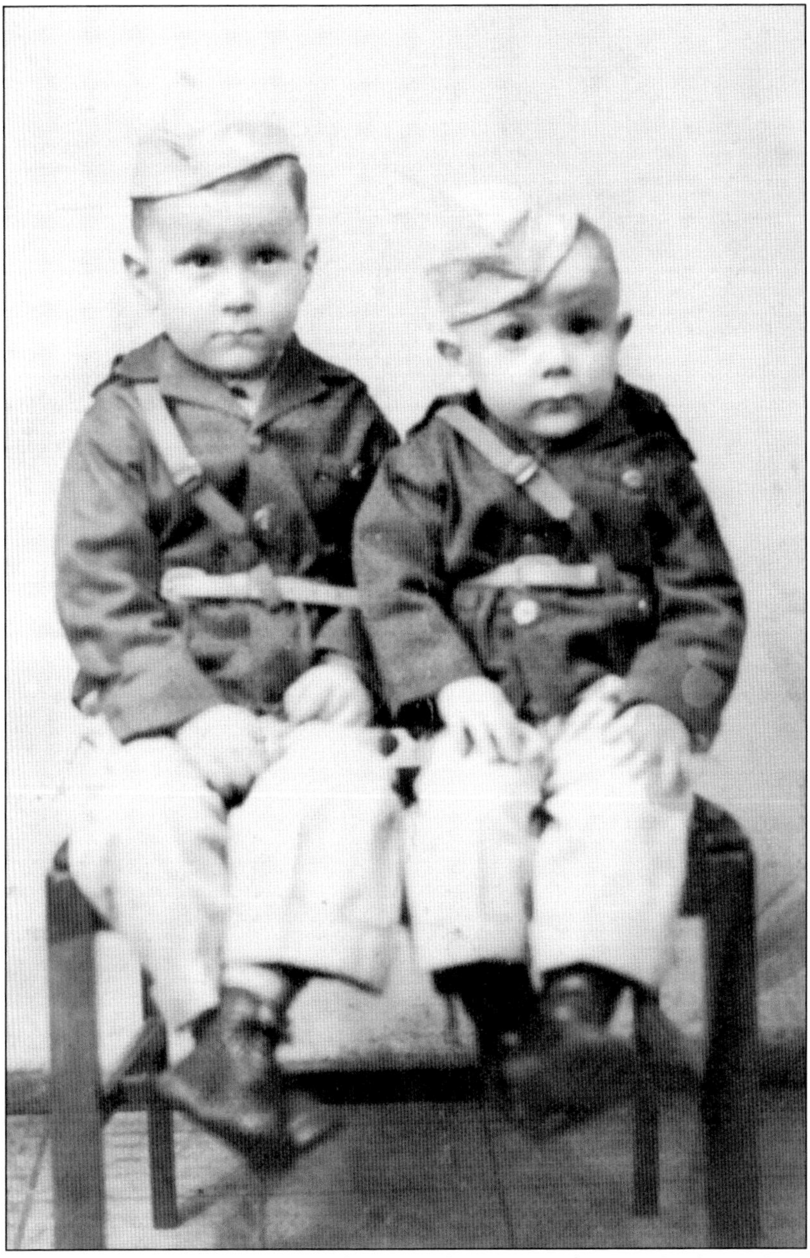

Dennis (left) and Kenneth Nunley were the sons of Warren and Grace Hickman Nunley. This photograph of the boys was taken around 1945, during World War II, when the boys were about five and four. It's possible that Grace made the boys' clothing as a symbol of patriotism, since Kenneth states that their mom made much of their clothing when they were young. The brothers played in the local creeks with marbles and rubber guns and participated in other games that local boys played in the mid-20th century. They lived in coal company houses, which had been moved above the ball field across from Soddy Lake and rented for $12 a month. Several years after this photograph was taken, there was a younger brother, Thomas, added to the family, who died when he was a few days old. Another brother, Rick, was born 10 years after Kenneth. (Courtesy of Frank Copeland.)

Cora Curtis was born February 16, 1883. When she grew up, Cora married Daniel Adam Lovelady (shown below) and the couple had 10 children: seven boys and three girls. Cora was a homemaker and helped her husband on their farm, where they raised cattle and horses as well as vegetables and other food for the family and animals. Cora died on June 26, 1952. (From the Rosella Neighbors Collection.)

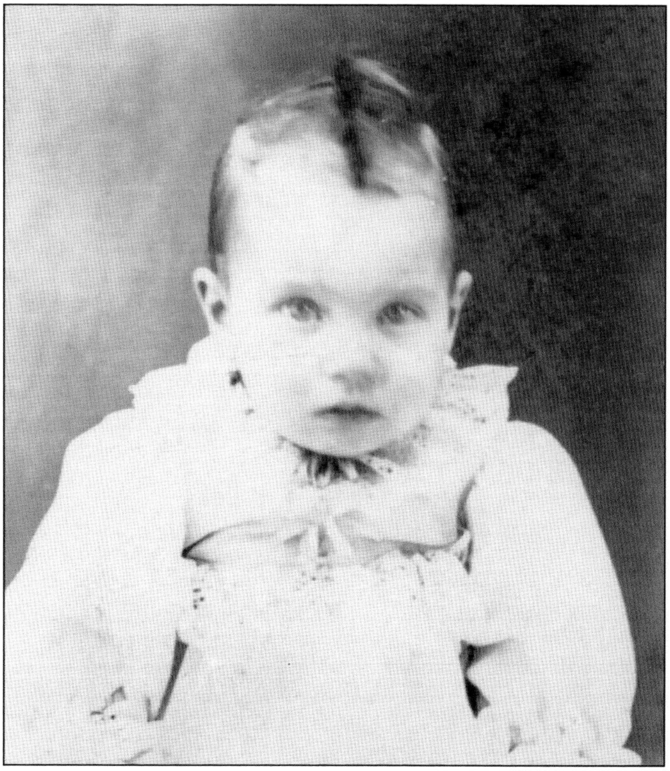

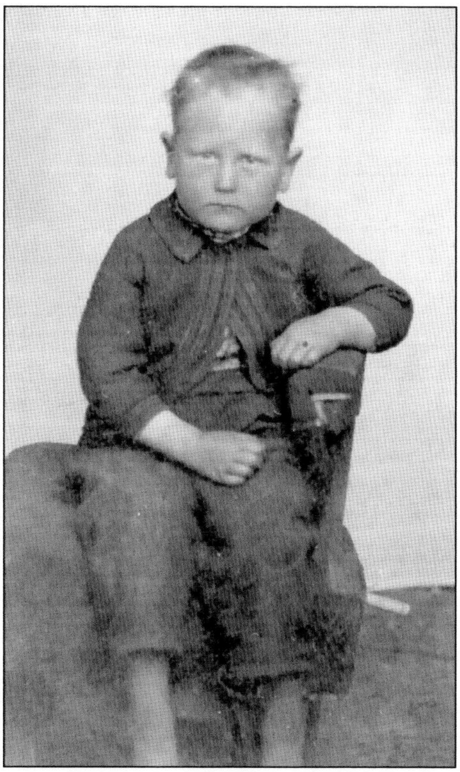

Daniel Adam Lovelady was born on November 6, 1871, and raised in Soddy. As an adult, Daniel married Cora Curtis (shown above). Although he was a farmer, Daniel also carried mail for the people of Daisy, Soddy, and Soddy Mountain. Dan transported the mail with his horse and a one-seat buckboard buggy. He died on May 3, 1954. (From the Rosella Neighbors Collection.)

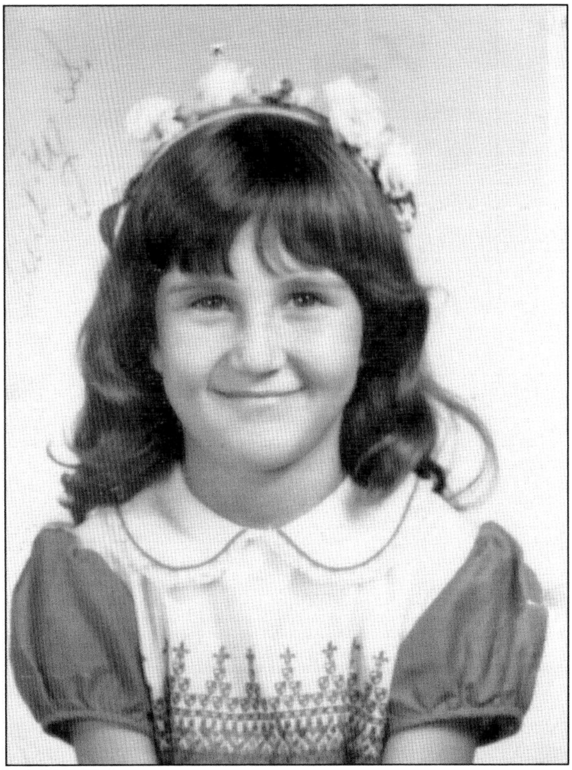

This eye-catching photograph of Audrey Ellen Sutherland (February 23, 1955–May 2, 1966) is one of the few reminders the family has of her. Audrey was one of seven children of Luther and Winnie Hendon Sutherland. Though there was never an exact cause of death for the 11-year-old, the death certificate states she died of encephalitis, an inflammation of the brain usually caused by a virus. (From the authors' collection.)

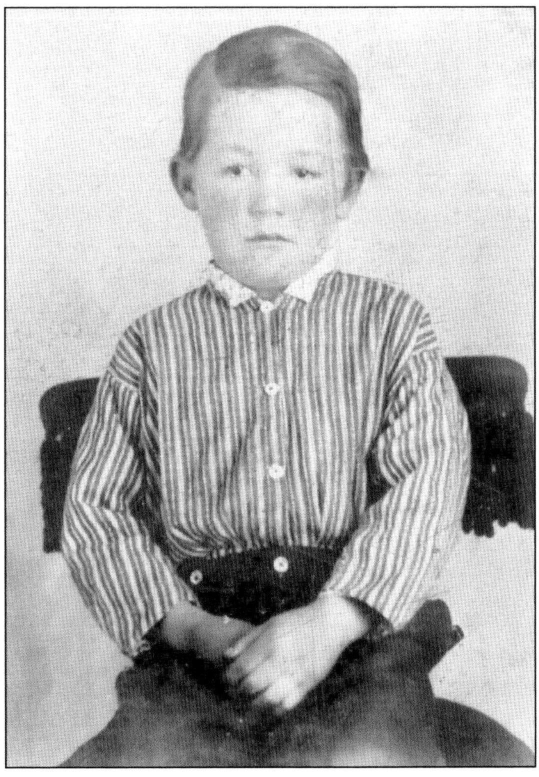

Charlie Sparks was eight years old when this photograph was taken c. 1881. Charlie's parents, "Bleu Doc" and Megan Carr Sparks, owned horse farms in Louisville, Kentucky. Charlie married Margaret Jane "Jennie" Harwood around 1890 and moved to Soddy-Daisy shortly thereafter. Charlie was a local justice of the peace for Hamilton County and also followed his father's footsteps by becoming a well-known horse trader in the area. (Courtesy of Madge Lockhart.)

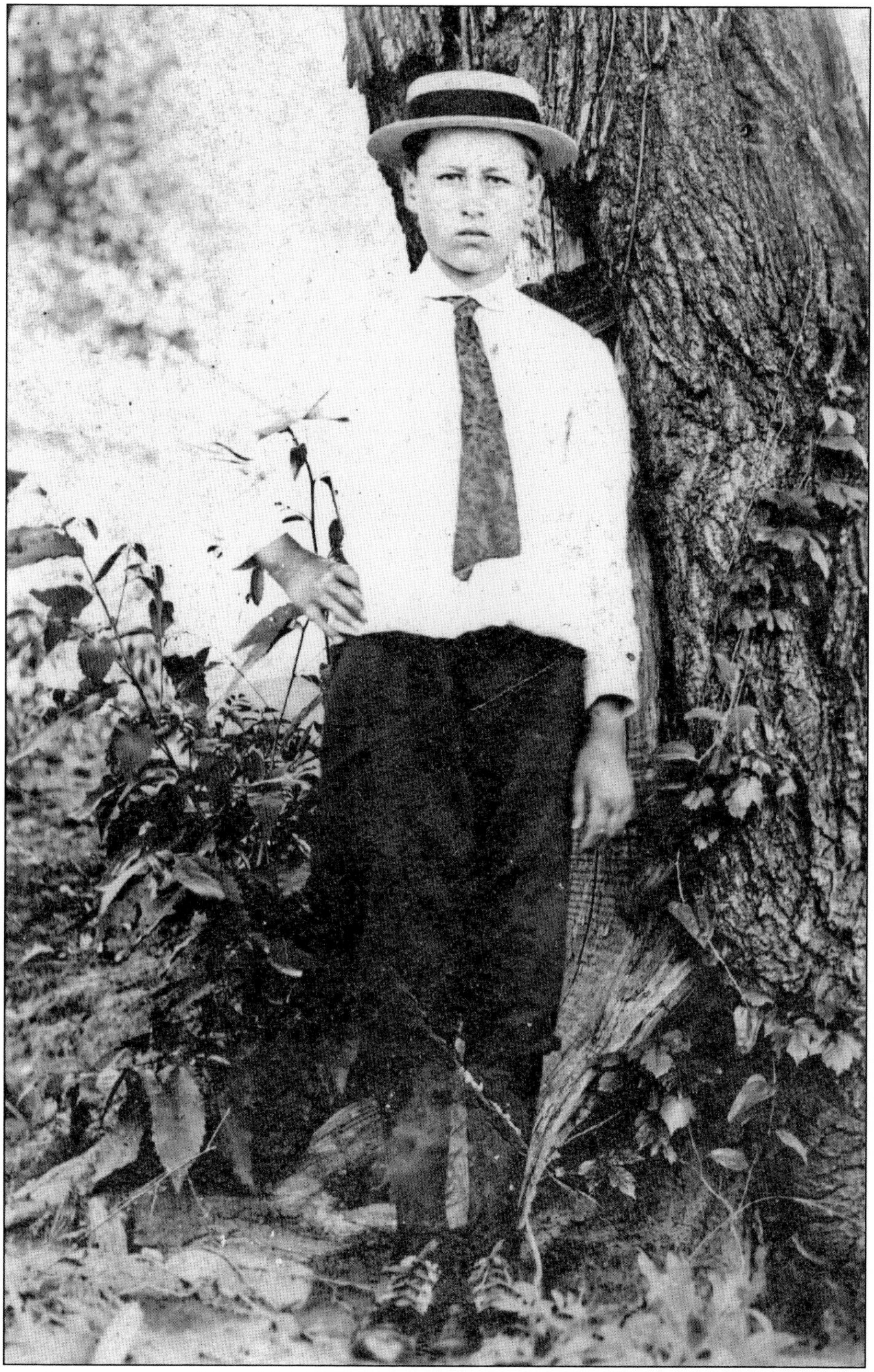

This striking portrait of Roy V. Millsaps was taken *c.* 1908. Roy is wearing clothing that was typical of the early 20th century. As a young man, he hauled coal off the mountain and later worked for the Texaco Gasoline Company. Roy had one son, whom he named Roy V. Millsaps Jr. (Courtesy of Bill and Patsy Hensley.)

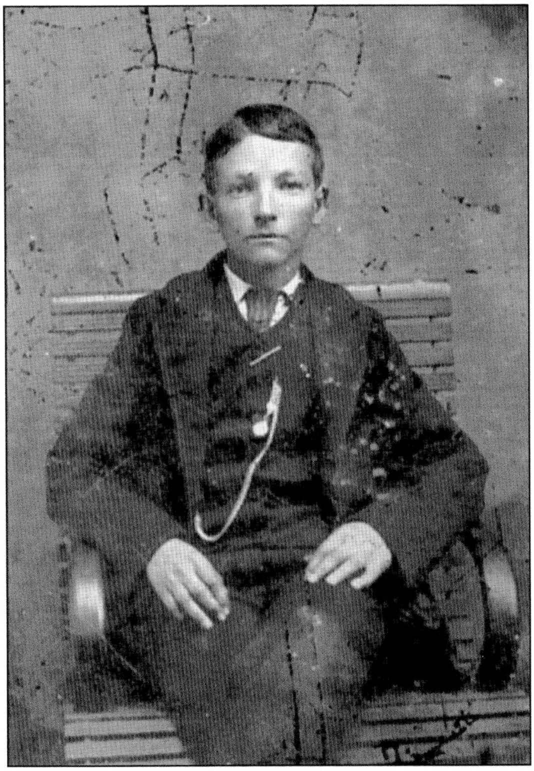

Bert Crites (July 8, 1872–September 23, 1937) was approximately 12 when this photograph was taken around 1884. Bert married Nora Norris (April 17, 1887–December 23, 1930) and raised four children. Though he may have had other occupations, he is best known for Bert Crites Ice Cream Parlor in Soddy. (Courtesy of Scott Brogdon.)

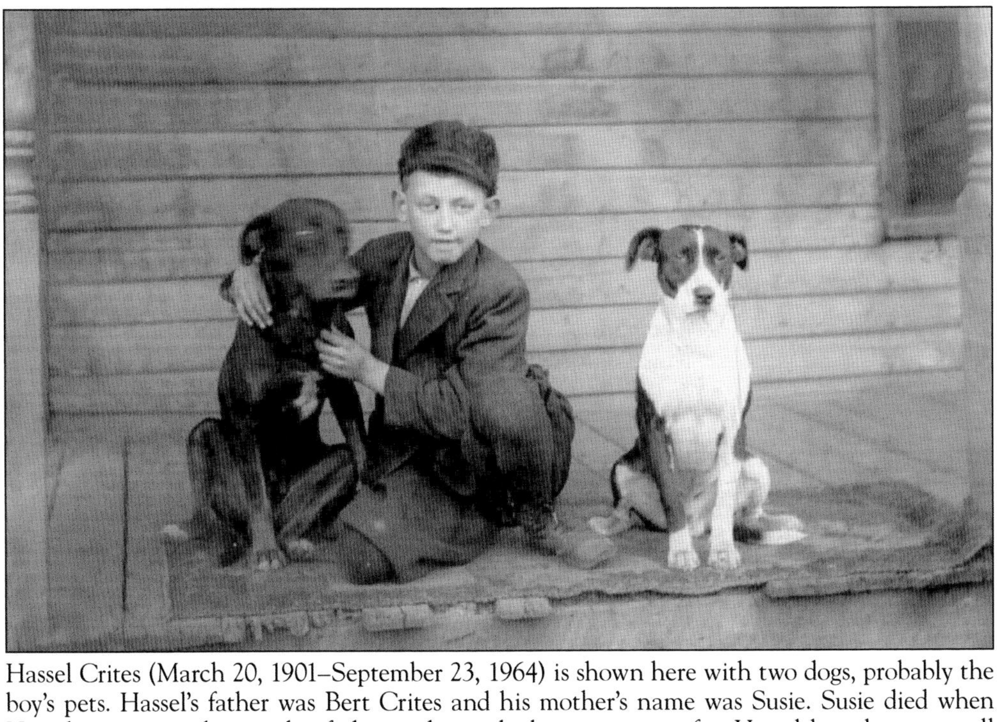

Hassel Crites (March 20, 1901–September 23, 1964) is shown here with two dogs, probably the boy's pets. Hassel's father was Bert Crites and his mother's name was Susie. Susie died when Hassel was young, leaving his father with two little sons to care for. Hassel later became well known in the area for running the theater owned by Dr. Hale. (Courtesy of Scott Brogdon.)

Nancy Cothran smiles cheerfully in her 1949 second-grade photograph. Nancy lived in Daisy with her four siblings and their parents, Walter E. and Bonnie I. Cothran. As an adult, Nancy married Charles Perkey and had two children, Tony and Lynn. Among other jobs she has had, Nancy has been a homemaker and has worked for the only shoe factory in Soddy-Daisy. (Courtesy of David and Clara Bowman.)

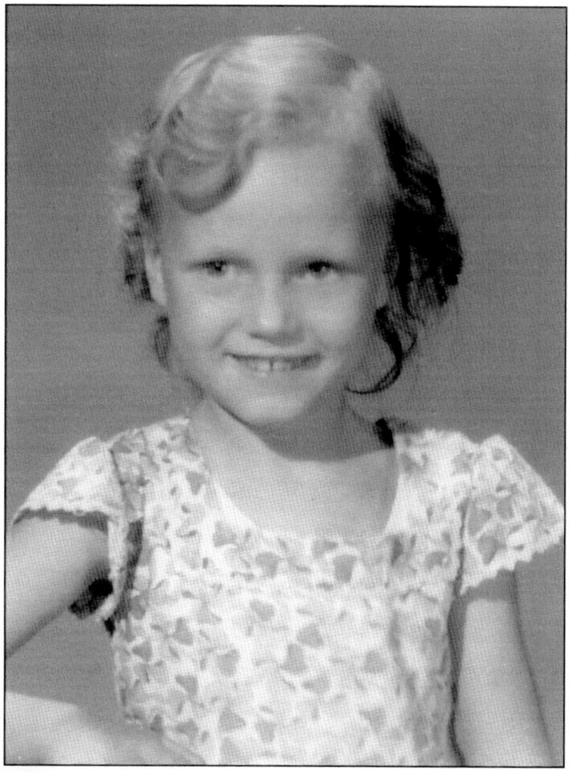

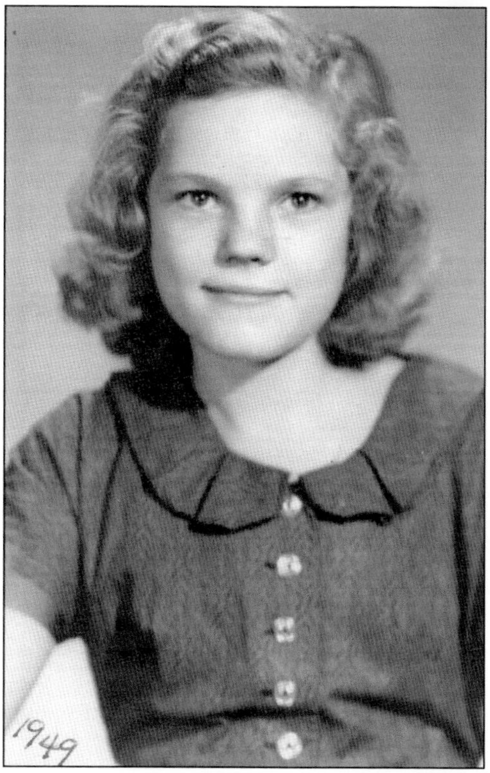

Clara Cothran maintains a beautiful pose for her fifth-grade photograph in 1949. She attended Daisy Elementary School. Clara's parents were Walter E. and Bonnie I. Cothran. One of Clara's four siblings, Nancy, is pictured above. Clara married David Bowman in 1963 at age 25, and the couple raised three children: Clay, Maria, and Marty. (Courtesy of David and Clara Bowman.)

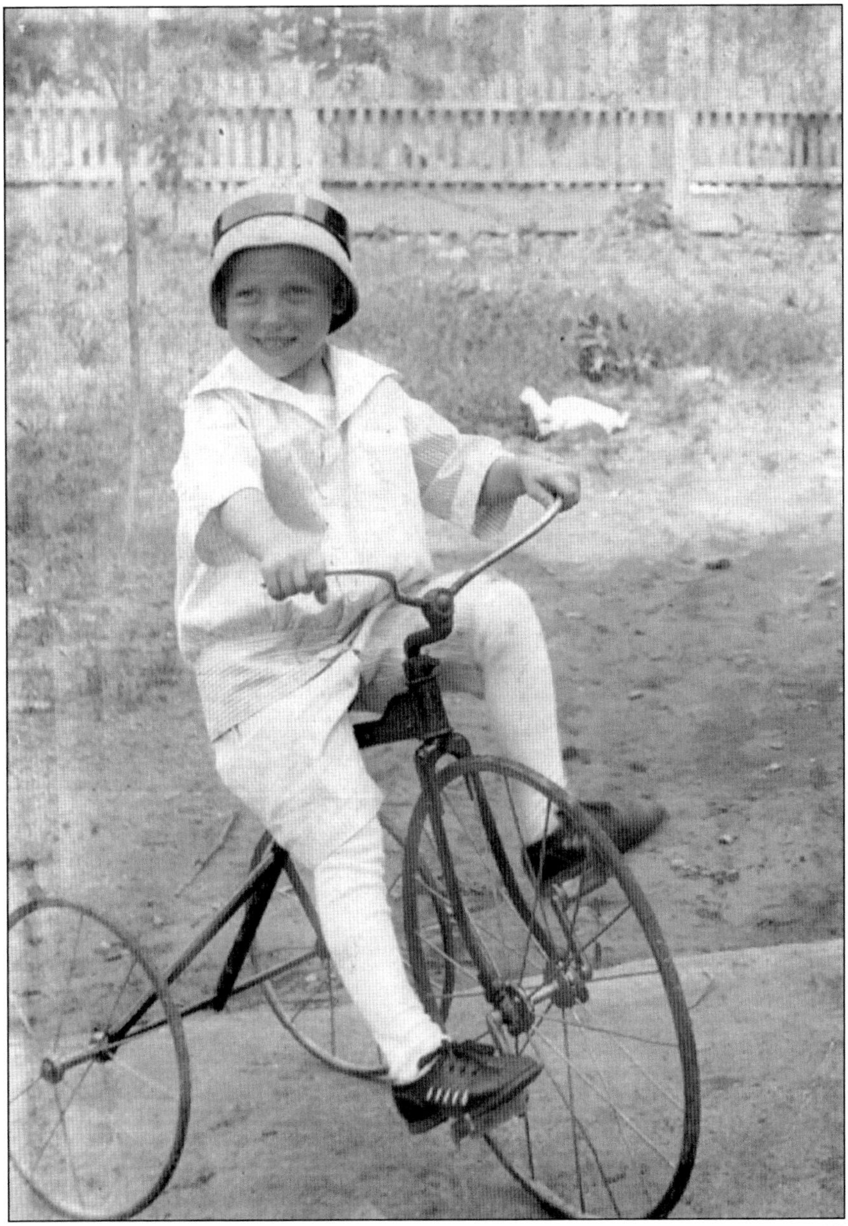

Elmer Bert Crites (August 4, 1909–August 20, 1983) is around six or seven years old in this lovely example of early-20th-century clothing and photography. Crites married Mayme Osborne (July 26, 1914–January 27, 2003) on December 15, 1933, and the couple had two daughters, Patricia Ann and Jossette Berta. Among his industrialist activities, Crites owned and ran a gas station and a restaurant and sold appliances for Sears and Roebuck and Standard Appliance Company. In the 1960s, he owned and operated Crites' Appliances in the Soddy Bank Building. Crites was a dealer for Norge Appliances, a popular appliance maker in that era. He retired in 1969. Crites's grandson, Scott Brogdon, now has a photography business in the Soddy Bank Building. Fortunately Brogdon is preserving historical information for his own family and others interested in Soddy-Daisy's past by collecting and displaying memorabilia, particularly photographs, relating to the history of the town. (Courtesy of Scott Brogdon.)

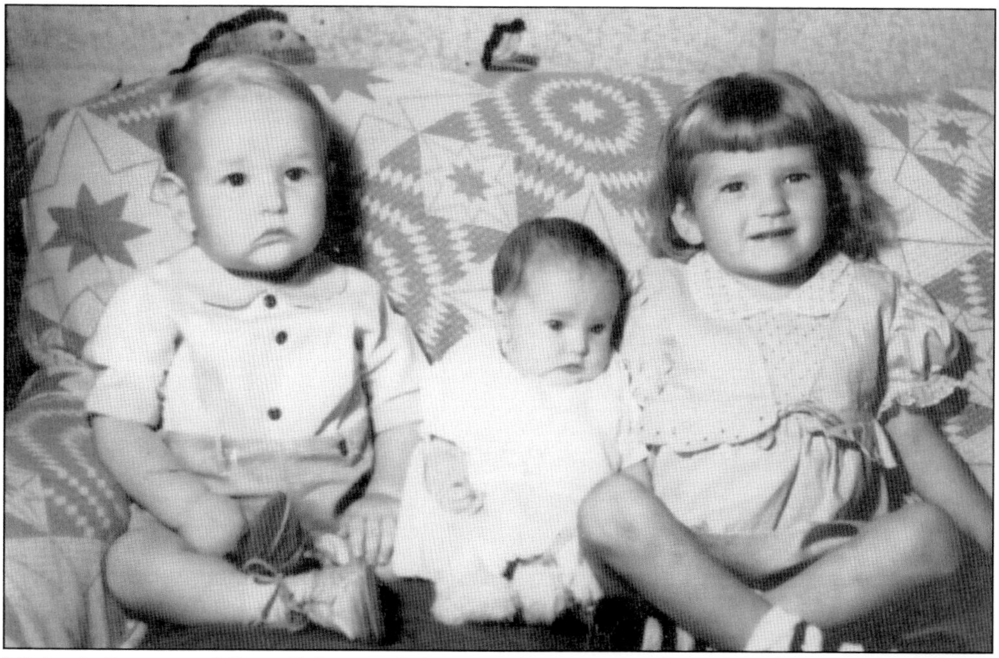

Michael, Susan, and Faye (left to right) were taking a nap when their house caught fire on March 15, 1951. The children perished, but an older brother fortunately survived the blaze. The children's parents were Sevier Adam and Pearl Eva Massengill Lovelady. (Courtesy of Ellis and Linda Sutherland.)

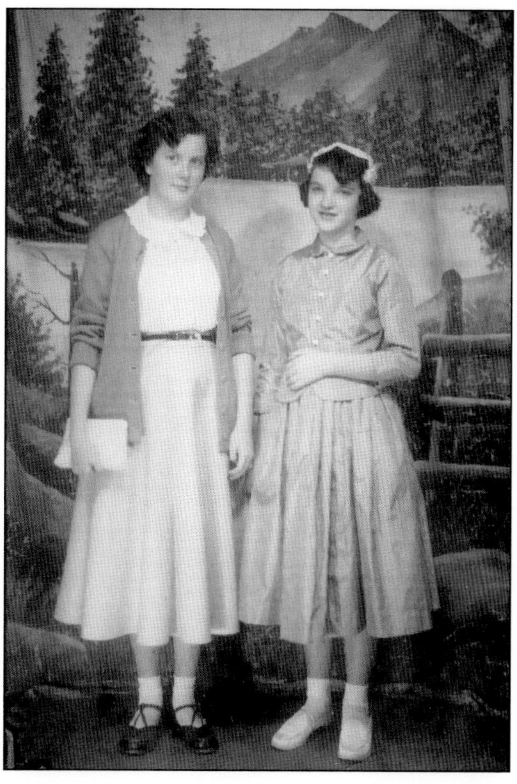

Kay Rogers (left) and Billie Orr were on one of their frequent trips to downtown Chattanooga when this photograph was taken c. 1954. The girls would catch a bus at Norman's Clothing Store in downtown Daisy and ride to Chattanooga, where they would watch a movie, eat, or just hang out. (Courtesy of Kay Williams.)

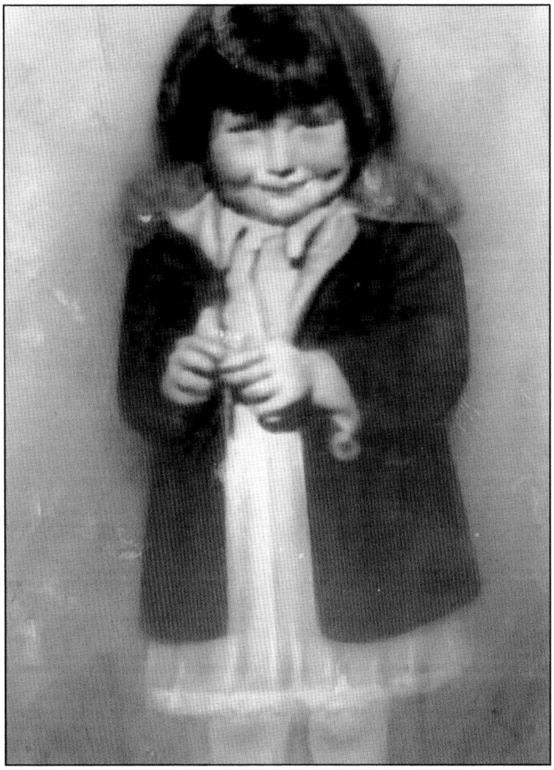

Anna Lee Lively (August 2, 1926–October 19, 1930) is shown here around 1930, shortly before she died of Bright's disease at age four. Anna Lee lived in Soddy with her siblings and parents, Ira and Molly Lively. Bright's disease is a kidney ailment that is treatable today but wasn't in the early 20th century. In 1900, one of every five children died before the age of five. (Courtesy of Rosa Lee Hambrick.)

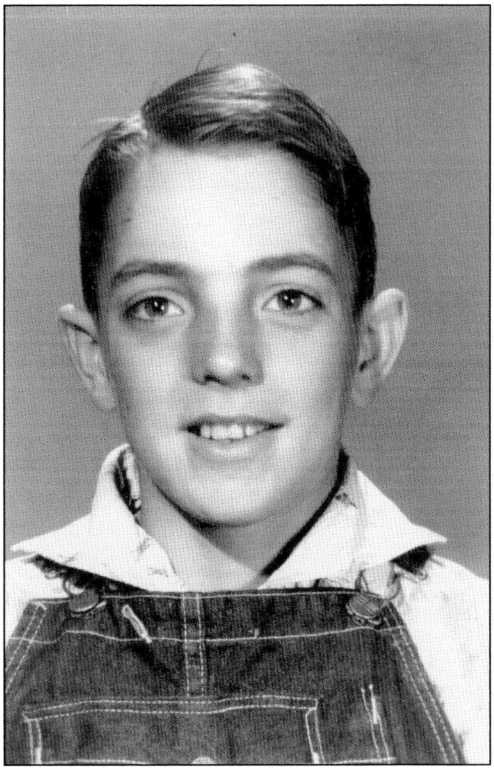

David Bowman smiles for his fifth-grade photograph at Daisy Elementary School in 1948. David was the son of Oscar D. and Jacqoyln Bowman. The family lived on Gann Road. David later married Clara Cothran Brown, and they raised three children, Clay, Maria, and Marty. (Courtesy of David and Clara Bowman.)

Eight

Athletics

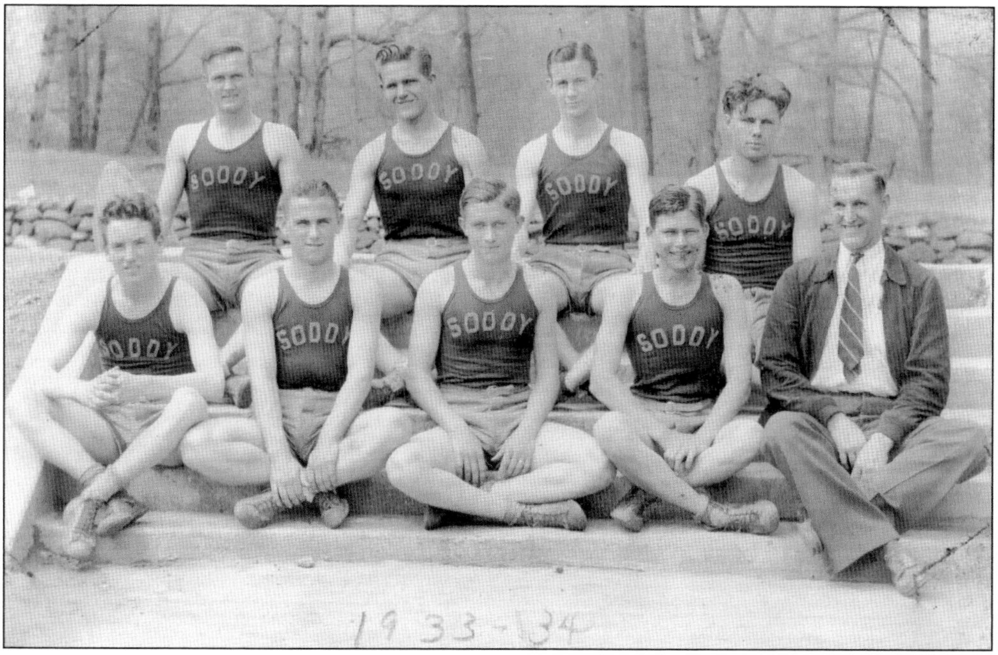

Athletes on the Soddy High School basketball team pose for this photograph during the 1933–1934 school year. From left to right are (first row) Lloyd George Roberts, Reese Clift, Cecil Lowe, James Clift, and coach I. K. Snyder; (second row) John McGill, Jimmy Morgan, Richard Bowling, and William Graves. (Courtesy of Soddy-Daisy High School.)

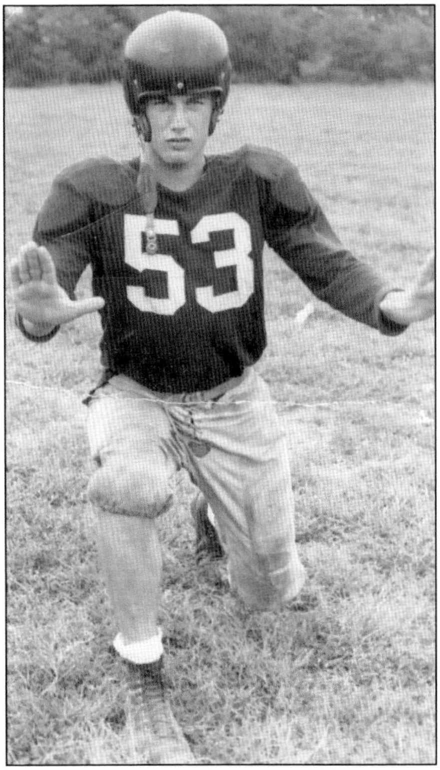

Tommy Levi played football during his freshman, sophomore, junior, and senior years. He is pictured here in football uniform during his junior year at Soddy-Daisy High School. The mighty Trojans won seven games and lost two during that football season of 1951–1952. Levi played for coach Harland Burnette and Frank Coffer. (Courtesy of Tom and Barbara Levi.)

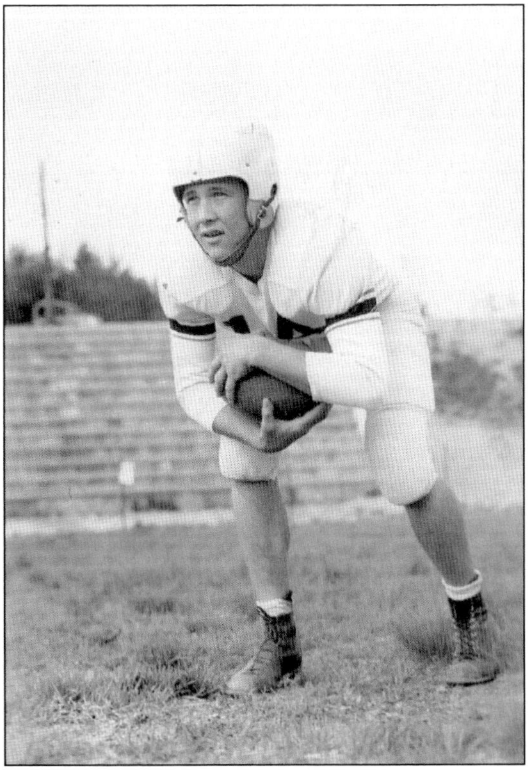

Don Elliott played football at Soddy-Daisy High School during his sophomore, junior, and senior years. During his senior year, Elliott won the Industrial Arts Award. He graduated in 1956 and went into the trade of carpentry. Elliott has three children: Debbie, Terri, and Matthew. (Courtesy of Tom and Barbara Levi.)

1947
Soddy-Daisy Trojans

DATE	TEAM	PLACE OF GAME
Aug 29	Bledsoe	Pikeville
Sept. 5	City High	City High
Sept. 12	LaFayette	Soddy-Daisy
Sept. 19	Notre Dame	Chattanooga
Sept. 26	Spring City	Soddy-Daisy
Oct. 3	Bridgeport	Soddy-Daisy
Oct. 10	Rockwood	Soddy-Daisy
Oct. 17	Marion County	Jasper
Oct. 24	Summerville	Soddy-Daisy
Oct. 31	Rossville	Rossville
Nov. 7	Tyner	Soddy-Daisy
Nov. 14	Whitwell	Soddy-Daisy

Soddy-Daisy Keeps All Pre-Game Ticket Sales For The City High Game.
Be Sure To Buy Your Ticket Before You Start To This Game.

A 1947 football schedule for the Soddy-Daisy Trojans lists many of the same schools the team plays against today. Of course, it also encourages people to "Support Those Trojans." (Courtesy of A. B. and Frankie McRee.)

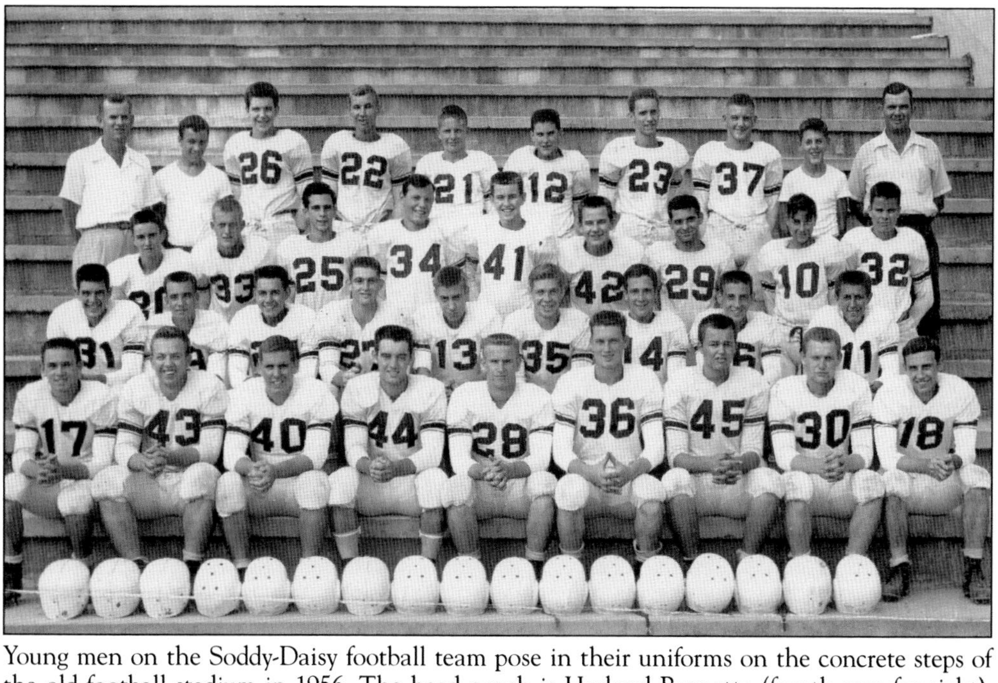

Young men on the Soddy-Daisy football team pose in their uniforms on the concrete steps of the old football stadium in 1956. The head coach is Harland Burnette (fourth row, far right). Assistant coach Frank Coffer is on the far left of the fourth row. (Courtesy of Soddy-Daisy High School; photograph by Ivory's Studio, Dayton.)

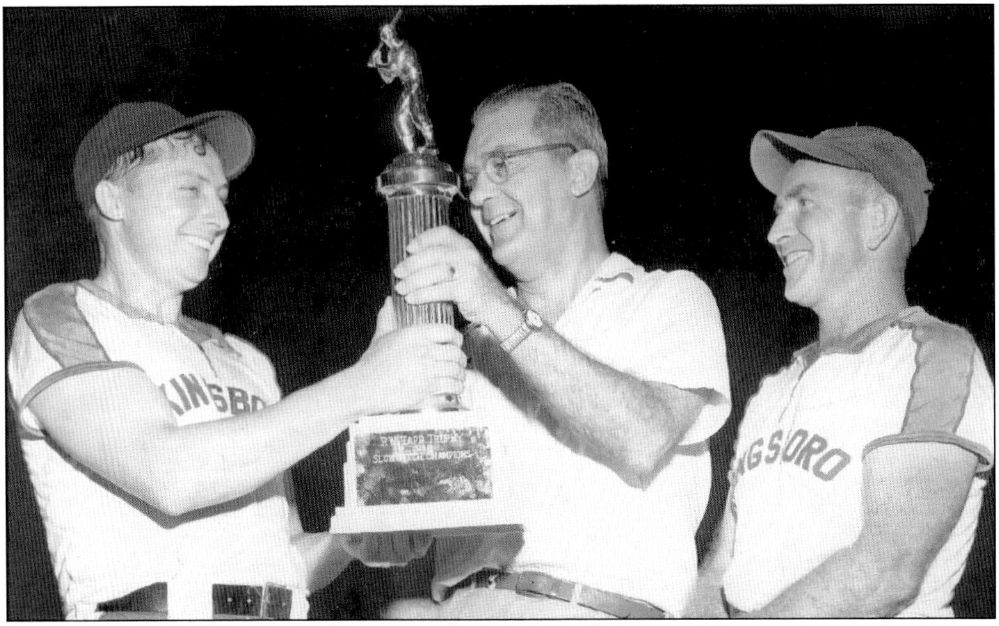

Charlie McAffee, Coach Krischbaum, and Paul Lewis (left to right) hold the trophy that the Kingsboro Silk Mill softball team received when they won the 1956 Slow Pitch Championship. That same year, the team went on to win the state championship for the amateur softball slow pitch league. (Courtesy of Buck Johnson.)

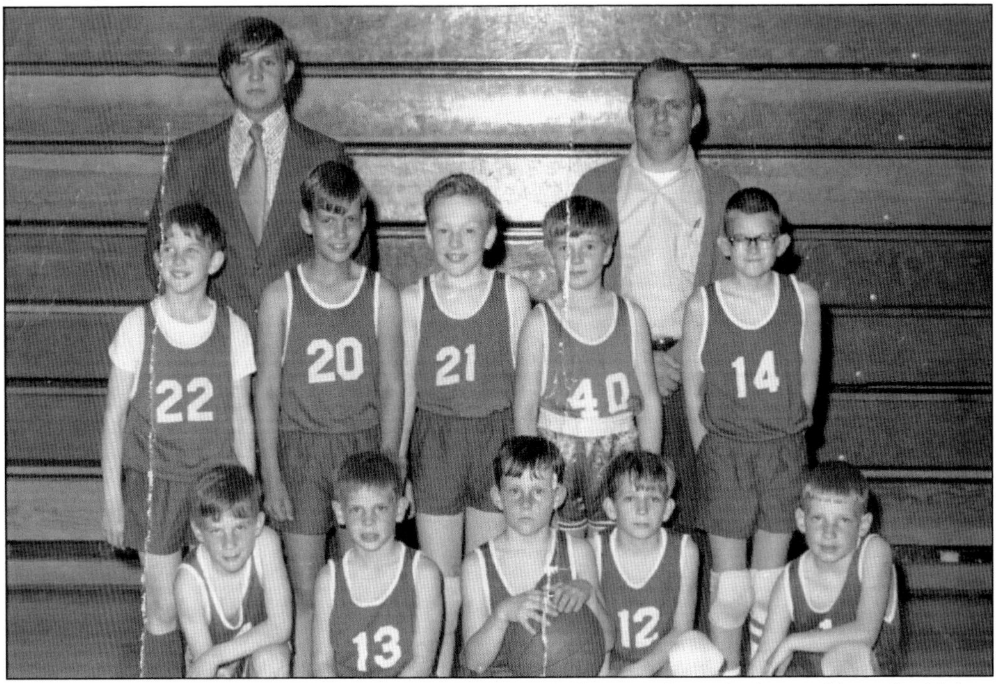

Frank Mulkey (back right) coached this boys' basketball team through the Soddy Kid's Club c. 1971. Kneeling from left to right are Paul Lasley, Rodney Smith, Patrick Mulkey, Jim Posey, and Jeff Jenkins. Standing from left to right are Ray Sutherland, Billy Uren, Paul Morgan, Jimbo Petty, and Reece Skillern. The man at left in back is unidentified. (Courtesy of Freida Sutherland.)

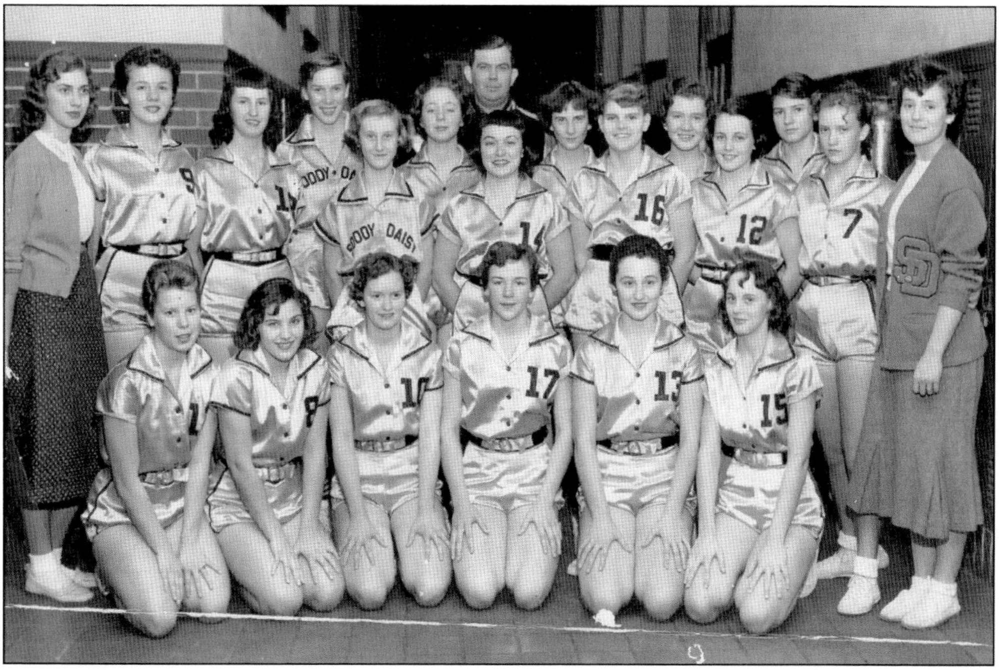

Pictured here on the Soddy-Daisy girls' basketball team from left to right are (first row) Velma Davidson, Carolyn Shattock, Rita Priddy, Sis Daughtrey, Sis Hixon, and an unidentified player; (second row) Carolyn Greene, Judy Varner, Edwina Arrowsmith, Myrtle Irwin, Judy Elliott, Beth Grant, Pat Holland, Sue Flerl, Norma Penney, unidentified, Bobbie Skillern, and three unidentified ladies. Coach Harland Burnette stands behind the girls. (Courtesy of Soddy-Daisy High School.)

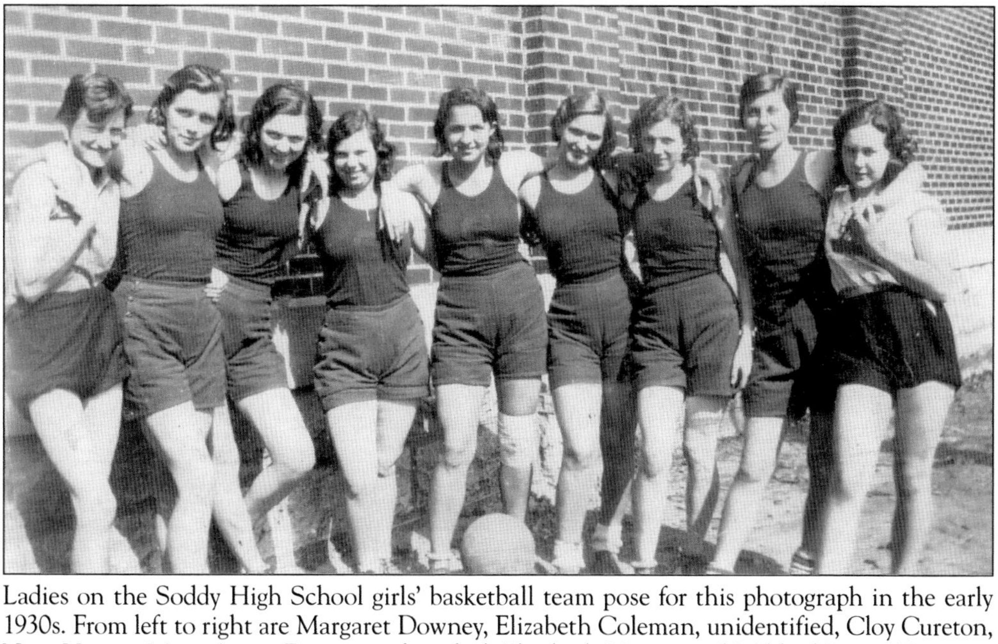

Ladies on the Soddy High School girls' basketball team pose for this photograph in the early 1930s. From left to right are Margaret Downey, Elizabeth Coleman, unidentified, Cloy Cureton, Nina Varner, Mary Agnes Evans, unidentified, Elizabeth Upton, and Mildred Price. (Courtesy of Tom and Barbara Levi.)

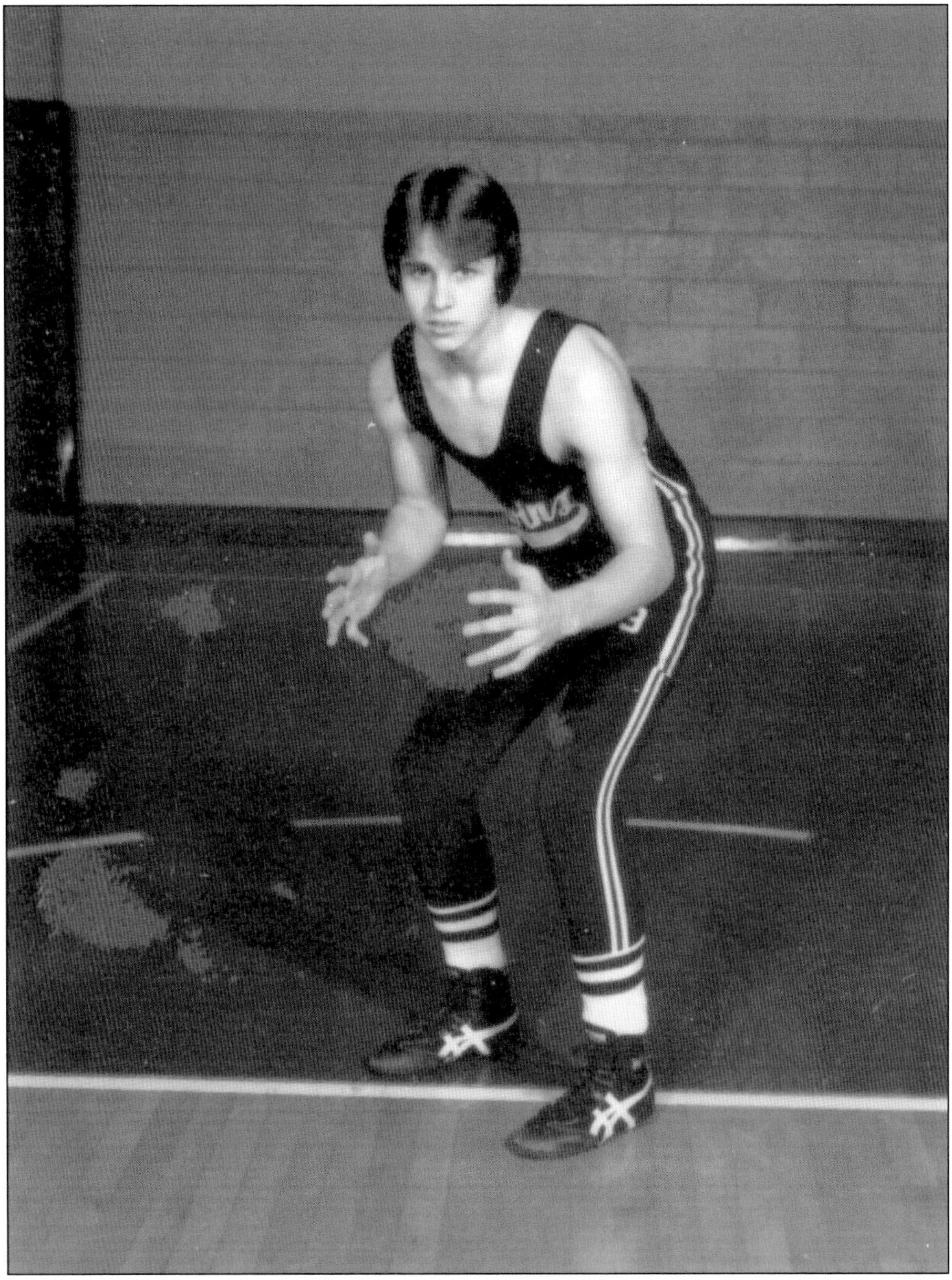

Harold Allen Johnson was on the wrestling team from his freshman year until he graduated in 1982. He also participated in several other sports, and many residents may recall when Johnson broke his neck sledding down the hill of the current Soddy-Daisy High School on Sequoyah Road. With time, friends and family helped Harold realize that God was offering a new direction to his life. Today Harold is a church planter and theological educator in the Czech Republic with his wife, Ginger Lynn Junek Johnson, and sons, Taylor and Hayden. The family serves under the International Mission Board. (From the authors' collection.)

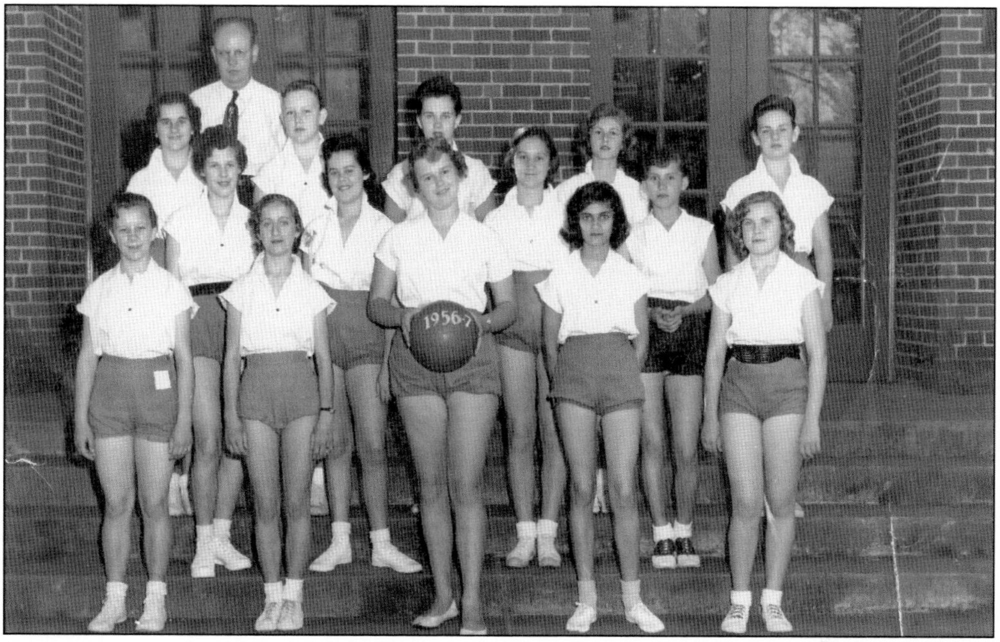

Pictured here is the 1956–1957 Soddy-Daisy High School girls' basketball team. From left to right are (first row) Catherine Copeland, Melba Bailey, Martha Hawkins, Juanita Edmonson, and Kay Merriman; (second row) Pauline Johnson, Joyce Roberts, Laverne Varner, and Georgia Greene; (third row) Judy Teague, Jeanette Morgan, Hollis Graves, Ina Daughtrey, and Marilyn Sims. The coach is Ansel Jordan. (Courtesy of Frank Copeland.)

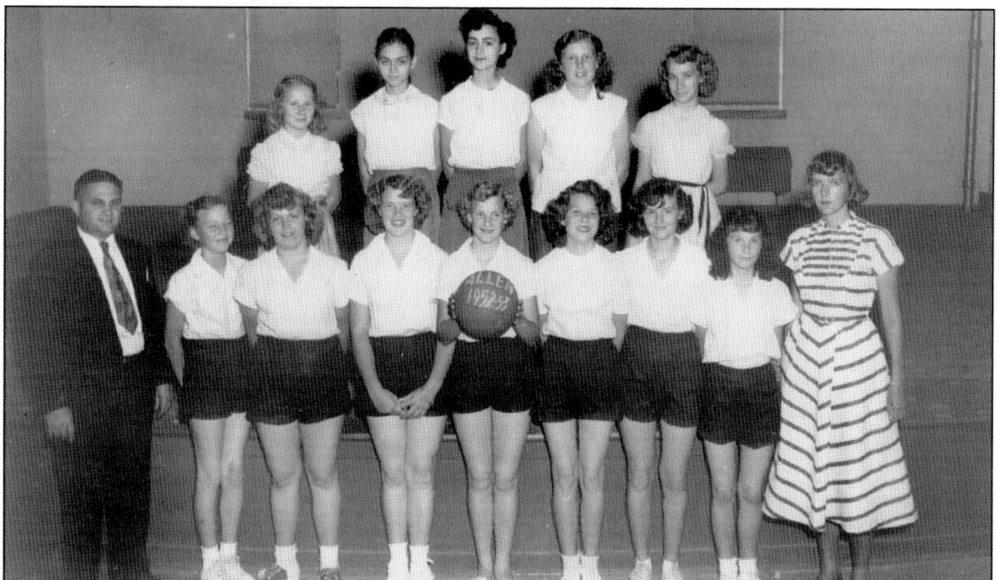

These young ladies, shown here with their sponsors, formed the first basketball team at John H. Allen Elementary School in the 1952–1953 school year. From left to right are (first row) Mr. Hale, Allene Hundle, Mary Ruth Millard, Joyce Watts, Peggy Nelson, Eva Mysinger, Barbara Smith, Mildred Mangrum, and Ms. McClure; (second row) Peggy Gamblin, Ruby Leffew, Virginia Leffew, Josephine Gravitt, and Katherine Davison. (Courtesy of David and Clara Bowman.)

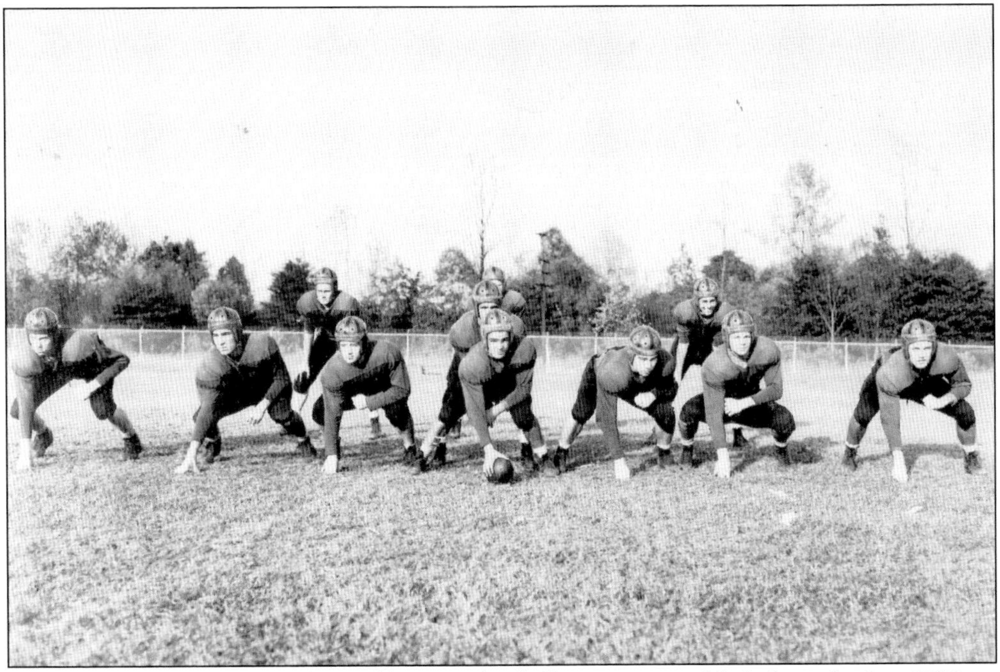

This vintage photograph of the Soddy-Daisy football team is most likely from the late 1930s or early 1940s, soon after the Soddy and Daisy high schools combined to create Soddy-Daisy High School. (Courtesy of Soddy-Daisy High School.)

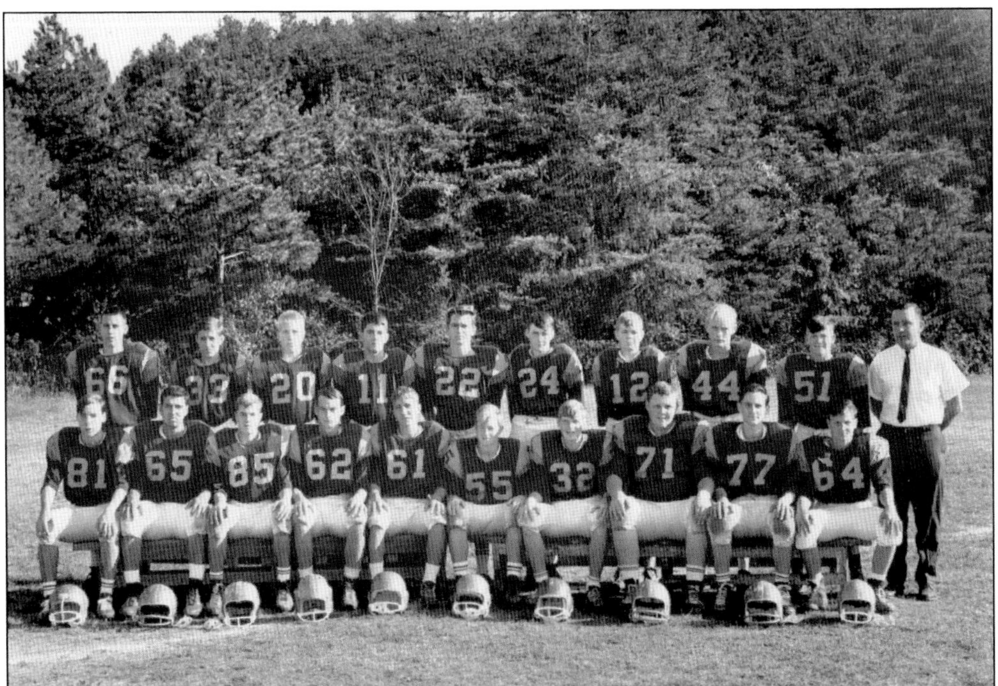

Soddy-Daisy Junior High School opened in 1961. Shown here is one of their first football teams, coach by Lynn Thompson. (Courtesy of Ellis and Linda Sutherland.)

Nine

COMMUNITY

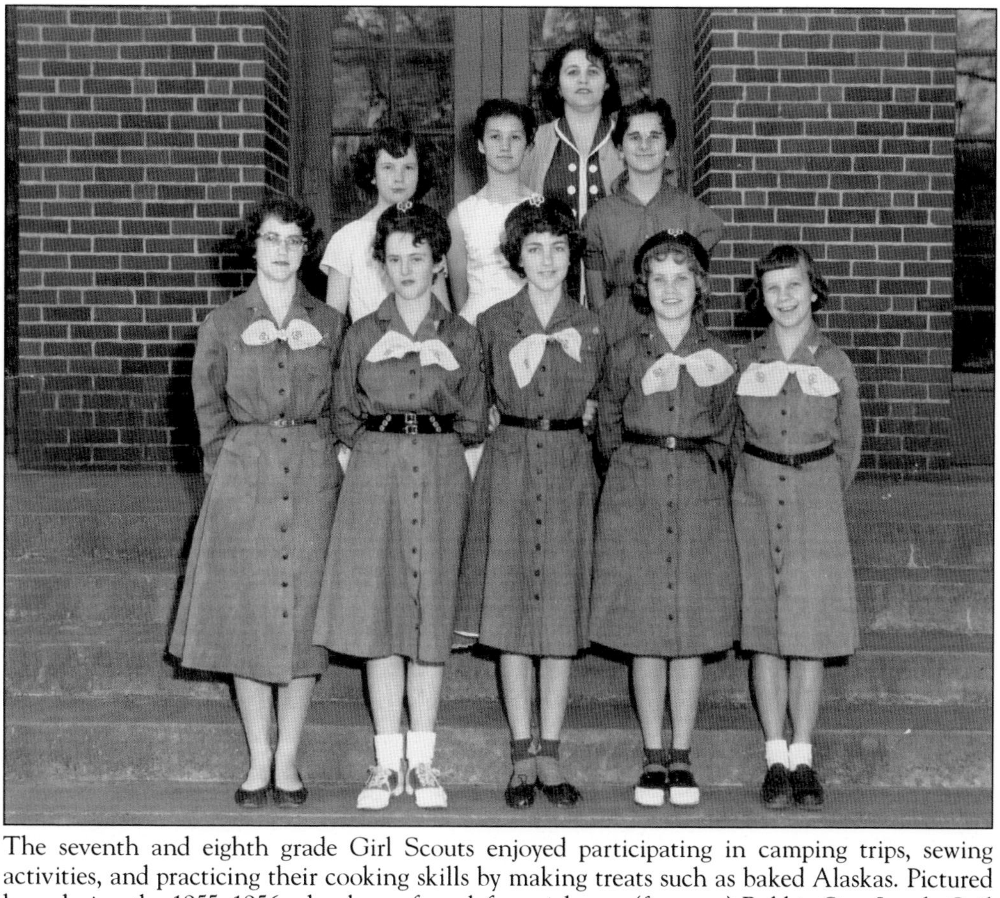

The seventh and eighth grade Girl Scouts enjoyed participating in camping trips, sewing activities, and practicing their cooking skills by making treats such as baked Alaskas. Pictured here during the 1955–1956 school year from left to right are (first row) Bobbie Cox, Lynda Gail Elliott, Raycelle Burris, Kay Merriman, and Catherine Copeland; (second row) Virginia Gill, Laverne Varner, and Judy Teague; (third row) leader Ruth Cox. (Courtesy of Frank Copeland.)

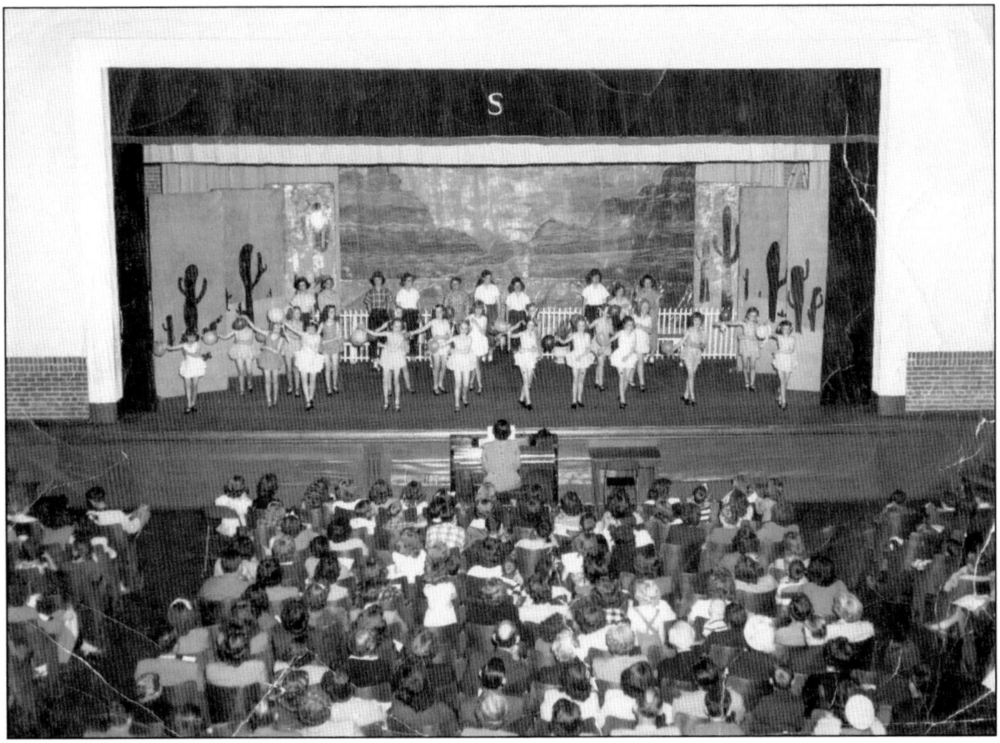

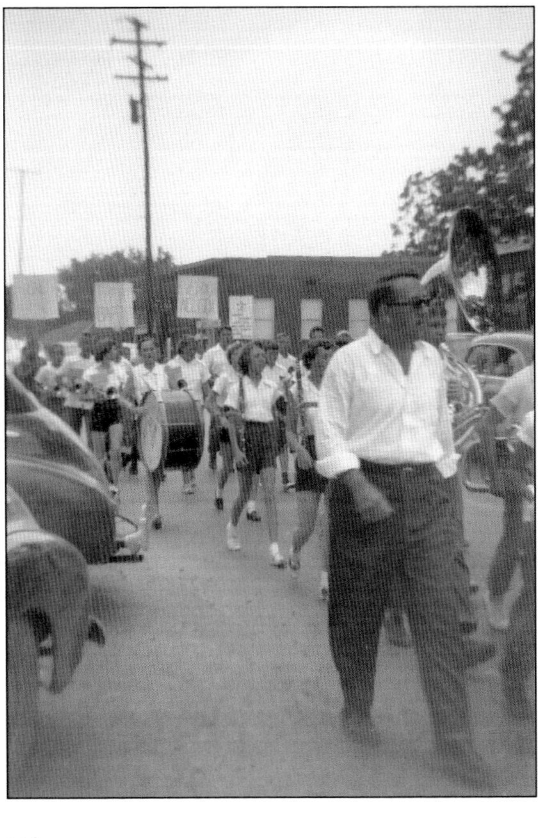

Dance students put on a program for visitors at Soddy Elementary *c.* 1950. The girls took dance classes at the school after school hours to learn tap and participate in the programs. (Courtesy of Freida Sutherland.)

This photograph depicts a typical Soddy-Daisy parade in the mid-1950s. Parades have always been popular in the community, and it appears from the signs that this parade (or at least this band) was advertising an event at the First Baptist Church. The parade is passing by a brick Currency Exchange building. In front is Mr. Hood, the band director. (Courtesy of Kay Williams.)

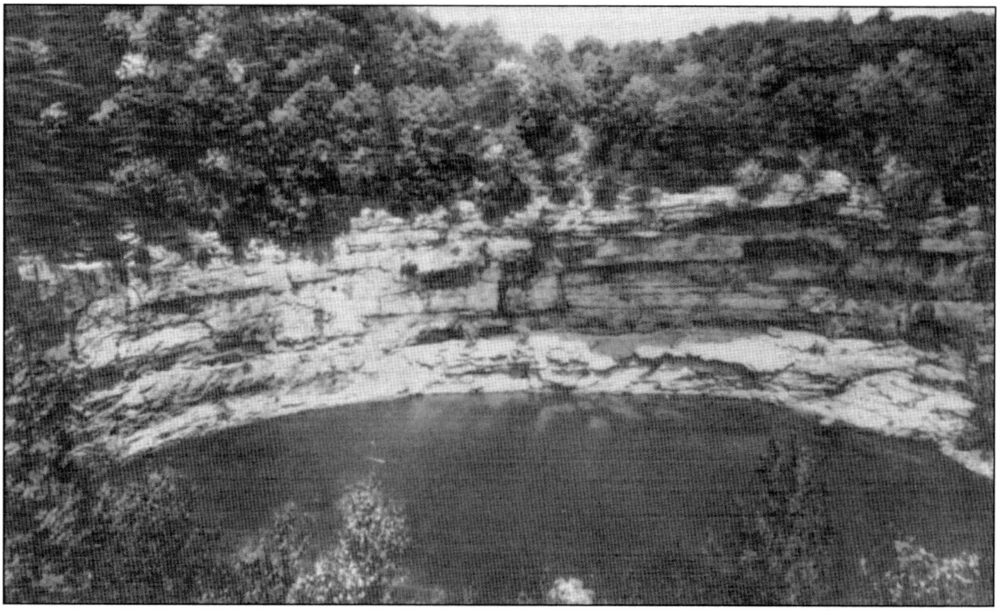

Named by pioneer settlers' Native American guides, Montlake is a geographical phenomenon that remains fascinating. The water is chemically pure and safe for drinking at all times, even though there is no visible inlet or outlet. According to the back of this postcard, speculations as to the natural causes of Montlake include a falling comet or a collapse of the subterranean structure. (From the authors' collection.)

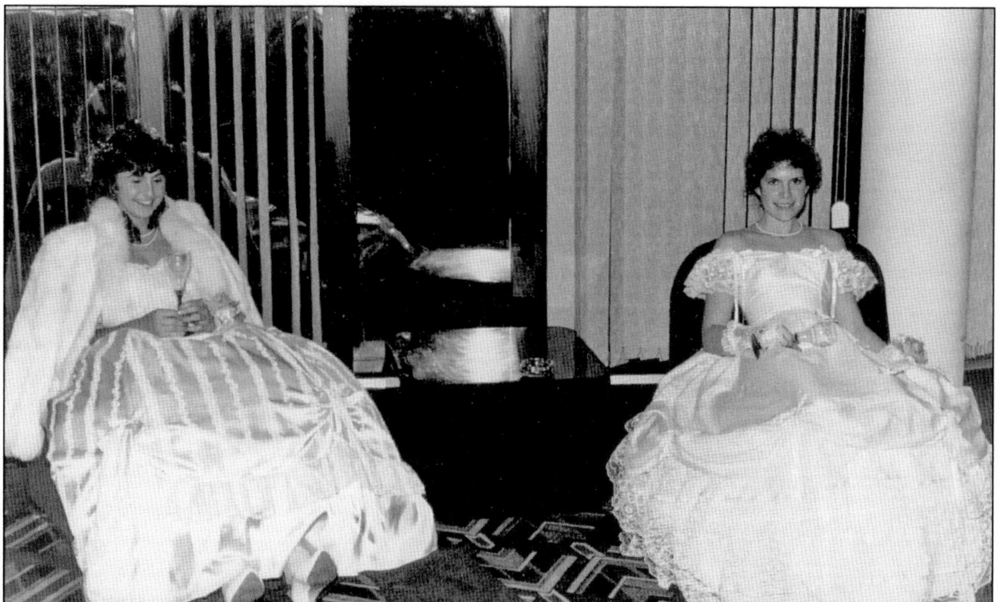

Sonya Annette Eustice, 16 (left), and Audrey Arlene Burton, 17, relax after the Soddy-Daisy High School Junior-Senior Prom on April 4, 1987, held at the Chattanooga Trade Center. Proms are an exciting part of life for high school students in Soddy-Daisy. Audrey Burton Headrick is now a wife and mother and is currently an attorney for the State of Tennessee. Sonya is a wife, mother, and author. (From the authors' collection.)

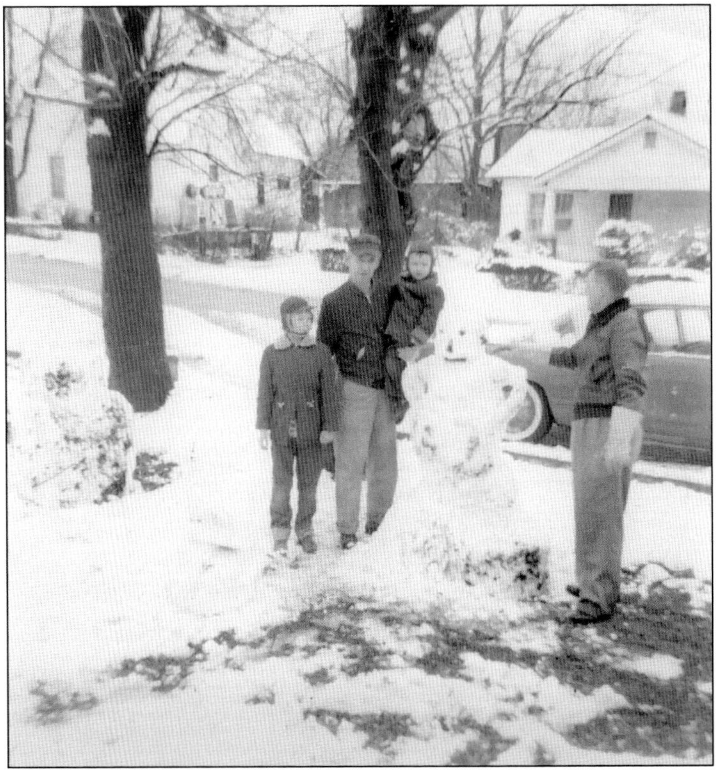

James Card stands next to his dad, Paul, who is holding his other son, Paul Wyatt Card. R. C. Martin joins the others in front of "Granny" Martin's house on Oakwood, behind where Kay's Kastle used to be located. The guys take advantage of a snowstorm in 1958 to make a snowman and enjoy some winter weather. (Courtesy of Norris and Mary Clift.)

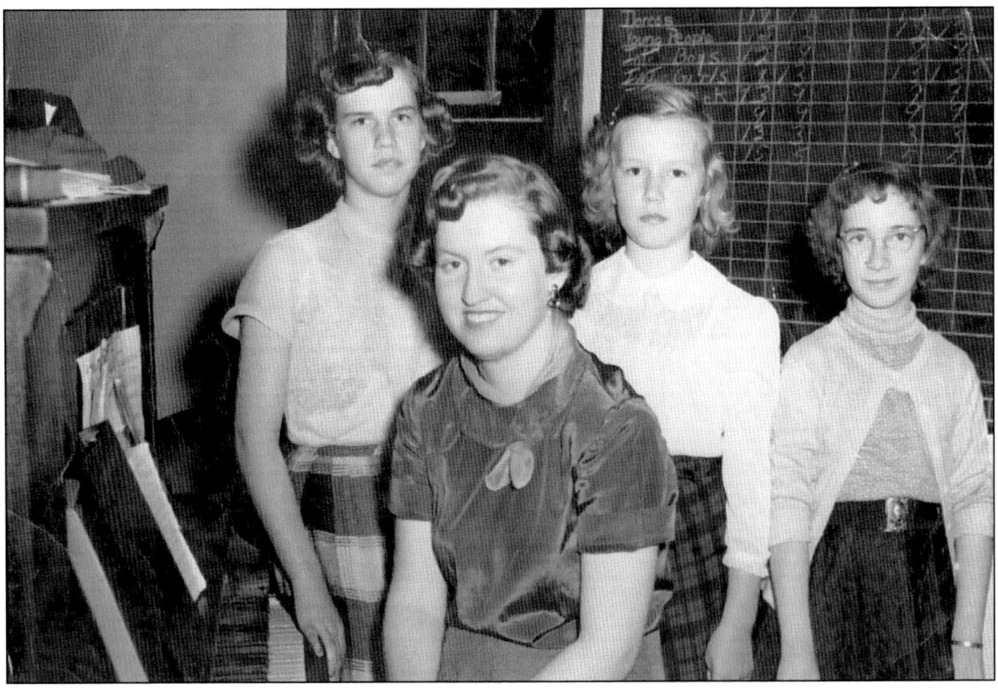

The Girls' Singing Trio, pictured here, from South Soddy Baptist Church performed at local churches during the 1950s. From left to right are Freida Lasley, Phyllis Pelfrey (the piano teacher), Jeanette Morgan, and Judith Ann Stuart. (Courtesy of Freida Sutherland.)

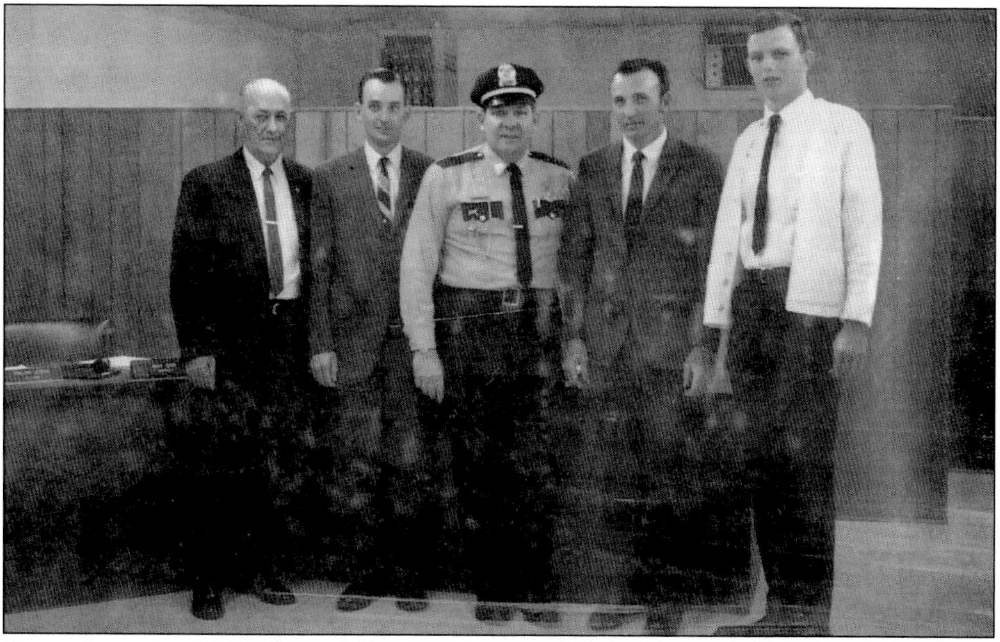

Since the areas of Soddy and Daisy were patrolled by the Hamilton County Sheriff's Department prior to 1969, the towns did not have their own police officers. The first police officers for the city of Soddy-Daisy are pictured here in 1969. These men are, from left to right, Bob Jett, Curtis Elliott, Police Chief Jim Baker, Ray Wilson, and Roy Penney. (Courtesy of Soddy-Daisy Police Department.)

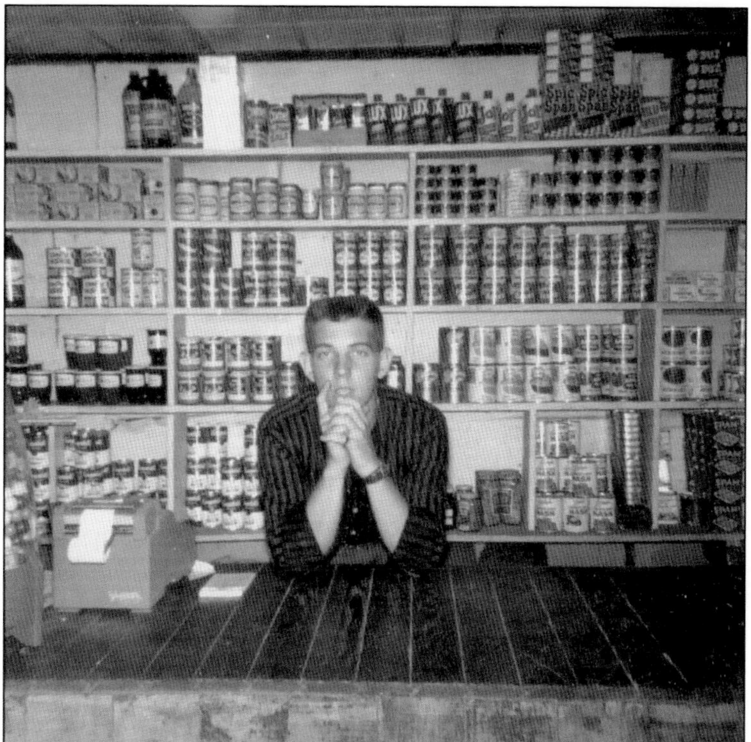

Duke Berry visits Rogers' Grocery c. 1957. On the shelves are various canned foods, including Dinty Moore beef stew, Campbell's soups, Van Camps chili, and Spam. Also available at the grocery were cleaning products such as Lux, Joy, and Comet. Notice the rocket filled with gumballs sitting on the counter by the register. (Courtesy of Kay Williams.)

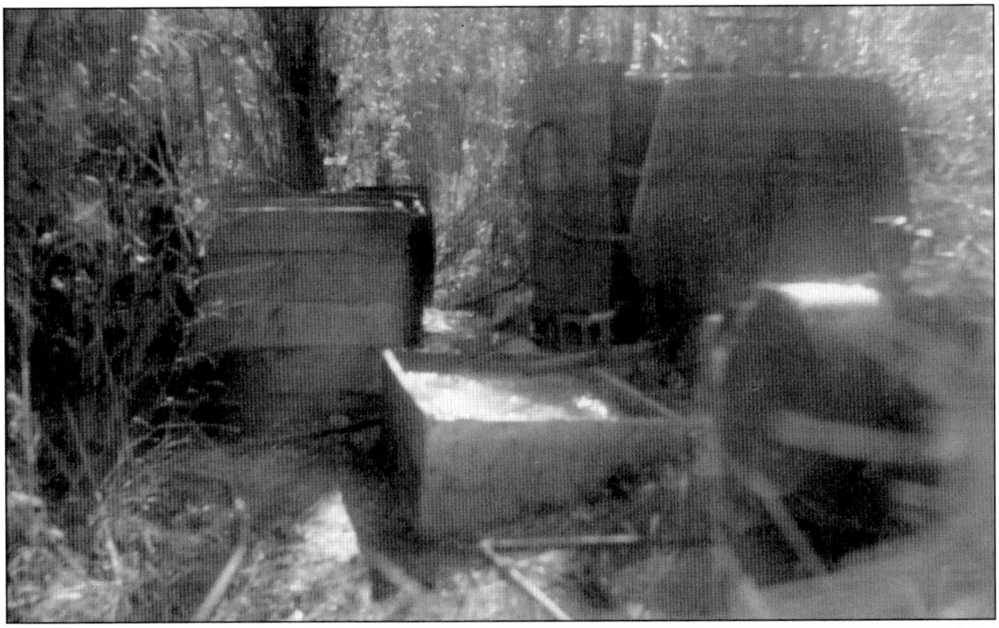

While many English words are of Latin, French, Spanish, or German descent, the word "bootleg" (hiding liquor bottles in one's boot leg) developed in America in the early 17th century. Pictured here is a moonshine still on Mowbray Mountain in 1959. The practice of illegally "bootlegging" or "running" whiskey and moonshine was widely practiced in the Soddy-Daisy area in the late 19th and early 20th centuries. (From the authors' collection.)

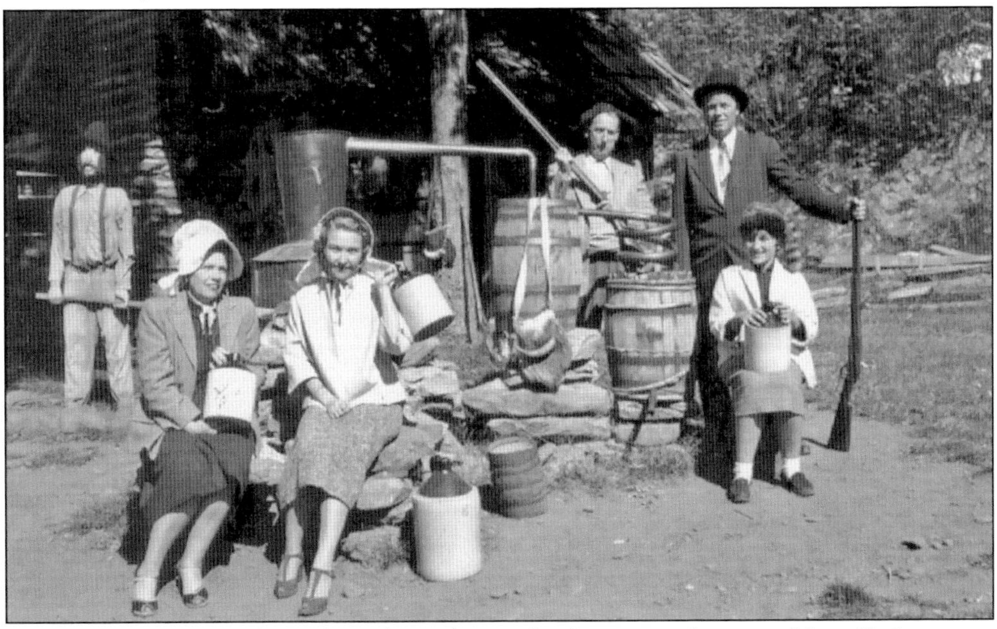

Though this family is only mocking the tradition of making moonshine at a fake still, there were many stills like this one in the area. Tradition has it that "running" moonshine is linked to the roots of NASCAR, since the bootleggers evaded police by driving very fast. Pictured here from left to right are a stuffed hillbilly, Inez Woosnam, Mayme Crites, Bert Crites, Bill Woosnam, and Jossette Crites. (Courtesy of Scott Brogdon.)

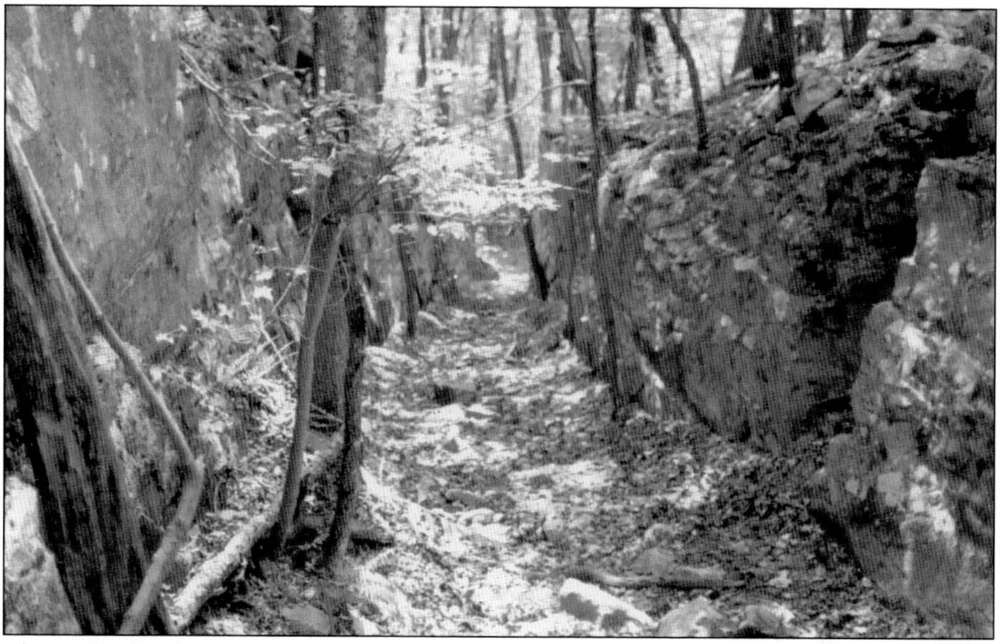

The Naires Road was one of the first foot trails from Hendon (on Walden's Ridge) to the foot of the mountain on the Dunlap side. The first travelers on the Naires Road, which may be a Southern derivative of "narrowest road," were Native Americans. In addition to traveling over the mountain for legitimate purposes, local people most likely used the road to transport moonshine. (Courtesy of Ellis and Linda Sutherland.)

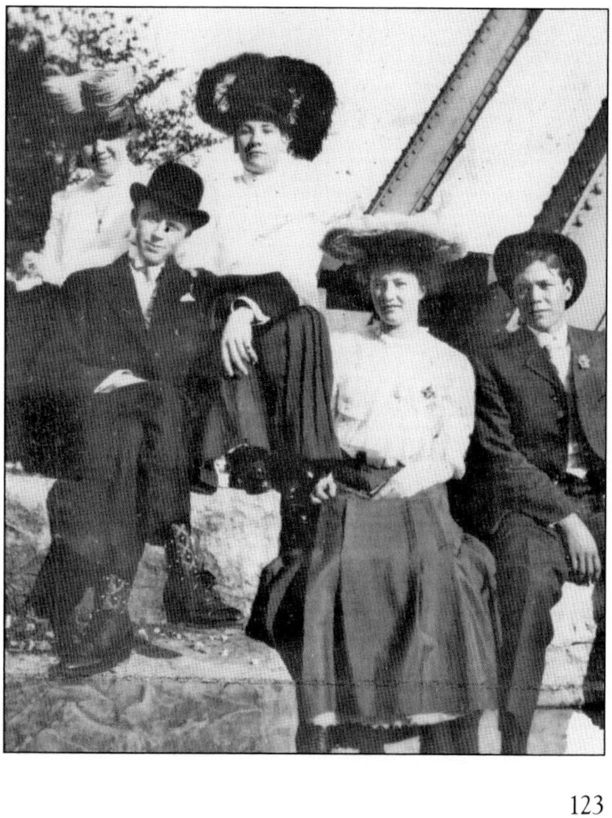

Seated on the edge of the iron bridge in Soddy from left to right are (first row) James Pickle, Gussie Hallett, and Joe B. Elliott; (second row) Mrs. James Pickle and Dolly Reese. The iron bridge was located at the foot of the mountain in Soddy on Back Valley Road. The bridge was torn down in the first half of the 20th century. (Courtesy of Tom and Barbara Levi.)

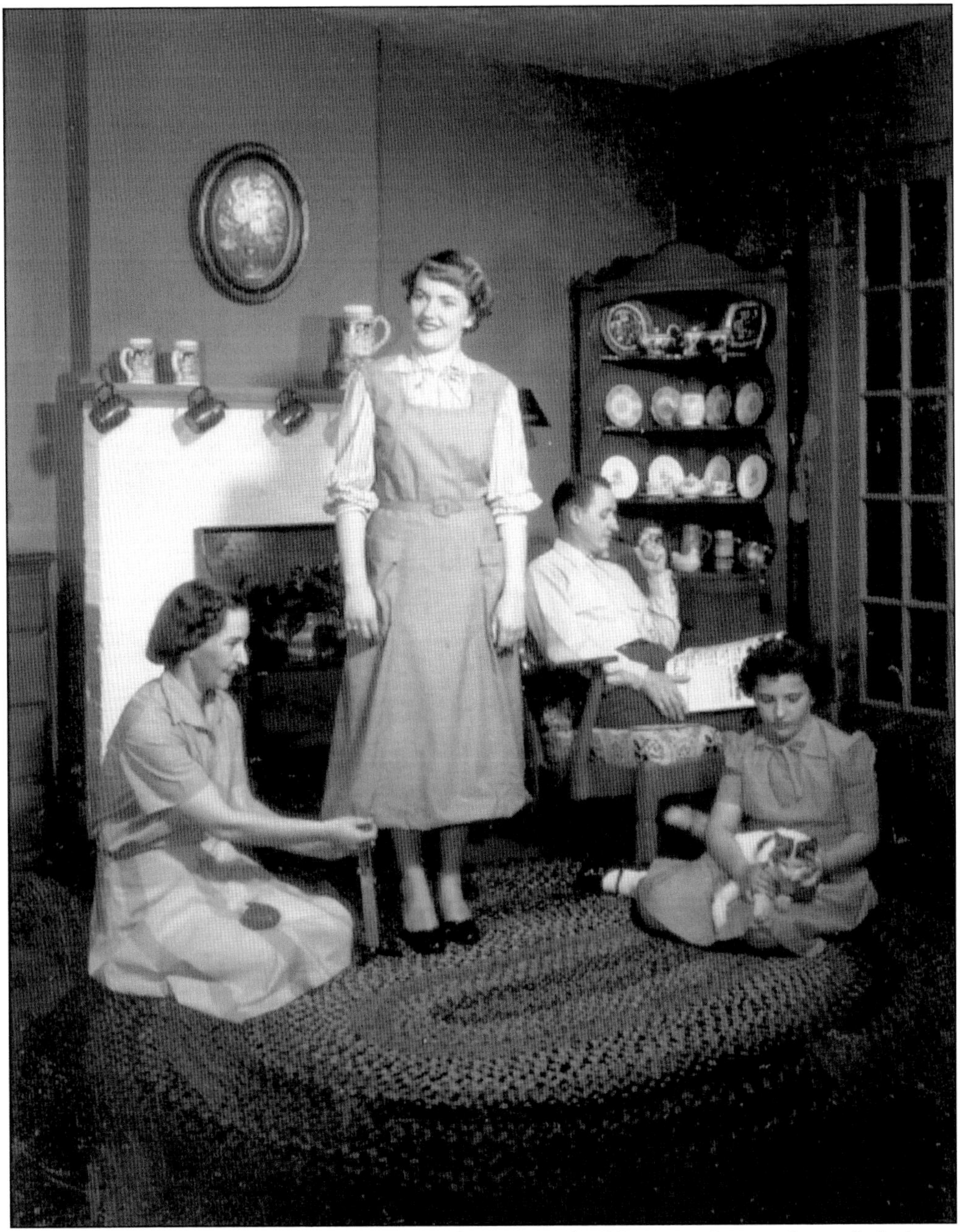

When Soddy teen Patricia Ann Crites was the National 4-H winner for textiles and clothing, she was listed in the February 18, 1952, issue of *Life* magazine. She also was featured on the September 1952 cover of *Farm and Ranch* magazine, shown here. From left to right are Mayme, Patricia, Elmer Bert, and Jossette Crites. The house in the photograph is still located in Soddy. (Courtesy of Scott Brogdon.)

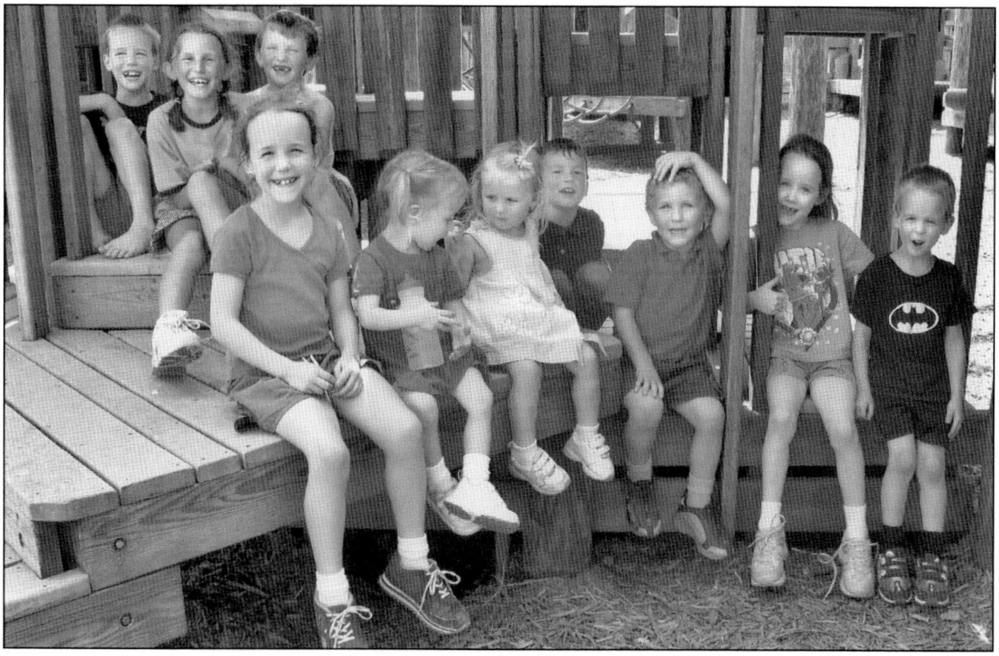

Construction began on Scramble Alley in 1995 and finished in June 1996. The cost was $120,000. The area is used for school field trips, birthday parties, and simply as a wonderful children's playground. Scramble Alley was built by a volunteer committee known as Friends of the Kids. Pictured here are local children and visitors to the area enjoying Scramble Alley on a hot day in July 2005. (Photograph by Sonya Haskins.)

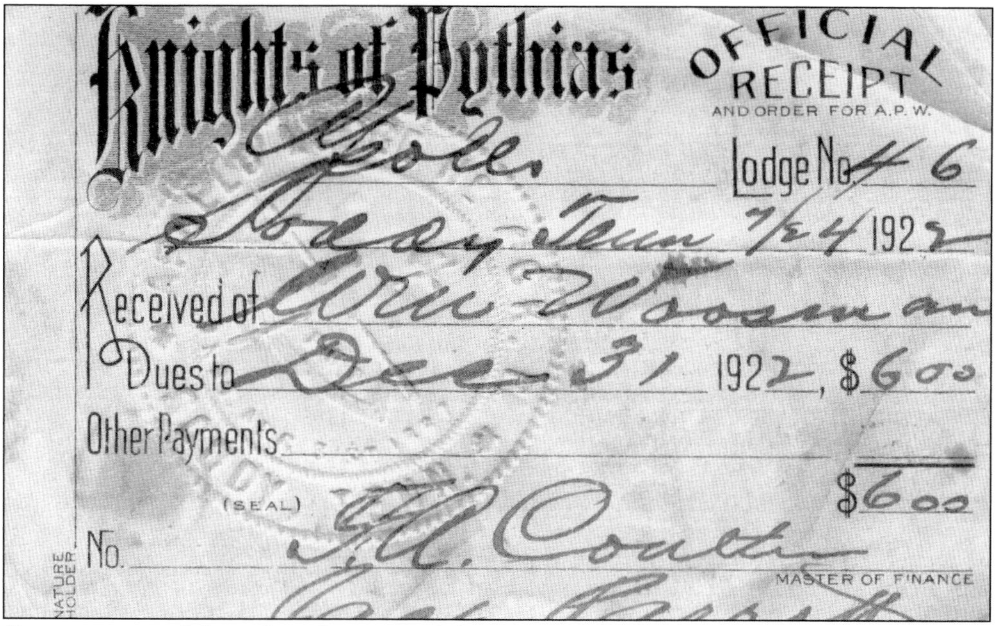

Knights of Pythias

OFFICIAL RECEIPT

AND ORDER FOR A.P.W.

Apollo Lodge No. 46

Soddy Tenn 7/24 1922

Received of Wm Woosman

Dues to Dec 31 1922, $6.00

Other Payments

$6.00

(SEAL)

No.

MASTER OF FINANCE

Civic or service clubs such as the Lions Club, Shriners, and Order of the Red Man have always been popular with the citizens of Soddy-Daisy. Shown here is a receipt from the Knights of Pythias, a civic organization of the early 20th century. This receipt for $6 is for the dues of William Woosman to the Apollo Lodge in Soddy. It is dated 1922. (Courtesy of Buck Johnson.)

About the Authors

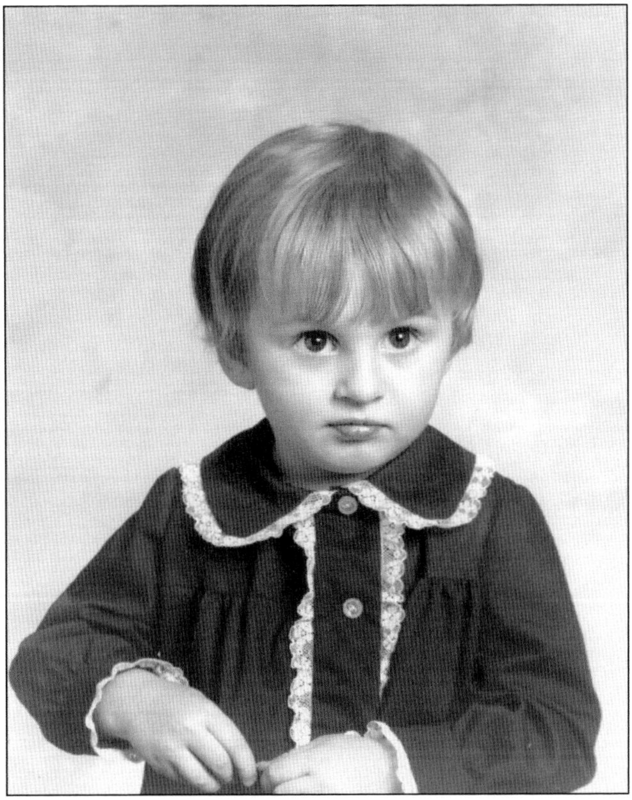

Sonya Johnson Eustice Haskins lived about a mile from Daisy Elementary School (where the municipal building is now) for most of her childhood. She attended both Soddy Elementary School and Daisy Elementary School in various grades, then she attended Soddy-Daisy High School for four years, graduating sixth in her class in 1988. Sonya frequently rode her unicycle to school and also rode in parades, a Soddy-Daisy bike-a-thon, and the Soddy-Daisy Junior Miss Pageant.

After graduating from King College (Bristol, Tennessee) in 1992 with a bachelor's degree in English, Sonya married Chris Haskins in 1994. They have five children: Sarah, Micah, Christopher, Daniel, and Hannah. In addition to their birth children, Chris and Sonya have taken in over 50 foster children since 2000. Among other commitments, Sonya primarily divides her time between teaching her children at home and writing. The family resides in Jonesborough, but they make frequent visits to Soddy-Daisy.

Sonya's other books in Arcadia's Images of America series include *Johnson City*, *Jonesborough*, and *Bristol*, all of which have been local best-sellers. She awaits the summer 2006 release of Images of Sports: *Bristol Motor Speedway*. Her work has also appeared in magazines such as *Writer's Digest*, *Guideposts for Teens*, *Decision*, *Physician's Practice Digest*, *College Bound*, *Educational Dealers*, and *Homeschooling Today*.

Sonya enjoys speaking to individuals and groups about history, homeschooling, and writing books. She welcomes opportunities to visit classrooms, churches, women's groups, and community groups and can be reached via the publisher.

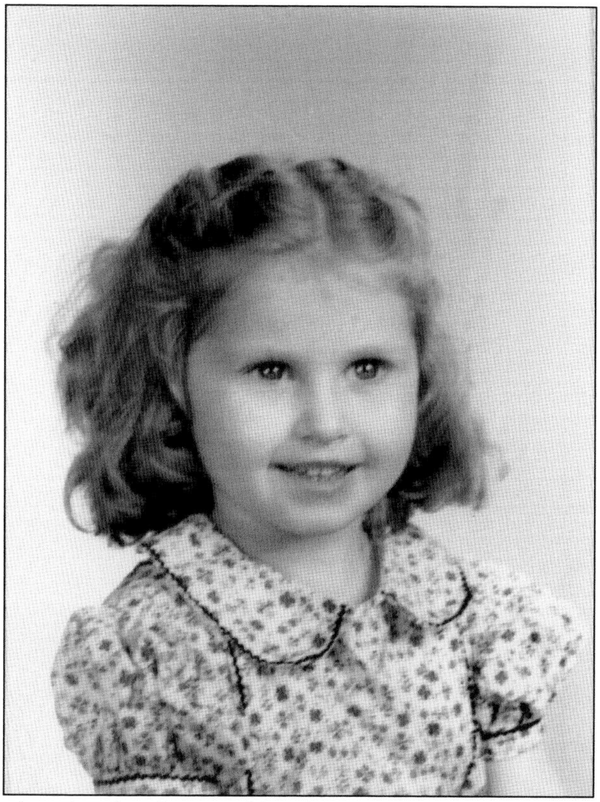

Cathy Johnson Hawkins has lived most of her life in Soddy-Daisy. She attended Soddy-Daisy High School in the late 1960s but left early to raise her daughter and now coauthor, Sonya. Cathy also has a son named Joe, who is now grown and works as an elevator operator for a grain company.

Cathy returned to school and earned a GED in 1983, then served as assistant manager of a local restaurant for several years. She obtained a CDL (Certified Driver's License) in 1989 and worked as a bus driver for Orange Grove Center for 15 years. Due to severe back disorder, Cathy is now restricted to lighter activities, such as coauthoring this book.

Cathy enjoys spending time with her grandchildren, doing Bible study, raising her dachshunds, and swimming when the weather permits. She has been married to Ronald Hawkins, known as "Hawkeye," for nearly 20 years. They live in Soddy-Daisy near Opossum Creek.

A member of Midway Baptist Church, Cathy has participated in Bible studies, has taught children's classes, and does extensive outreach with people who are homebound. She also enjoys writing songs and singing them among the congregation.

BIBLIOGRAPHY

Haskins, Sonya A. *Johnson City*. Charleston, SC: Arcadia Publishing, 2005.

———. *Jonesborough*. Charleston, SC: Arcadia Publishing, 2005.

Parks, Joseph H. and Stanley J. Folmsbee. *The Story of Tennessee*. Norman, OK: Harlow Publishing, 1973.

Smith, Steve. *The Good Old Days (Continued . . . Part II)*. 1992.

The authors also obtained numerous bits and pieces of information and/or verified information through census records, church records, letters, newspaper articles, and various small publications that have been written by people in Soddy-Daisy or the surrounding communities. The documents we used to verify or find information included in this book date back to the early 19th century.